Breaking the
Gender Code

breaking the
GENDER
CODE

DANIELLE DOBSON

Dedication

For Alex, Leo and Luca, my phenomenal learning partners.

This work is also dedicated to all the women and men who have used courage, tenacity and determination to make a stand for what they believe in and to share their vision of a different future, and to the disruptors and innovators who have risked their reputations, financial security, and physical and psychological health in pursuit of the gender equality cause. I am grateful for the opportunities they have helped create for many women and men to make choices rather than accept a predetermined future based on outdated Gender Codes.

First published in 2020 by Danielle Dobson
codeconversations.com.au

A catalogue entry for this book is available from the National Library of Australia.

ISBN: 978-1-922391-07-0

Project management and text design by Michael Hanrahan Publishing
Cover design by Peter Reardon

Disclaimer

Contents

Part Four: How to write and execute your own code

Introduction

Do you feel like you are never doing and being enough? Would you like to understand more clearly what 'doing and being enough' means? What difference would that make to your daily life? Would it give you more space and energy to do what matters to you without feeling guilty?

Whether you work full-time, part-time, or flexibly across the week, and no matter how pressured your role is, at times it can feel as though everyone constantly wants things from you and the days are just too short. Trying to be the glue that holds everything together is hard at the best of times and impossible when sometimes you are the one falling apart. Would you like a solution and to feel as though there is a point where you will have a sense of balance?

Could it be that the things you are trying to achieve, thinking they will save you—work-life balance, me time, having it all, happiness, leaning in, leaning out, shattering the glass ceiling—are actually getting in the way and stopping you from having what you truly want?

You may be working too hard to formulate plans and strategies, to find the perfect time management system and build efficiencies into your day. Are you becoming caught up in "Perhaps I just need to do more tasks, more meditation, more activity, drink less wine, get more sleep, do a course, join a networking group, sign up to the gym?"

You may make some changes and create a rhythm which you maintain for short periods, but pressure builds up until you are on that treadmill, running five times faster than you planned to.

You are not alone. Your problems are typical, but fortunately there are solutions.

What is causing this? How did we get here? Who is responsible? When did it all become so hard?

1

It's time to change the way you are thinking and acting

If you want something different, it is crucial to understand more about society and identify the established cultural beliefs and stereotypes that have become truth, to see them for what they are: myths and stories.

With mostly good intentions, structures of power have evolved to make sense of the environment and manage the people who live within it. We all live within certain structures—gender, race, colonial relationships and class—which provide the set of rules of how to belong, embedded into our cultures over millennia that have formed the codes we live by.

The code that impacts the lives of women struggling, striving and straddling is the Gender Code.

When you accept, understand and break the Gender Code, you can explore its rules and expectations. You can question whether the externally created expectations of past millennia are relevant to you today and how you may be subconsciously perpetuating them and subconsciously creating your own personal pressures and barriers. These barriers may be getting in the way and preventing you from feeling that what you are contributing is enough.

This book puts the Gender Code under the microscope. It scrutinises the equation of productivity + busyness = worthiness and it dismantles outdated motherhood myths.

Rather than living according to what you assume society expects, you will be able to question the norms and choose for yourself what makes sense and fits with your values and purposes.

This book also describes key attributes and values of incredible people—just like you—who move through the many challenging stages of leadership and life, curious and open and learning from their mistakes, living with courage and compassion whatever the difficulties and struggles.

Rewriting the old story

With information, insight and practical tips, I would like to help you rewrite the old story of juggling everything to achieve an unattainable 'balanced life'. New possibilities are revealed so that you can create a different relationship with work, family and community. You can choose to focus on what is most important to you and build your resilience so setbacks do not derail you — so you are able to cope and bounce forward.

You have enough internal resources right now. This book shows that all that you do now is valuable and that being a parent or carer is not only having a positive impact on how humans flourish but is also a powerful career asset.

You don't need more of anything

What helps is to be who you truly are and use that as a driver, to give yourself permission to claim and step into your personal power. With this power, rather than straddling two worlds of career and life, you can create your own new, evolved world: one that works for you, rather than against you.

The genesis of the Gender Code

Sitting in a cosy cabin on Lake Washington in Seattle, October 4th, 2017, the sun streams through the window, creating a warm spotlight on my body. The companionable silence is punctuated by occasional speed boats on the lake and chirping birds. The smell of freshly ground coffee provides a sense of comfort and familiarity in a foreign place.

My coach Pam and I are two days into our three-day intensive business coaching course. It is 9 am and I feel like I have hit a brick wall.

My head is clouded, my stomach is in knots and I am out of ideas about how to ramp up my business. The whole point of my being here is to build my coaching practice. I performed a massive feat of family related logistical gymnastics to get here and I am starting to question myself, wondering if I have made the right decision.

How did I get here, to this crux in my life?

Twelve years earlier I had thought I knew exactly what it took to be successful. I was committed and worked long hours, immersed in my roles. I was driven by achieving financial security, and also wanted a warm, lovely home and to be able to give any future children the best education possible.

When I became a parent in my early 30s my priorities changed. Concentrating completely on work was no longer what I wanted. I wanted to be an engaged and present parent, and realised that if I continued working at the same pace, in my mind, I would be a half-arsed finance professional and a half-arsed parent. Not good for a 100 per center—my preferred way of operating. I needed to decide which was more important and chose to focus on parenting.

I was fortunate to be in a privileged financial position where I could take a career break so I stopped working. In terms of purpose and meaning, increasing shareholder wealth and bonuses for senior executives paled in comparison to investing in raising a healthy, happy human. My only view of the workforce and my place in it was all or nothing, so I decided to take the lead support role: lead parent, home CEO and supportive spouse.

One week I was immersed in the corporate world in America and the next week I was a mum. I had planned a fortnight's break before giving birth, but my son decided to arrive just after Thanksgiving, eight days early, the first sign that I was no longer in complete control. However, I felt it was where I was supposed to be, and my mission was to raise healthy, happy human beings.

Initially I viewed myself as a significant contributor to the marriage partnership and was able to use my strengths to achieve desired outcomes. We had a shared mission of running a home and raising children. My husband (let's call him Fred) had the breadwinning and career portfolio and I had everything else. I was the quintessential corporate wife with the added bonus of having worked in my husband's firm for three years in a senior finance capacity, so I knew the operations, politics and pressures from an insider's perspective.

When my main focus was kids, family and community, I felt valued. It was exactly where I wanted to be.

Fred was travelling 80 per cent of the time and, with three young sons aged one, three and five years old (the second and third were lucky shots between business trips), I was struggling to accept our situation. The cracks in our marriage were becoming chasms. I felt pressure to be hyper-responsible for everyone and everything and he only felt responsible for contributing financially.

I had assumed that being a parent would be a shared mission, but the reality was in stark contrast and difficult to navigate.

Following a family relocation to Beijing for a year, our marriage ended, and Fred and I established a new partnership to raise our sons. While he provided financial support for the boys, I needed an income to support myself and cover the shortfall in the monthly maintenance. I had to become a breadwinner as well as the primary care-giver—to create something out of nothing and start from ground zero to build a business. It was important to me to have the flexibility of working when and where I wanted in order to be the parent I envisaged.

I struggled with the transition, because I had not really accepted that my model and definition of fulfilment needed to change. So I dragged myself towards paid work kicking and screaming, because I needed to be financially independent. I did not want to end up one of the growing number of women facing an uncertain financial future in their 40s and beyond. I needed to start earning and rebuilding my career. However, my heart belonged to the old model I had built my life on: I was convinced that it was not possible to be successful at work and be the parent I wanted to be.

I needed help.

I invested in myself professionally by becoming a coach and also financially by being coached by the best coach I could afford. This trip to Pam's home base in Seattle was the start of our one-year apprenticeship programme.

Pam could see that I was struggling and she said "You have got to get to know the people you want to support and coach better. What is going on for them? What are their biggest challenges? How can you help them?"

These few questions blew up my world and I decided that the people I wanted to support and work with in my coaching practice should be women who lead in their careers and also take on the majority of the parenting responsibilities — lead parents.

This was the birthplace of The Wonders of Women Leaders market research project.

Everyone has a unique context

I set out to understand my clients' particular perspective and how being a leader, taking on responsibilities in both major areas in their lives, affects their wellbeing. I also wanted to know how being a parent detracts from or enhances their performance as a leader and how being a leader enhances or detracts from their parenting capacity. Rather than focusing on two separate worlds, I wanted to see what works well across all areas and what strengths they bring and build in both.

To honour and respect the inspiring people who shared their confidences and insights with me, I have quoted them throughout the book, but I have not attributed names and titles in most circumstances to protect their privacy. There were well over 100 conversations and I formally interviewed and recorded 52 people (including four men) working at different levels in finance, banking, petrochemicals, the automotive industry, government, engineering, education, medical and health, recruitment, hospitality, not-for-profit, science, information technology, coaching, and journalism. The majority — 70 per cent — work full-time and a quarter work flexibly across the week and are paid for three or four days.

While I started by interviewing women who are parents, I expanded the criteria and included men and women highly recommended by the research participants for their outstanding leadership and caring. Over 60 per cent had two children, 15 per cent had three or more children and 9 per cent had no children.

The burning questions

Although I worked from a list of questions (which is included in the Appendix), often the conversations would move in different and deeper directions. Starting simply, I would ask what a good day looks like and what gets in the way, and from there we would move to discussing the biggest challenges as a leader and a parent, what works well and what influences decision-making. Typically I would also ask about sources of support, how to build connections and community, ways to transition between work and home, helpful things they wish they had known years before and their greatest hopes for leaders of the future.

Confidential conversations

The people I spoke with all have demanding roles and often back-to-back meetings for weeks ahead, so I was grateful for the energy and attention they dedicated to this project. The appetite to share was huge, and the interview gave them a confidential space to be seen, heard and acknowledged without an agenda and with no performance outcomes attached. They felt safe to be honest and open.

What is really happening?

Of the many themes that emerged from the interviews and further research, I have identified the five that are key. Some themes were acknowledged and discussed, while others were not so obvious and deliberately or subconsciously hidden.

1. Leaders are lonely

I knew women are under pressure to do more with less but I did not realise to what extent they suffer. Some women leaders are lonely, and feel their wellbeing is not a top priority to anyone around them. They are trying so hard to be everything to everybody and to be hyper-responsible, and it is costing them. It is costing them in terms of their health, wellbeing, sense of values and contribution and the opportunities to progress in their careers.

2. Women are trapped

Women seem to be feeling trapped in a myth, believing that they should aspire to have it all, and depleting themselves in the process. They are so conflicted between working and parenting that they feel overstretched as they juggle, and feel judgment, shame and guilt.

3. Women are not feeling Wonder Woman worthy

What also emerged was that most women I spoke with place a high value on setting everyone around them up for success and human flourishing, yet are unaware of the extent of the positive impact this has. From the outside they look like Wonder Women (which inspired the original title of the project), performing at high levels of productivity and achievement, but not one felt she was worthy of the superhero title. They feel that the way they live and operate is just what they do and what they and society expect.

They find it much easier to see brilliance in others than in themselves.

4. What is surprising about parenting

Everyone I spoke with said that becoming a parent changed them fundamentally. This was no surprise, but what was surprising was how much their contribution at work and their leadership style changed for the better, and how it impacted the people around them. The experience of being a parent was integral in helping them to further build their self-awareness, empathy and self-regulation—important emotional intelligence skills. They also built or strengthened other talents such as flexibility, adaptability, critical thinking, prioritisation, efficiency and creativity. These critical skills are desperately needed in the workplace, leadership and all areas of life.

5. Gender disparity is a massive hurdle

What also kept coming up were observations and experiences around gender disparities, pay inequality, discrimination and inappropriate treatment of women in the workplace. These disparities extended to home life and the unequal distribution of unpaid work.

Where did all of this come from? It all seemed so unfair. All I knew was that I wanted to fix it.

What began as The Wonders of Women Leaders market research project morphed into a grounded theory research mission. I searched, inquired, interviewed, read books, articles, blogs, magazines, social media, attended events, joined various networking groups and did everything I could in an effort to understand and make sense of the gender disparities most people experience on a daily basis—disparities implanted in our cultures over millennia: the Gender Code.

Universal truths

While most of the people I spoke to have leadership roles, the themes emerging from the research are universal truths which we can all identify with. I don't know exactly where you are at right now, but I guarantee that if you join me and read this book, my insights will help you see things through a different lens; you will understand you already have everything you need, and that giving the best you have is enough. You will be equipped to create solutions and step into a new world filled with opportunities for you and everyone you love, living life on your own terms.

part one
WHERE ARE WE NOW?

1 What is happening to us?

"Trying to be good at everything or trying to be there for the kids and also trying to get everything done in the business. It's really challenging. It's trying to be all things to all people, and I think as a mother you've got the kids, the husband, the dog, the job—everyone wants a slice of the action. No matter who feeds the dog, it's me she stands in front of when she's hungry."

It is clear that women are under immense pressure and feeling overwhelmed.

The mental health struggle is real

Women (and men) can feel quite isolated and disconnected as a consequence of the relentless pursuit of productivity and busyness. Dedicating your all to work and family administration and jampacking your days may result in little or no energy for outside activities such as exercise, friendship and the extracurricular opportunities which give perspective and balance.

You may feel it in yourself or see it in others anecdotally, but when lived experiences are combined with the following data from studies, it packs a powerful punch.

The Women's Health Survey

In 2018, a survey involving over 15,000 Australian women conducted by not-for-profit organisation Jean Hailes found almost half had been diagnosed by a doctor or psychologist with anxiety or depression. 67 per cent reported having felt nervous, anxious or on edge several days a week over the four weeks before the survey. Over a third reported that they were unable to carve out any time for themselves on a weekly basis.

Are you surprised to learn this?

Wellbeing Survey

Findings from a sample of 1,000 female and male leaders, compiled by the *Global Leadership Wellbeing Survey (GLWS)* and published in October 2018, showed that females report lower wellbeing overall and specifically in their home, social and personal lives compared to their male counterparts.

The data showed that women experience more self-doubt at work and compromise more in their careers. In their home, social and personal lives, women feel stuck on fast forward and would like a slower pace and more tranquillity, and are more likely to experience guilt about neglecting their non-work responsibilities—devoting attention to their children, family and friends.

Can you relate to any or all of this?

UK and Australian studies on chronic stress

UK researchers from the Universities of Manchester and Essex discovered that chronic stress is 18 per cent higher in mothers who work full-time and are raising one child, and 40 per cent higher in full-time working mothers with two children.

This theme is backed up by Australian studies. Rae Cooper, Professor of Gender, Work and Employment Relationships, University of Sydney, speaking on the ABC Radio National programme on 6 February 2019, agreed that women in Australia working full-time while parenting two children are the most stressed people in the workforce.

Do you have times when you suffer from chronic stress? If so, how does it manifest itself?

What is it costing us?

The relentless work of the daily juggle is taking its toll on women's physical and mental health. Women are trying to achieve everything on their endless to-do lists and, in the process, suffering from sleep deprivation and exhaustion. This impacts cognitive functioning, impulse control, emotional intelligence, empathy and engagement and keeps them persistently overwhelmed and on the edge of burnout.

It is affecting our relationships

It has a knock-on effect too on relationships with kids, partners, direct reports, colleagues, leaders, family and their community. The women I interviewed expressed frustration and remorse at not having the space or time for conversation, nor having time to spend with the important people in their lives. They admitted they often lose perspective and balance and that work takes centre stage. They understand that the pace they operate at is not sustainable and feel tired and stressed, which drains their energy, sense of joy, and personal and professional fulfilment. On a bad day it feels too hard, like they are on the verge of a nervous breakdown, and the lack of support and respect can result in a sense of not coping.

Where is the off switch?

Women confided that they want to find a way to switch off and contain their stress. They are losing themselves in the daily grind and feel they can't trust their instincts—some can't even remember a time when they could trust their instincts. They are worried they might be setting a bad example to their children.

Feeling depleted day in, day out means that the ability to live, connect and lead is severely compromised.

It is generally not recognised, but what women with many roles are doing is exceptional. So often they feel frustrated and it is understandable if they want to give up. Words of recognition may help, but if they are working and not getting any recognition at all from anyone it is easy to think "Oh my God, I'm exhausted all the time; this is the end of me."

Do you have these thoughts and feelings?

Do you wonder what is driving all of this? What are the specific challenges you face?

2 Why is working and parenting so tough?

"You actually need a certain amount of sleep to lay down memories, and I reckon the sleep deprivation post children is nature's way of making sure you have more than one child, because you don't actually have enough sleep to lay down the memories of how bad it was for the first six months."

Asking the research participants what their biggest challenges were, the number one that emerged was achieving a sense of balance, a problem shared worldwide by anxious mothers.

Does this ring true for you?

Balance—wanting it, finding it, keeping it

Thinking and feeling you have the balance right overall of time and energy, work and family is difficult. There's always that pull.

"You want to spend more time with your daughter, and your daughter might want to spend more time with you. And when work's busy, you want to spend more time at work. You're enjoying it. You've got things to do. So it's just trying to get that balance between it all."

Working and having leadership responsibilities and being a mother —it is hard to balance it all. You have a career that you want and you want to continue progressing in, but how do you do that without

17

impacting the kids? So the kids think all you do is spend time at work and not with them.

How much of the quest is driven by outside-in thinking, where our external world influences our choices, behaviours and actions the most, how much by inside-out thinking, where our internal world is more influential? Or is it a combination?

Is there more to balance than we currently believe? Is working hard to seek it actually an elusive quest?

Let's look more closely at balance

After putting balance under the microscope and examining what it really means, seven interrelated sub-themes emerged. These provided more depth to the problem and a way to understand why women are under so much pressure.

1. Why do we feel we are not doing enough, being enough or choosing well?

The constant question that women ask themselves is "How am I doing and is it enough?" When we don't feel we are good enough or successful enough this influences our choices, behaviours and wellbeing, so it came up frequently with women who are not content unless they are delivering to an even higher standard.

It is hard to separate your family responsibilities from your professional ones. You want to be there for your children and family, yet you are committed to your work, too.

Women feel as though it is really hard to feel like you are doing everything well. It can feel like you are constantly compromising on something. There is a real pull for your time and presence. Your children want you to be energetic and present, so if you're exhausted and a bit preoccupied, they sense it straight away.

Are you constantly making choices about what is right? Wondering whether to spend half an hour with your children and the important people in your life? Just to be with them or doing something productive? It is tough, constantly trying to work out how to use your time wisely and be present, and also trying please everyone.

One person I spoke with said her son's memory of his childhood was that his parents were not available and that she was never home.

2. Why are we doing more with less?

How do you deal with the challenges when you are constantly stretched by endless tasks and activities in a fast-changing world? You may find there are constant pressures to absorb more and more tasks in your day at work and beyond. Do you find yourself researching and setting up opportunities for others to flourish and succeed, upskilling at work, absorbing departing team members' tasks, and taking on additional responsibility for yourself and others?

> *"Flexibility is such a nasty word. In the name of flexibility we are giving our lives away, we are working after the children go to bed, we work before they wake up, we work to the point that we lose our mind in order to meet this flexibility. We can't do it all. It doesn't work that way."*

Attempting to do everything when there are finite resources and an endless list of tasks and activities that seem to grow and reproduce is challenging.

You may have days that drain your emotional well when things are really busy or frantic at home and at work. You may have a week that is really full-on at work by anyone's measure and it is high pressure. And then the same week you realise that your son or daughter really wants you to attend assembly because he or she is receiving a prize. These are the weeks that women are struggling with and could do without.

3. Why everyone depends on us — being everything to everyone

This was a consistent theme that mothers relate to, which impedes their sense of balance. So many women find it incredibly challenging to fill several roles simultaneously and be the all-seeing, all-knowing oracle with all the answers to everyone's needs, frustrations, disappointments, problems and desires.

This ranges from answering the question, "Where is my [insert difficult to find but obviously positioned object here, from socks to book to keys]?" to refereeing sibling arguments and managing the weekly family timetable, as well as being the sounding board at work for personal and professional challenges — and everything in-between.

Women are also adding aging parents to their list of responsibilities, which takes a toll personally and professionally. Include a child with high needs, a challenging teenager, testing toddler, developing pre-schooler or a mix of other family and child dynamics and the pressure escalates.

You may experience this too when you are trying to be everyone's person and, in the process, your own needs are forgotten.

4. Why don't we want to let anyone down?

A common challenge in the balance equation is over-committing regardless of personal cost. Letting people down is not an option. But the deeper insight that emerged on this topic was actually a question of who are we letting down? Is it more that we feel we are letting ourselves down and not meeting our own high expectations?

Letting someone down is unfortunate and, when your work really requires 120 per cent of you and it leaves nothing at home, it is really difficult. But it happens; you can't avoid that all the time.

5. Having to deal with the unexpected

Even the best time management system designed by seasoned professionals cannot insure against unexpected obstacles, and the entire day can be determined by the flow of key periods such as the morning routine.

If things happen and you've got a child who is sick or doesn't want to go to school then it all falls to pieces. Or if you're running late because you can't get out the door. What happens in the morning with the kids does actually have an influence on and impacts the rest of your day.

Then throughout the day if key stakeholders do not operate as expected and additional effort and attention are required and deviation from the well-designed plan occurs, the pressure is dialled up several notches.

"...everything's okay until it falls off the rails. I had a meeting and as I sit down I get a phone call from the after-school care. My son had slipped over, smashed his teeth, smashed his face, there's blood everywhere.

"I've got to get back home. I've got to get the car. I've got to go pick him up and then arrange a dentist's appointment. And then I had the auditors coming at noon, which I had to be at. So it's those tough things when you've got it all planned. You've got it all scheduled and then someone's sick or something happens and it throws your nicely little organised plan all out."

6. Why it is so hard to carve out time and space?

You may dedicate a good portion of the day and a great deal of energy to setting everyone around you up for success and creating the conditions for them to flourish: preparing meals, ensuring family administration tasks are performed, devising plans and communicating logistics and projects, corresponding with people responsible for activities, and, at work, encouraging feedback, gaining perspective, direct reporting, supporting and encouraging colleagues—the list is endless and often at the expense of your own opportunities to rest, recover or play, which affects your sense of balance.

Finding your own time, time for yourself or down time, can be very hard. You leave work, you might still think about work all the time, but when you get home then there's dinner to cook, washing to do. You need to do something for your kids, help with homework, and offer some coaching. Then you go to bed, and then it all starts again six hours later.

"I would say that that need to always do something or be doing something is worse now that I've had kids, because I think not that you don't have you time, but generally it's really hard to get space for yourself, like that brain space.

"You've got either the kids or work, and sometimes one will be before the other depending on what's going on with work and what's going on with the kids. Generally you're the last person as the mum. You sacrifice for everybody else. It's hard to wind down."

7. Why aren't we honest about not coping?

An energy-draining challenge is the fear of being judged, of giving the impression of struggling with work priorities and family responsibilities.

How many women put on a brave face and wear the mask of doing it all well for fear of being considered incapable of high-level performance?

"As female leaders, there's a few of us within the senior team and also at management level that are mums and carrying out particular roles. A lot of our roles in our organisation, people would probably be challenged by balancing work and life.

"The reality is we don't talk about it with each other. I know how I feel about it and, if it came up with somebody I don't work with, I might be quite comfortable saying "You know what? It's such a juggle. It's really hard to be everything to everyone," and I personally really struggle and I feel like I'm not doing enough at home and I'm not doing enough at work.

"I don't share how challenging things are at work because I feel like maybe I'd be judged or it's not okay to bring those things into work. Even though I wouldn't mind if people did it to me. We communicate problems when they get to breaking point, and we don't encourage working mums to talk about things before they become a problem."

This problem is not confined to the workplace. It also plays out in mother and baby groups.

Jamie was struggling after the traumatic birth of her first daughter. Nothing had gone as planned: she had had an emergency caesarean section, was torturing herself trying to breastfeed and her family support network had fallen away unexpectedly. She was surrounded by seemingly perfect women and seriously questioning her ability to cope.

"They didn't want to talk openly about how hard it all was. We don't naturally know what to do when we become a mother, but we have these high expectations. I felt so much pressure. I had to challenge the group so I owned up and said I was struggling. It was like everyone let out a sigh of relief, and from then the conversation changed. We were more honest about all of the problems."

The fear of judgment is a consistent mental and emotional barrier for women who are parents and operating at any level. How much of the judgment originates from the externally driven stories, myths and models built over a lifetime?

What our Bad Moms have to say

Curious for more perspectives — and the Hollywood version — as part of my research I watched the 2016 movie *Bad Moms*. Admittedly quite a lot happens in a short period of time and the changes in the characters seem to occur at warp speed, however there were several key moments most mums can relate to.

The three main characters are mums are bonding in a bar following a harrowing day for the main character, Amy. Her hyper-organised, high-performing life explodes after a series of events outside her control and she experiences a breakdown of sorts.

In the movie their solution to the pressure is to swing the pendulum from hyper-responsible to the opposite, and Amy decides it is time to violate all of the Good Mom stereotypes. She is initially vilified for not living up to the ideal, but ultimately respected for her honesty and openness about how difficult it really is to be perfect. This way of facing pressures may not appeal to everyone, but perhaps you have fantasised about it. I know I have.

3 Why it matters that women are suffering

"We need females; females will save the world. That's why they always say we would have less war in the world if we had more female leaders. More times than not, females don't feel right doing the wrong thing."

When you are overwhelmed it is easier to be judgmental and, as a result, reactive. In these moments it is difficult to have clarity, and when you don't have clarity it is hard to be creative and think differently. You keep looking outside yourself to find answers to your problems. You try to change your external environment by looking at your stressors, which may be people, tasks, job role, physical surroundings—anything or anyone causing you distress. Then you find a way to eliminate the perceived stressors or make them easier to deal with.

Are you actually trying to avoid the uncomfortable feeling of not being in control? When women are tired, stressed or overwhelmed, instead of resting and recovering or investing positively in wellbeing, they may do more to get back a sense of control. This creates a downward spiral of heaviness and energy drain.

What is the impact?

Working hard is fertile ground for perfectionism, productivity pressure, and expectation gaps, carrying the mental and emotional load, parental guilt, shame and judgment. Living this way handicaps you. It may mean that you are actually fighting with one hand tied behind your back.

It is easy as a woman to lose yourself in the struggle to juggle work, partner, children, parents and friends. When you lose yourself and feel disconnected, energy levels are lower and the ability to contribute decreases. When you don't feel you are contributing to the best of your ability, gaps form in terms of your expectations of yourself and other people.

A gap can grow to a chasm if you don't feel valued and aligned with what is most important to you. If left unchecked, the chasm can fester and lead to the greatest disconnection of all: loneliness in a sea of people, disconnection from those you love.

Can you release the pressure and connect?

It is essential for you to stay connected and build a solid foundation to experience joy, focus on the things that are most important to you, find perspective and balance, switch off and minimise stress.

A sense of freedom, general ease and fulfilment gives you the energy to invest in your health. Take a breath and slow down. Create time and space for relationships. It makes a difference in all your leadership roles when others see and recognise your value.

You have a crucial role to play in the world now and in the future. Using all your experience, you can have an exponential influence on your children and the world they will inherit, your families and the relationships you build with them, people in your communities whom you support and who support you, and your colleagues at work. You have an exciting opportunity to be a leader in the future of human flourishing.

It is important to understand that wherever you are is absolutely okay. It is exactly where you need to be right now. Whether you feel the important parts of your life are serving you well and you are serving them equally well, or you feel persistently overwhelmed and need support, or somewhere in-between, I want you to know that it is fine for you right now.

But you don't have to stay there. You can choose something else.

It is time to look at expectations through a different lens and reveal the Gender Code.

part two

HOW DID WE GET HERE? LET'S TALK ABOUT THE GENDER CODE

4 Man hunter, woman gatherer?

"Gender is a combination of cultural, social, biological and psychological elements. Gender is how we look, act and feel."
Dr Sarah McKay[1]

Why the Gender Code exists today

It is 3:05 in the afternoon, March 2018, and I have shut out the noise of the outside world. I am in my natural-light-starved, Lilliputian office using only a desk lamp for illumination. I am focused and centred, interviewing Elli, the 21st participant in my research project.

Elli is the chief financial officer of a major infrastructure project and a non-executive director. She is in her fifth decade and has had extensive experience in the finance, banking and commercial worlds. There is strength and wisdom in her words. She has overcome traumatic professional and personal challenges, burnout and breakdown.

Elli illustrates the plight of many women in similar roles, and also gender inequality with the story of a lunch she had been to the day before for a government financing body with $90 billion of funds managed within the state. The guest presenter was a female fund manager who said she was essentially the only female fund manager anywhere, and

---

1 *The Women's Brain Book: The Neuroscience of Health, Hormones and Happiness,*
 Dr Sarah McKay, pg 14

when she asked a chairperson why his organisation did not have gender equality on the board, he replied "What do you mean? We've got one."

The lunch guests laugh, but Elli's response was "No, don't laugh. It's not funny. Oh shit, we've got to fix that."

This really got my attention. Why do decision-makers and people in charge of important financial projects laugh at how few women are in leadership positions? The people with the money have the most power. Elli was right, and it became an 'oh shit moment' for me too.

How do gender and gendered behaviour play a leading role in the workplace and beyond? What are the barriers about? How did they get there? Why are they so difficult to break down?

What has caused gender differences?

What are the contributing factors causing distinctions between genders? Are they related to testosterone levels or physical strength? Are they related to childhood experiences? Perhaps there are differences in our brains that can solve the mystery. Maybe evolutionary biology can help us understand.

Or is there a lot more to it?

Why the myths about our evolutionary past hold us back

I thought that nature had reasons why men seem to wield more power and influence than women, that our genetic make-up explains why most women seem better at caring for children than most men and were designed to be more capable nurturers. I completely bought into the hunter-gatherer myth that men are generally more suited to breadwinning and women to providing support and managing the family—guilty of believing and conforming to the Gender Code and harbouring internalised misogyny!

Not that I thought men and women could not exchange roles. It was a case of playing to the strengths of the individuals for the benefit of the whole. Nor did I believe that men or women are superior in terms of intelligence, work ethic or morality—just better at different tasks.

Everything changed when I discovered a book by Angela Saini, *Inferior: How Science Got Women Wrong—and the New Research That's Rewriting the Story*. Angela puts many of the gender myths shaped and perpetuated by current and historical scientific understanding under the microscope, and the insights are life-changing.

While there continues to be debatable research on the differences between sexes, some researchers have a transformative perspective on women's minds, bodies and our evolutionary history. There are new theories suggesting the differences in women's and men's brains are statistical anomalies, driven by the fact that each human is unique, and Angela's research has unearthed some inconvenient truths about sex and gender.

After decades of meticulous research and testing girls and boys, her work, and that of others in the same field, confirms that there are few psychological differences between the sexes. The differences identified are substantially encultured and not innate.

This research into our evolutionary past reveals that the division of labour and roles according to sex and gender and domination by males is not part of our DNA. Some argue that it is programmed biologically into human society. Rather than adhering to a gender code, we were once an egalitarian species. Further research is busting another ancient myth that women are naturally less promiscuous than men.

Given the potential backlash and benefits of the findings, the research is thorough and evidenced-based. It completely challenges age-old concepts and beliefs about the meaning of being a woman. The long-held view is that women are subservient, weak and unable to excel in anything outside the home. Many patronising, 'soft' adjectives have been employed to distinguish women as the gentler, more empathetic and, the old favourite, fairer sex. However current scientific research—and personal experience—show that individual women are as intelligent, strong and strategic as men. And they always have been.

This reinforces the imperative of sexual equality.[2]

"When it comes to family and working life, the biological rule seems to be that there were never any rules. While the realities of childbirth and lactation are fixed, culture and environment can dictate how women live just as much as their bodies do." Angela Saini[3]

---

2   *Inferior: How Science Got Women Wrong—and the New Research That's Rewriting the Story*, Angela Saini, pg 10 and 11

3   Ibid., pg 119

Who is keeping everyone alive?

Was the hunter-gatherer belief a way science asserted male dominance and kept women in a support role?

The hunter-gatherer theory was popularised in the 20th century and still subconsciously forms the foundation for the way families are structured, although people who refer to it often do not understand where it came from and how incomplete it is.

Hunting is considered the most significant activity in human evolutionary history. The assumed associated skills are working collectively in teams and groups, developing strategy, being innovative and creative, building tools and weapons, and developing language. Obviously catching prey and delivering food led to the logical belief that men were able to provide nourishment, thus hastening human development.

The focus is often on the hunters and their critical importance. What about the rest of the tribe, the gatherers? Research conveniently swept under the carpet shows that gathering was probably a more important calorie source than hunting!

Research conducted on the !Kung hunter-gatherers in Africa and published in 1979 by Richard Lee, organiser of the 1966 conference 'Man the Hunter', pointed out that gathering activities resulted in as much as an estimated 66 per cent of the food in the tribe's diet.

The women in the group were predominantly responsible for organising shelter, preparing meals and playing a support role in the hunts even while pregnant and raising children.[4]

It would have also been necessary for mothers and gatherers to keep their children alive in a natural environment with no playpens or child locks—a pretty incredible accomplishment! Mothers and gatherers would also have been responsible for teaching, passing down customs, warning about possible dangers in the environment, and using language—all intellectual challenges essential to survival and human flourishing.

Share the load to survive

It is estimated that the harsh realities of living and survival would have compelled women and men to share workloads and be flexible.

---

4   Ibid., pg 109

Everybody learns everything in hunter-gatherer societies; consequently there is less division of labour.

Although the division of labour concept has not been popularised over millennia, it is definitely possible. If your life, the life of your family and your tribe's survival depend on having tribe members playing to their strengths, then the choice based on sex chromosomes of who hunts and who gathers is a matter of survival.

> "In our ancient past, thousands of years ago, it's even possible that men would have been far more involved in childcare and gathering while women would have been hunters." Angela Saini[5]

Why your support environment dictates your level of mastery

Environment played a huge part in people's roles. If the environment was dangerous for hunting, women were less likely to go as it was more important that a child not lose their mother than their father or another male. The survival of the tribe is more dependent on the mother's survival, and having family and village members willing and able to care for children was vital in terms of the roles women filled.

> "If the culture does not provide enough support for women in terms of childcare or other work, a woman may simply be unable to put in as many hours as a man to perfect her skills, making her a less useful killer." Angela Saini[6]

This understanding of how our ancestors perpetuated the hunter-gatherer belief system to support the aims of people in charge of knowledge and maintain the status quo is very powerful. However the reality is completely different, for if the culture—family, work, community—does not provide support to raise children and care for other tribe members, women are less able to develop mastery in their work, perfect their skills and contribute at a high level in any sphere.

In short, biology and physical make-up are not barriers to meaningful work or a reason to be the main carer. Women are not naturally suited

---

5 Ibid., pg 114
6 Ibid., pg 118

to caring any more than men are, but were trained to care using available internal and external resources.

This is valuable to know right now as women progress in leadership positions and take on increasing workloads. We were never meant to do it all on our own. We have been trained to do it!

It takes a village—collaboration and cooperation 101

Since women did not evolve to raise children single-handedly, it is not the primary responsibility of the mother to be everything to her children.

Logically it is possible to understand this, but are the old messages and Gender Code still in charge? If the women are out hunting, who looks after the kids and does the important human flourishing and caring jobs?

If childcare is not the sole responsibility of mothers, who else can be relied upon?

There is more and more evolutionary scientific evidence from anthropologists to conclude that cooperative breeding is important to understanding the human story. Evidence is shifting the focus to the importance of 'alloparents'—people who play central roles in the lives of other people's children.[7]

> "There needs to be more support for mothers, working mothers. And, interestingly, why are we always classified as working mothers? Nobody is classified as a working father.
>
> "Even that title or that description implies that we have the primary care. And so there should be more support around childcare for working people, and that would allow it to be more equitable."

Why we need to understand the pyramid system

With this knowledge of science and evolution and what is possible, the question is why society became less egalitarian and how we got where we are today.

Exploring this conundrum drew me into the world of patriarchy.

---

7   Ibid., pg 105

In the interviews, patriarchy was regularly referred to in terms of gender inequality. Not always perpetuated by males, patriarchy is a system of control followed by both men and women. Markers include individualism, oppression, dominance, rigid social rules and aggressive allegiances to tribes.

I tend to think of patriarchal structures as pyramids where there is room for only one person at the top. More inclusive systems can be represented by circles. Knowing what is structural and not personal helps to understand and learn.

"I had to educate my husband about patriarchy and male privilege, because it's not something that came to him easily. He kept thinking privilege means that you've got access to some private clubs or something. I'm trying to explain the concept of privilege to him: 'You have a privilege not of your asking. But there is a system that's benefiting you without you asking.'

"I was so thankful we had two daughters because my husband can start to see now. 'Oh, it's different for the girls.' They are treated differently when they go out. And he's now become very alert to it, but I had to help him see it."

There are many well-meaning, loving, professional, educated men and, if you can start to deepen your important male's perspective and change his mindset around patriarchy and privilege, it will help you with challenges in the workplace. Most men in the workplace may be like your partner, without any bad intentions, however not understanding privilege — and patriarchy is a real challenge.

Change is happening slowly. I spoke with men who have been outliers throughout their careers and have not been part of boys' clubs, even though they know they exist. Why? They see the benefits of having diversity rather than "We follow the rules and it's about who you drink with, who you are friends with." One male's perspective is that over the last 15 years or more there has been a more marked shift in the workplace with how people want to work. And there are a lot of males now who actually don't like the boys' clubs either.

Why the pyramid was built

Family dynamics provide a solid foundation that sets us up for success or failure in future relationships, friendships, school experiences, workplace and group belonging, and way of operating.

Most people have known gender expectations and bias either in their own or friends' families. Factors influencing family culture and stereotypes include position, class, race, experiences, financial means and religion—mainstream religious texts which perpetuate the patriarchy. (Only 36 per cent of Australians are religious, yet the stereotypes remain.)

Traditionally females have been considered more fragile, in need of protection and less able to determine their own financial future.

What does patriarchy have to do with this?

Gender power imbalance perpetuated for millennia is based on the human desire to protect resources, which is fed by the fear of losing out to others and feeling diminished.

As our societies moved from subsistence living and became denser thanks to the domestication of animals and the development of agriculture, allowing us to store our resources, specialised groups controlled by men started to form.

"…as they accumulated land, property and wealth, it would have become even more important for men to be sure their wives were unswervingly faithful. A man who could not guarantee his babies were his own wasn't just being cuckolded, but also risked losing what he owned. Mate-guarding intensified." Angela Saini[8]

Could it be that women have been viewed as weaker, less intelligent, less capable and less sexually promiscuous for millennia primarily to ensure the males in the family are able to hold onto their resources? In many cultures, women are still classified as the property and possessions of their fathers, husbands, brothers and sons. Women in ancient Egypt had more rights and relative freedom than women in Victorian Britain.

Women in the ruling classes were the most protected from outsiders and inappropriate suitors. Their chastity was fiercely guarded as their families had the most to lose financially and socially from illegitimate offspring.

---

8   Ibid., pg 146

Studies and statistics reveal that negative mate-guarding behaviours can range from vigilance to violence by both males and females, but predominantly males.

Why Charles Darwin got it wrong

Rather than shedding light on the importance of the contribution women could make to science, the Enlightenment shut women out, further strengthening the patriarchal code. Women were expressly excluded from joining scientific organisations, investing in scientific learning and being part of important scientific experiments.

Charles Darwin, one of my heroes, believed wholeheartedly that women were intellectually inferior and less evolved than men. In *The Descent of Man*, Darwin reasons that males are superior as they have to work harder and be more attractive to earn a mate. He focused primarily on the animal kingdom, observing the lion and his mane and the peacock's colourful feathers. Reasoning that competing male animals had been forced to become warriors and strategic thinkers, Darwin felt men had developed more than women physically and mentally.

Looking for evidence to substantiate his theory, Darwin found that the most renowned philosophers, artists, scientists, politicians, religious leaders, historians, sportspeople and adventurers were men, which made it easy for him to conclude *"The chief distinction in the intellectual powers of the two sexes is shewn by man attaining to a higher eminence, in whatever he takes up, than woman can attain—whether requiring deep thought, reason, or imagination, or merely the use of the senses and hands."*[9]

I have learned to forgive Darwin. It was the culture of his time, which shows how cultural norms of the past and related myths based on incomplete research and belief systems initiated, controlled and perpetuated by people in charge inevitably skew the interpretation of science. It also illustrates how history always reflects the society that the writer/scientist/artist has come from and to a large extent, their personal values. This is vital to understand in an age of limitless information forming people's 'truth'.

---

9 Ibid., pg 15

What about the bonobos, Mr Darwin?

Darwin did not know about bonobos though. In most primate groups, the males exert physical power over females and weaker group members and are aggressive, but this is not the case in bonobo monkeys.

You can learn a lot from bonobos about sexual interaction, promiscuity and connections. Although, like humans, female bonobos are approximately 20 per cent smaller than the males, they dominate and control the males by banding together. If a male bonobo starts to harass a female, all the other females will attack him.

This keeps the males in line—and they need a female ally to survive, which is the opposite of the human situation where the male will deliberately isolate a female from her network to gain control over her. This can be done by moving away and creating geographical distance, or through emotional influence and manipulation. In some cultures the separation is embedded in the ethnic code and wives are obliged to live with the husband's family after marriage, which isolates them and makes them easier to control.

Perhaps women should be more like bonobos: stick together and live on their own terms. What an impact this would have on domestic violence, financial and emotional abuse and subjugation.

Perhaps the patriarchal system understands how powerful women are working together and this is why it is so intent on dividing and conquering.

Blame the female brain

The pattern of exclusion continued as science explained differences between genders. For centuries there has been a huge focus on brains, and given the female brain is typically smaller than male brains, it was used as a reason to justify male superiority.

Gina Rippon in her book *The Gendered Brain* describes Gender Code-driven brain beliefs as myths. In the early days of brain research, *"... indignities have been heaped upon it as being the cause of women's inferiority, vulnerability, emotional instability, scientific ineptitude—making them unfit for any kind of responsibility or power."*[10]

---

10 *The Gendered Brain: The New Neuroscience that Shatters the Myth of the Female Brain*, Gina Rippon, pg xii

The interpretation of science provided an explanation for why women were more suited to nurturing roles and being mothers and carers. With these special, natural qualities (driven by their brains), women were also more suited to being the supporters and companions of men in all of their personal and professional pursuits. And who was conducting the experiments? Who was drawing the conclusions and disseminating the information? Who had the most to gain from the results?

Experiments and technology improved, however the focus of the research tended to be on how female and male brains are different rather than how they are similar. Studies were set up to prove the stereotypes and designed in accordance with the convincing list of differences.

"If a difference was found, it was much more likely to be published than a finding of no difference, and it would also breathlessly be hailed as an 'at last the truth' moment by an enthusiastic media. Finally the evidence that women are hardwired to be rubbish at map reading and that men can't multi-task." Gina Rippon[11]

Now with more women working in scientific fields and more open-minded experimentation taking place, there is opportunity for a more balanced view. However, the stereotypes dictated by the code still linger. They are easier to believe.

How powerful religions strengthen the code

Most Western religious texts are written from the male perspective and perpetuate patriarchal thinking. Our value systems are based on Christian values, a powerful source of authority and influence. In the Old Testament, Eve is credited with tempting Adam with the forbidden fruit, which results in their being expelled from Eden.

Ferrying my sons between soccer games one Saturday morning, we were having a discussion about the historical accuracy of the Bible. I was explaining how the stories are more for guidance than a strict code of conduct when my youngest suddenly said "Yes, you really have to question whether the Bible is true, Mum, because there are people called Mark, Paul, John and lots of others who wrote it. They are all men. There

---

11 Ibid., pg xiii

are no women's names in the Bible writing the stories. How could it be 100 per cent true?"

I hadn't even thought of that myself, though I was raised Catholic. Thrilled with his insight, I said that a group of men had decided which stories written by other men would be included. How could it be accurate when 50 per cent of the population was not represented? They all agreed!

There is also evidence emerging to support the idea that women were instrumental in the early Christian church. Not only were they more active in supporting Jesus while he was living than is commonly believed but they played a pivotal role in keeping Christianity alive during the period when the Romans were persecuting anyone associated with the new religion.

It wasn't until AD 313 that Christianity was awarded legal status in Rome, and then women's importance was conveniently written out of the popular narrative. Without downplaying the role of women in Christianity, it would have been difficult for the Romans to sell the belief system to their patriarchal society.

Not everyone could have intended to support and strengthen the patriarchy and ensure women remained in an inferior position. Some must have simply adhered to the code that had seemed to work for millennia. If it didn't seem broken, why fix it?

Why it is crucial for you to understand the Gender Code

If we accept that human history started as a collaborative, egalitarian society, where we operated in an interdependent manner using our strengths for the good of the group in order to survive and flourish, there was little room for ego or self-serving behaviour.

As people moved from subsistence to farming, gathering and storing resources, society changed, building structures and creating roles in addition to hunting and gathering. There was a need to protect resources—property, possessions, people, knowledge and egos—which facilitated the systems of male control. Women, given our reproductive abilities and ability to affect the distribution of resources in terms of offspring, became subject to mate-guarding.

Mate-guarding became embedded and codified into cultures. Women were the physically weaker sex, requiring protection from mate-hungry males. Pre-marriage virginity, female monogamy, female genital mutilation, exclusion from paid work, modest dress code to cover female features, separation from female support networks and family after marriage were all baked into cultures to mate guard and protect property.

Mate-guarding is often masked by religious doctrine, and anyone who ventures outside the norms and defies the code is vilified. Effectively, the superpowers of shame and judgment punish whoever dares desire a different future or creates a new model. It is an insidious societal stigma related to separation and divorce and what happens to the family resources.

Despite scientific advances and the Enlightenment, gender stereotypes have been strengthened. Science was used to explain male superiority and female inferiority, and opened the door to gender essentialism and neurosexism, a term coined by psychologist Cordelia Fine.

Since women were excluded from politics, science, history, art, finance and philosophy, decision-makers only represented 50 per cent of the population.

Why we need to break down the pyramid

This structured hierarchy lasted for centuries and led to dependence, the patriarchy's preferred way of operating. However, hierarchical structures and motivations of leading and traditionally respected and trusted religious orders, banks, schools, universities, and finance and legal professionals have been challenged over the past 50 years. Trust has been breached and the institutions called to account.

Thus our society has moved from dependence on hierarchy and respected leadership to independence, similar to moving from childhood to adolescence. It is a time of questioning, challenging, awkwardness and, hopefully, growth.

Why it is time to adapt command and control

The days of command and control leadership are ending, and we are in an exciting phase where the world is creating a more sustainable model of leadership, valuing empathy, compassion, selflessness, adaptability and collaboration. We are focusing more on people's strengths and working toward and for the greater good.

As we transition towards investing more in sustainability, wellbeing and relationships, and valuing what is important to us and our planet, we are protecting and acknowledging our symbiotic relationship with the natural environment and placing a lower value on individualism and elevated egos. Our survival depends on working together collaboratively and in an egalitarian society.

This is important for you to know as you navigate the daily challenges related to all of your responsibilities. Most women already have the skills and attributes needed to work collaboratively and these are sharpened when they become a parent or carer. With a shift in perspective, and refocusing our current view of working and caring, we can understand that being a woman with caring responsibilities is a powerful leadership and career asset.

> *"If nature teaches us anything, it's that those species flexible enough to adapt to changing environments are the ones that survive."*
> Kelly Lambert[12]

---

12 *Unfinished Business: Women Men Work Family*, Anne-Marie Slaughter, pg 154

5 How the Gender Code plays out in your life today

You may think that gender equality has improved over time and especially in the last two years since #MeToo. The landscape has definitely changed: our expectations for equality have increased and inroads are being made. However the stereotypes are so embedded into how we think, feel and act that lasting change will take time. We need to pay particular attention to how the Gender Code operates in our lives today and how it is cultivated.

My first insight into the rules and expectations governing our daily environment was through a training video, *Invisible Rules: Men, Women and Teams*, by Dr Pat Heim, an expert on how men and women behave differently based on gendered norms. A senior executive in a male-dominated industry shared important elements that provide a guide not only in the workplace but in all relationships.

Having a discussion or solving a problem?

A woman may ask "Which pair of shoes should I wear?" Her partner replies "Those." She responds "What about these?" He says "It's been 20 years. I've never got it right. Why bother to ask me if you don't like the answer?"

Have you ever been a similar situation — not necessarily with shoes?

The fact is that because the question is wrong, the answer is wrong. She's not asking her partner to pick a pair of shoes; she's actually asking for a shoe discussion. If he enters into a shoe discussion, he has answered the question correctly. He is not actually being asked to choose a pair of shoes.

Transplanting a similar discussion to the workplace, a woman may ask a man "What do you think about this problem and these solutions?" And he says "That solution." Then she asks someone else who prefers another solution. And the first person says "Why did you bother to ask me?"

This scenario may play out across both genders, but stick with me.

The man thinks the woman is asking him to solve a problem, but she is actually just asking his opinion, and this can consume a great deal of emotional energy and jeopardise reputations, working relationships and workplace culture.

However, if the woman simply says "Business problem: I'm looking at these three options. I'm going to make the final call, but what are your thoughts?" she is being clear and succinct and he will not think he has given the responsibility of solving a problem, but the freedom to offer suggestions.

That goes a long way to explaining why male partners risk getting the shoe question wrong every time. The correct answer is actually a question: "Well, what dress are you going to wear? What handbag are you going to take?" The shoe discussion ensues and then she chooses.

There is a great deal to learn about being clear with communication and articulating process and outcomes with these examples. Right now, though, we are focusing on how gender plays a part in the default operating system.

How do we learn the Gender Code?

It all starts early in life with childhood play behaviours and the strong influence around gender socialisation, and continues to the workplace and beyond.

Most activities that boys engage in are competitive, whether it's cops and robbers, Nerf gun wars, football, soccer, tip or tag. Everything has rules and there is always a hierarchy. Boys learn very early that there are winners and losers, and if you are at the middle or lower end of the hierarchy/pyramid you lose more often than you win. Or, if you are like my eight-year-old and insist on playing with stronger, fitter, faster boys several years older, you lose almost all the time. You then have to use your non-physical strengths to compete.

Childhood play behaviour teaches boys and then men to look, learn, move on and focus on the next win.

The gendered games girls tend to play are mostly process and relational games such as dolls, drawing, acting and beading, so there is usually not a clear winner or loser.

Contrast boys and traditional boys' games: if they are playing football, they tend to pick the best players for the team based on the skills required to win. They may choose the biggest, roughest person to be on the team, because they are the biggest, roughest person, and not because they have exceptional social skills.

Girls are usually taught to nurture, whereas boys generally receive the message they need to take care of themselves and deal with challenges. This pattern of behaviour and expectation may continue throughout life, even though boys and men may also be compassionate and empathetic and know how to hold a sensitive conversation.

This is gender essentialism and how the Gender Code operates right now. It is not ideal or even fair, and I am confident of a more egalitarian future when we ask if the codes still make sense and then make choices that recognise what individuals contribute.

The Gender Code in my own life is clear. My sons reflect to the letter what the Gender Code can build for boys and men. They excel at taking physical risks—another element in the gender socialisation process—experimenting and learning, and building strength, self-confidence and resilience.

Thinking about your experiences, does this make sense?

How does it play out in your family? Are you gender blind?

One of the interviewees introduced me to her concept of gender blindness:

> "Australia is still far too male-orientated. Positions of power are
> still male-dominated because of the demands. If you want to have

a family, the child raising, caring, home duties fall on the female shoulders. There's an unequal distribution of housework, not work. Companies are getting it, but it is not happening in the home and that is the problem that women face. That is, in a nutshell, because of fathers, brothers, uncles, sons not carrying their weight."

Amanda grew up with three brothers and two sisters in a stereotypical environment. The boys gardened, mowed the lawn and washed the cars. The girls did the cooking and cleaned the bathrooms. Everything was done along gender lines. When Amanda met her husband's family, there was none of that and she was amazed. Her husband, one of three boys, would wash up and he set the table, tasks her brothers would never contemplate doing.

"Clearly he's my bedrock because he's gender blind and it's the best thing ever."

Amanda believes that the more men become gender blind, the greater the positive impact on homes and families will be, and that this will open up more opportunities for a woman to put in as many hours as a man in the workplace to perfect her skills and progress to pivotal leadership roles. The three leaders Amanda has most respected (who are male) have daughters and no sons.

I was shocked but not entirely surprised to realise the distinctions in how home work in families is acknowledged and rewarded. Domestic tasks traditionally viewed as women's work, such as washing the dishes, cleaning or preparing meals, are paid less if at all.

By contrast, outside or yard work, washing the car, mowing the lawns, building projects traditionally viewed as men's work are usually remunerated more handsomely, reinforcing the belief that work men are trained to do is more important and valuable than the work women are trained to do.

How do childhood play behaviour and conditioning play out in the workplace?

Most workplaces have an organisational chart detailing the roles and responsibilities of their people. There is usually one person at the top—the CEO or equivalent—then the executive level, senior/middle management and their teams. If you were to draw an outline shape of the organisational chart, what would it represent?

A triangle? Or a pyramid of hierarchy?

Boys and men are consciously or subconsciously trained to identify the hierarchical structures, find their place in them and move up (if they wish). Along the way they learn the rules of the game and how to move on from loss to the next win/opportunity/promotion. They are attuned to the strengths and weaknesses of the people they are competing with.

Women who have been trained in the gendered way are not prepared for this system. Their training has been more about process, relationships, collaboration, more of a circle.

Do circles fit with pyramids?

Women do the unpaid work at work

If women have been gender trained and their family dynamics dictated that girls are expected to do the inside work with little or no payment, is it any wonder that females in workplaces tend to do the unpaid work: tidying the kitchen, organising food, cleaning up after others?

If we can accept that the gendered way of operating for males is to focus on opportunities and progression up the pyramid and that this is expected and rewarded, is it any wonder that they do not usually do the unpaid tasks in the workplace? There is no training or expectation that they should.

What is your meeting etiquette?

In a meeting, two men may be confrontational, but go out for a beer together afterwards. If this happens with two women, is that discussion over when they leave the meeting? Are they likely to drop the loss and look towards achieving the next win?

Why is this important?

If you accept that, although it is not fair or ideal, it is the state of our current culture and you are the product of your upbringing subject to constant change and updating, then that may help you respond in terms of perspective and effective communication.

When you think about your own upbringing, how has your experience of being a woman influenced you? Does it determine how you treat girls and boys and how you parent/care for your own children?

Understanding the Gender Code can help you make decisions and take action in terms of parenting or caring for children. You may already operate an egalitarian household. You may think there could be some tweaking. If you choose to, you can start building equality into your family system and structure.

Your children and your family will benefit.

How does the Gender Code influence the gender pay gap?

A retired female partner in a financial services firm found that after 10 years, women doing the same jobs were paid 20 per cent less than their male colleagues. She admits with exasperation and disappointment that she has been a player in the system that underpays professional women.

A major reason she offered for the gender disparity issue is how men and women approach going to an appraisal: most males say they scored 10 out of 10 on this, 5 out of 5 on that and 6 out of 6 on that, exceeding expectations in everything. They also focus on the key tasks and performance areas where they exceeded expectations. There is less focus on the areas they failed in, and the fact they didn't do 10 other things they were meant to is not even mentioned.

A woman will say "Well, I didn't exceed expectations. I wasn't exceptional", even though she may have exceeded some expectations. Or "Well, I didn't quite hit my management mark here and I didn't quite hit it there, but did I okay in that. Overall I met my expectations." So the perception is "Yes, you met expectations. Good." Tick the box, fit the bell curve.

If we think of the traditional appraisal system with a 1 to 5 rating criteria, if more women tend to be in the middle range and more men on the right-hand side of the box.

If salary increases each year are determined by the 1 to 5 rating system based on where people come on that bell curve, the average pay increase for people who have met expectations is 2 per cent and, for those who exceed expectations, 4 per cent.

With this same pattern of behaviour and rating system, with the woman believing she is only meeting expectations, after 10 years, the male is being paid 20 per cent more.

Do you meet or exceed your work expectations?

"The fact that her expectations are higher than average is not so good for performance reviews."

The main obstacle is that women are working a system designed by men for the gendered male way of operating. The traditional performance review system is all about pushing rankings down and fitting the bell curve from exceptional to meeting expectations.

If women say they met expectations there is no additional administration or need to do anything. It is easy. Unfortunately, the system was never designed to push ratings up, so if someone says "I meet my expectations" in the review and their expectations are really high, they are likely to walk out with 'Met expectations'.

One of the many challenges for women is the Ginger Rogers and Fred Astaire analogy. Ginger Rogers had to do everything just as well as Fred Astaire, but do it backwards in high heels. They were both great dancers, but doing it backwards and in high heels must have been a lot harder.

"And the challenge is that women often have to, or feel they have to, over-exceed to be considered a peer."

Not only does the traditional performance and pay review process favour the male gendered way of operating, valuing self-promotion and higher confidence or bravado, but it is at odds with the way women place incredibly high expectations on themselves to achieve and be considered successful.

Women are often criticised for underselling performance or not marketing and celebrating successes. You are encouraged to speak up, let everyone know what you have accomplished and request promotion. But there is a great deal more to the challenge that is more complex to overcome.

Whose expectations are they?

Do women really believe the high performance hype? Do we believe we need to perform at the same perceived level, raising our own expectations of ourselves in the process?

I believe it is more that we don't feel as though what we do is exceptional, just a tough challenge and a combination. The women I spoke with seemed from the outside to be Wonder Women, helping others and performing at high levels, but as mentioned earlier, not one believed they were worthy of the superhero title.

Contributing to pressure are the variables based on personal life, mindset, family dynamics, sense of identity, world view and, essentially, the messaging we listen to most.

And where else does male high performance hype show up? Does it play out in relationships, in sport, as a parent, as a leader in the community? Where else do women accept the myth of men exceeding expectations? And what is it costing us?

How do we close the expectation gap?

A senior executive of a male-dominated petrochemicals company redesigned the performance review process to reflect actual performance, reducing the influence of the Gender Code. When he moderated the scores of all the teams, some men who had claimed they were exceptional were middle of the road and some women who rated themselves as middle of the road were exceptional. He adjusted the scores and salaries accordingly.

The approach he recommends is if an organisation has 50 per cent women in the workplace—and many places have not achieved this yet—it is important to actually benchmark and scale and rate people's performance. It is necessary to calibrate, and a critical step in the process is to ensure that more than one manager is saying "I think they're exceptional," as unconscious or conscious bias may be at play.

The company also started reviewing people as a peer network, identifying them and what they did that made them exceptional.

"Everyone should know that person's exceptional, because that's the case. If they're kicking it out of the park, people will know they're kicking it out of the park."

This way of conducting reviews and career development is more difficult in a smaller workplace. It's difficult to compare three people, but in a larger workplace the differences are more easily identified.

Let's listen to Miss Triggs — speaking up and being heard

Many studies show that women don't ask for promotions and opportunities, but expect to be approached and asked. My view is that this is another myth and a form of confirmation bias.

As most workplace environments and systems have been set up to favour the gendered male way of operating, men who have trained their whole lives to be successful within the patriarchal structure feel confident and are therefore more likely to know their value and ask for a promotion.

Women have less confidence and take fewer risks, but one should not assume women are risk-averse. Psychologist Cordelia Fine's research reveals that women take risks and compete in more familiar contexts.[1]

Risks for women who challenge to be heard, acknowledged and understood are deeply rooted in the Gender Code. For millennia, public speaking has been the domain of men. Mary Beard explored this in *Women and Power: A Manifesto*. Looking at how we are indoctrinated to hear women and women's voices contributes to the confidence gap in terms of 'speak up' challenges. We are trained to believe that a low-pitched voice indicates manly courage and a high-pitched voice indicates female cowardice. The deep voice of authority is usually male; whereas in a woman we *"do not hear a voice that connotes authority; or rather they have not learned how to hear authority in it."*[2]

Mary highlights this with a cartoon created by Riana Duncan 30 years ago. It depicts a meeting of five men and Miss Triggs in a boardroom with the caption *"That's an excellent suggestion, Miss Triggs. Perhaps one of the men here would like to make it."*

Can you identify with this situation?

Many women in senior leadership positions have experienced this situation. A woman makes a suggestion in a meeting, which is met with deathly silence from the other, predominantly male, group members.

1   'The Myth of Gender Essentialism', ABC Radio National *Big Ideas*, 6 September 2018
2   *Women and Power: A Manifesto*, Mary Beard, pg 30

A few minutes later, in the same meeting, a man makes the identical suggestion, which is met with appreciation and action. The woman is left dumbfounded. People are not prepared for her authority. This can diminish confidence and the will to take risks, but can also motivate.

Women can't handle the pressure

There is an age-old assumption that women are more emotional than men. It is used as a weapon and an explanation as to why women are not as suited to leadership positions or higher levels of responsibility and are considered less capable than their male counterparts. Being sensitive and showing emotion is perceived as a sign of weakness in our culture—unless of course you are an influential male and give an emotional, rousing speech.

Perception is everything

One of my most surprising discoveries was the gendered perception involving emotions. Lisa Feldman Barrett is a Professor of Psychology at Northeastern University, respected for her groundbreaking research revealing that, contrary to popular cultural and scientific beliefs, emotion is not hardwired in our brains. Emotion is formulated and constructed as we experience and make our way through life.

In her book *How Emotions are Made: The Secret Life of the Brain*, Lisa describes how she and her team found that the definition and perception of emotion vary culturally far more than was originally thought.[3] Essentially, we create our emotions depending on what happens to us, what we are exposed to, what our experiences mean to us, who influences us and how we are trained.

When she and her team asked people to describe themselves and how emotional they felt they were, it was no surprise that women described themselves as more emotional and men agreed. However when tracking people's day-to-day experiences, asking how they felt, assessing facial movements and measuring physical changes, overall there were no differences between men and woman.

---

3 'The Creation of Emotions', ABC Radio National *All in the Mind*, 9 July 2017

"You see some people who are more emotional than other people, but on average men and women don't differ." Lisa Feldman Barrett[4]

So why do we perceive women as more emotional?

We predict people's emotions from their facial movements, based on our own experiences and determined by how much we adhere to the Gender Code.

Lisa found that when a man scowls, people assume that if he is angry then something must have happened to make him angry and his expression conveys the state of the world. When a woman scowls, people assume that she is emotional.

So if men experience negative emotions they are externally driven, whereas women's emotions are internal and consequently their fault or even their choice. Therefore women are trapped in a 'double-bind' situation: either overly emotional, which is seen as a weakness, or not sufficiently emotional and violating the stereotype.

"Then we are considered to be cold and untrustworthy and unlikeable."
Lisa Feldman Barrett[5]

Can you spot the Gender Code in your world?

Art imitating life

Do you notice the Gender Code playing out clearly in all areas of life? It is everywhere and here is an example.

In the kids' movie, *Cars 3*, the lead male character, Lightning McQueen, at the tail end of his racing career, is struggling after a crash. His sponsors appoint a young female trainer, Cruz Ramirez, and Lightning assumes Cruz's ambition is to become a race car trainer rather than a successful racer and is initially unkind and unappreciative. Cruz explains that she had wanted to be a racer, but though she had the skills she lacked confidence in her ability and she gave up: *"The other racers looked nothing like me... It made me feel like it was a world in which I didn't belong."*

She asks Lightning how he believed he could be a racer and he replies *"I don't know — I never thought I couldn't."*

---

4   Ibid.
5   Ibid.

That revelation screamed gender socialisation differences. Cruz had internalised messages about not only what she could and couldn't do, but who she could or couldn't be, while Lightning, with total confidence, believed he could accomplish what he set out to achieve without gender or cultural barriers.

Do you want to take the red pill or the blue pill?

If you have seen the 1999 film *The Matrix*, you will understand the coloured pill analogy. The lead character Neo is offered two pills, a red one and a blue one. If he swallows the red pill it will reveal the harsh realities of his world, but if he chooses the blue one, he will remain oblivious to the truth.

I chose the red pill, although that was not intentional.

Without understanding the cultural and gender expectations in my own life, I was unquestioningly perpetuating the myths. The patriarchal system had worked so well for those in charge for so long, why question it? Why not accept that boys will be boys and girls should be good? Isn't it easier to maintain the status quo?

Questioning long-held beliefs that constitute the model of your masculinity or femininity and essentially who you are can be scary. Saying that I was conducting a research project deconstructing and understanding the Gender Code made some people distinctly uncomfortable, while others lost interest. Some men became defensive, some thinking they might be to blame and others that they might somehow miss out or be diminished. These challenges are structural and not personal.

While it is difficult at first, a different reality is possible for women and men. When you question and understand the state of play, you are on the path to create a new world.

Let's sum it all up

If you like tables, I have created a comparison of reported gender differences that apply across pretty much all cultures.

This does not pertain to all women or all men. Women and men differ as individuals for many reasons, and we are influenced by nature, nurture and neuroplasticity.

This is a general summary presenting what I found from my research. If you keep an open mind, you can reflect on it, start to change the conversation with increased awareness and choose whether or not to do things differently.

Focus area	Male — typical	Female — typical
Childhood play The socialisation process begins to establish gender norms.	Games tend to be structured and competitive, have a hierarchy, rules and a clear outcome with winners and losers. Players lose about 50 per cent of the time. Players deal with losing, learn from it, move on, focus on the next win and build a strategy.	Play tends to be process and relationship based — no winner or loser — and competition can be seen as a relationship breakdown. Play doesn't allow for practising to lose. Play competition and clashes are taken more personally: is it about me? Is it my fault?
Rules and expectations	The male hierarchy structure provides order — this plays out in organisations with org charts. The rules of the workplace are written for the male way of operating.	Relationships and women connecting with each other — flatter structures. The rules of the traditional workplace are not drawn up for the female way of operating.
Approaching challenges/tasks	Goal-focused — what is the goal, find the solution and solve the problem.	Process-driven — discuss the problem, what are the options?

Focus area	Male — typical	Female — typical
Job appraisal	I am a 10/10 superstar — dial up expectations and don't highlight unsuccessful areas. Self-promote, push up the performance rating and expect to be moderated down. Perception is that expectations were exceeded and ahead of the bell curve. Exceeded expectations may attract a 4 per cent pay increase.	Perception is met, but didn't go beyond expectations. Personal expectations are higher to start with. Less self-promotion. Perception is that expectations were met. Meeting expectations may attract 2 per cent pay rise. A period of 10 years with consistent increases results in a 20 per cent difference in pay across genders.
Problem-solving	Desire to solve. Shoe discussion.	Desire to discuss. Shoe discussion.
Social codes	More acceptable to be aggressive and a wider range of behaviours. Aggressive = adhering to the code.	Different rules: aggression and assertiveness are not acceptable. Aggressive = violation of the code.
Workplace competition	In a meeting men may be highly competitive, even aggressive but, after the meeting is over, go off and have a beer together. Letting go of the loss/win and looking for the next one.	The discussion is not over and will probably continue. Less likely to let go of the loss and move on.

Focus area	Male — typical	Female — typical
Success and failure	Success due to own skills, strengths and abilities. Failure due to something in the external world.	Success due to the external world — I was lucky, someone helped me. Failures due to me — what have I done wrong? What is wrong with me? I am not good enough. Solution — draw a box around it, drop the loss and don't drag it around — it was this boss, this time. Evolve and learn from the loss.
Competition	Constant — not personal, but playing the game. Business is a game — not about me. Take risks. Segment and partition. Embrace competition.	One to one — best friend. Competition can be damaging to relationships. Avoid competition. Women perceived as risk-averse — not given as many opportunities. Example: "Get out of the tree, you might fall", which is code for you are more physically fragile. Current scientific research reveals that women are not more fragile.

Focus area	Male — typical	Female — typical
Self-promotion	Bragging is a survival skill — ego. Talk about successes. Talk about potential and track record. Open and clear about aims.	Good girls don't brag. Don't talk about yourself too much. Expectation is if I am good and work hard I will be recognised. People should know what I want — read my mind. Second-guessing and questioning internal voices — driven by fear of disconnection when it is all about connection.
Communication process	Pull the problem inside. Process the problem/question/challenge internally. Find a solution. Express externally. Internalise and verbalise. Perceived to have lost position of power when asking for discussion based on the hierarchy rules. Bottom line first and then backfill.	Share the problem externally. Process externally. Speaking, sharing and processing with people builds relationships. Process, then arrive at the bottom line.

Focus area	Male — typical	Female — typical
Body language	Open body stance generally. Stand firmly in place. I belong here — which can sometimes be bravado. Example: male bikers on the road riding two or more abreast. Males spreading their legs on planes.	Socialised to be thin, beautiful and quiet. Can sometimes shrink and be conscious of taking up space. Women in meetings — especially small women.
Negotiating	Don't ask, don't get. More likely to make a bold proposal. Four times more likely to negotiate than women. More acceptable to be tougher — expected behaviour with no negative outcomes. Example: graduate males asking for positions.	Concerned about asking due to potential social consequences — may seem aggressive. Cooperative negotiation — let's talk with the boss rather than let's fight the boss (unions) — positive outcomes with less aggression. Example: graduate females expected to be asked to fill positions based on merit.
Emotions	More likely to mask.	More likely to show.

6 How the Code sets your personal expectations

Myth: "a popular belief or tradition that has grown up around something or someone; especially: one embodying the ideals and institutions of a society or segment of society."[1]

What are you up against?

There will be no shortage of experts, both amateur (family and friends) and professional (inspirational speakers), willing to help you release the pressure and feel like you are doing and being enough. Well-intentioned partners may suggest you slow down; concerned family may tell you not to be Wonder Woman; others may call you a perfectionist and ask you to go easy on yourself or get help. Experts may suggest a seven-step process to empower you to progress in your career and relationships.

Advice does not usually help unless it comes from deep understanding of your daily struggle—and tips and strategies that work for other people may have little impact on your world. You may also be suspicious of the motives of others who would like to help you release the pressure when it is clear that they will benefit more than you will.

It is frustrating to be told that you just need to ask for more, promote yourself more, be more confident, more direct and negotiate more, when

---

1   https://www.merriam-webster.com/dictionary/myth

you are already at capacity. This also reinforces the belief that your own choices and focus on having it all create your exhaustion and depletion, as though having it all were an indulgence or a privilege rather than the determination to do your best to contribute.

Understanding the rules of your environment—the code and set of expectations that form the culture of your friendships, family, community and workplaces—is important as these shape your thoughts, emotions, choices and behaviours. They may protect you though, and provide a sense of reliability that helps you operate and interact, and adhering to codes reduces the fear of being viewed as an outsider. The 'this is the way it has always been done' approach makes life easier, even if it limits you.

Cultural expectations may also be a barrier when the knock-on effect prevents honesty, openness, rich conversations, innovative thinking and creative solutions, and kills any meaningful connection.

The Gender Code may be telling you that you do not feel you deserve a thriving career, flourishing children, strong relationships and positive wellbeing at the same time. You may believe you are not smart enough, slim enough, experienced enough, fit enough—not worthy of an ideal of fulfilment or success.

This is the breeding ground for perfectionism that places a high value on productivity and a low one on care. It prevents relieving the pressure, building stronger relationships and progressing in your career.

part three
WHAT ARE THE GENDER CODE PERFORMANCE PRESSURES?

7 How does the Gender Code feed your personal code?

"If we can let go of the mountain of assumptions, biases, expectations, double standards and doubts that so many of us carry around, then a new world of possibilities awaits. We may lose our status as superwomen, but we have everything to gain." Anne-Marie Slaughter[1]

The crucial first step is exploring the origins of the environmental challenges and barriers to progress and inequality we face as women. Personal expectations, thoughts and stories are our internal code source and how we build our identity.

Once you concentrate on the Gender Code and your personal code, you can choose how to respond, whom to listen to and which direction to take. Decide what makes sense for you and what you wish to adhere to; you may accept and embrace parts of your personal code, but there may be parts you are not so keen on and new parts you would like to add.

---

1   *Unfinished Business: Women Men Work Family*, Anne-Marie Slaughter, pg 169

Let's shine the spotlight on expectations

"I think my own personal expectations of myself are my biggest challenges. I guess most women in leadership are quite goal-oriented people, and I find it's sometimes hard to meet my own expectations and that's quite frustrating."

Do you believe the expectations you place on yourself and on others are reasonable? Or unrealistic? If you acknowledge, understand and question your expectations, you may realise that they are creating barriers to success. But you will certainly find freedom, space and joy by using your strengths, capabilities and wisdom.

What does enough look and feel like?

Parenting and work are the two biggest challenges where you are on show—analysed, judged and criticised. Who you are takes centre stage, and sometimes it feels as though the eyes of the whole world are watching, just waiting for you to trip up.

Do you feel you are driven to work hard towards an imaginary future, where everything is as it should be—all the ducks in a row, everything balanced—and only then will you able to allow yourself to be fulfilled and satisfied?

"When I have lost weight... when my kids are in school... when my kids have left school... when my boss leaves the company... when this project is done... when I pay off the mortgage... when I get a divorce... when I find a more supportive partner... then I can have what I want and everything will be great."

With this approach, the experiences, wins, connections, opportunities for growth as you pursue success may not be acknowledged or valued. The focus may be on the destination, the prize, the achievement, the next thing, the social media, and picture-perfect moment.

Could you also be trying to engineer Utopia for yourself and everyone you care about? A place where no one experiences pain or discomfort and everyone is high up on the happiness scale? Would that give you the sense that you are doing well enough and feel good enough?

Are you veering from inner peace to panic attack?

Trying to fulfil all your roles based on your own expectations of the ideal, you can go from over-functioning, giving everything to everybody and working yourself too hard, to under-functioning, falling in a heap exhausted and no good to anyone, least of all yourself and needing a retreat in Bali to recover.

Rather than veering from inner peace to panic attack, what would it be like to live more of your life in and around the centre and not riding the pendulum from one extreme to the other? How would it be to have the confidence to believe you are doing and being enough?

It is possible, but first we need to explore the barriers and performance pressures.

What are the barriers?

Research and experience reveal that people create different types of barriers based on the culturally created Gender Code and internally driven personal expectations. There are three key barriers: presentation, self-perception and resources.

1. **Presentation barrier**

   The thought process may include "I am not successful as I am not slim enough, attractive enough, young enough, feminine enough, energetic enough, fit enough. I don't have great shoes."

2. **Self-perception barrier**

   The internal conversation may sound like "I am not successful as I am not sociable enough, direct enough, confident enough, nurturing enough, intelligent enough. I am too outgoing, too emotional. I am a woman. I am a working parent. I don't deserve my success."

3. **External resources**

   This is based on the view that if there were more external resources, life would all fall into place. The thought pattern when a roadblock is hit may be "I don't have enough support, money, time, opportunities."

Do these apply to you or women you know?

These limiting thoughts may be experienced individually or simultaneously and may even all feed off each other. I find I combine two and three and in the past had a higher weighting on three. As soon as I hit a wall my reaction was "I don't have family support and am doing this whole thing on my own as a single parent. No wonder I can't do…"

What are performance pressures?

Barriers and pressures tend to work together and can create a continuous cycle of feeling like there is more to be done. People all have different experiences and perceptions, and what is normal and acceptable for you may be completely foreign to someone else. Whatever you believe is your personal truth and how you have built the person you are. However some of these 10 interrelated, common themes may contribute to your high expectations:

1. Perfectionism

2. Productivity

3. Caring

4. Having it all

5. Working harder

6. Mental load

7. Emotional load

8. Judgment

9. Parent guilt and shame

10. Time poverty.

What is your pressure point? Perhaps only one of these applies to you. Or maybe several and perhaps even all of them. Would you like to explore them?

Where to from here?

Feeling like you are doing and being enough sounds both logical and straightforward. Perhaps you are now internally driving the pressures and barriers originally created externally, and what needs to change is your thinking.

Imagine how liberating it would feel to free up your thinking and increase your impact. Perhaps the new world of possibilities Anne-Marie Slaughter refers to is one with clarity and energy, richer conversations, stronger relationships, feeling valued and a deeper sense of connection with yourself and the important people in your life.

Sometimes when you are focused on being everything to everyone while trying to make it look easy, it can be difficult to see what is right in front of you, and to understand what you are tolerating and what you could access.

In the next seven chapters of the book, we will delve deeper into the performance pressures and help you to understand more about your pressure points and how you can think differently about them. At the end of each chapter is a tried and tested 'pressure release' practice for you to experiment.

8 Perfectionism pressure

"Perfectionism is by far the biggest stone that we carry around on our X sex chromosome. I work with a lot of men and they're just not as bought into everything needing to be perfect, and have a ribbon around it and then give it to someone. Until we can get rid of some of that, then we just can't really thrive, because we're constantly handicapping ourselves, to be honest."

The Gender Code has provided fertile ground to cultivate the pressure to be perfect. How much do we internally drive the myth to be perfect?

What effect does perfectionism have not only on the perfectionists themselves, but also the people they work and live with?

What do we need to do in order to dial it down?

Let's unpack and understand perfectionism

Do you call yourself a perfectionist? Do people think you are one?

Ask any group of women that question, and a few will claim the title. It is important to explore this view women have of themselves.

What is a perfectionist and what does it mean to be a perfectionist?

Dictionary.com defines a *perfectionist* as:

Noun

1. *a person who adheres to or believes in perfectionism.*

2. *a person who demands perfection of himself, herself, or others.*

Thesaurus.com had no antonyms for perfectionist. Synonyms include:

- Purist

- Quibbler

- Fussbudget

- Nit-picker.

Words related to perfectionist are:

- Anal personality

- Anal retentive personality

- Over-achiever.

It seems most descriptors are quite negative or unattractive. I struggle to imagine a group of women owning up to being a fussbudget.

Surely there is something positive about being a perfectionist if so many women claim to be one?

Perfection however is defined as:

Noun

1. *the highest degree of proficiency, skill, or excellence, as in some art.*

2. *a perfect embodiment or example of something.*

3. *a quality, trait, or feature of the highest degree of excellence.*

4. *the highest or most nearly perfect degree of a quality or trait.*

Perfection seems a great deal more appealing based on this. It makes sense for high achieving people to work towards the highest degree of excellence, so where does the negativity come from?

Searching for antonyms, it was obvious:

- Flawed

- Imperfect

- Inferior

- Poor

- Second-rate

- Wrong

- Inexpert

- Unknowledgeable

- Unskilled

- Imprecise.

It all makes sense. No high functioning, driven woman would ever wish to be considered flawed, second-rate, unskilled or unknowledgeable! I wonder if we are flogging ourselves trying not to be the opposite of perfection!

And the stigma attached to perfectionism may be dependent on interpretation—and the person claiming the title.

Do you want to be perfect or excellent?

What if people are striving for excellence rather than perfection, but being labelled perfectionists? Surely trying your best always, having high standards and working towards mutually beneficial outcomes is a form of excellence. Why apply yourself to a task if you do not plan to be excellent? I sought input from Brené Brown, the leading researcher, who refers to perfectionism as a form of numbing and armour preventing us from being seen.

"Perfectionism is not the same thing as striving to be your best. Perfectionism is the belief that if we live perfect, look perfect, and act perfect, we can minimise or avoid the pain of blame, judgment and shame. It's a shield. It's a twenty-ton shield that we lug around

thinking it will protect us when, in fact, it's the thing that's really preventing us from flight." Brené Brown[1]

How do you know if you are in perfection mode or excellence mode?

"Excellence seems more positive. Perfectionism always has a negative turn to it. If we see a person's a perfectionist, it's almost isolating them. We think all of those connotations, hard to work for, hard to communicate with, hard to reason with. It is striving to be our best in order to do our best work versus there's a person who can't deliver."

A perfectionist is set up for failure as the goal posts keep moving. Conversely, excellence can be a way to learn, improve, challenge and engage without the limits of perfectionism.

Are you an unintentional perfectionist?

I looked at my own experiences of operating as a perfectionist. The most obvious was when my three boys were four and two years old and 14 days old—and Fred left for China on a two-week business trip. I was determined to keep it all together with virtually no support other than a babysitter for a few hours twice a week and meals supplied by generous friends.

I thought I was pursuing excellence, however on reflection it was the perfectionism which came crashing down around me—the perfectionist's worst nightmare.

My two-year-old contracted school sores, but was trying to cuddle the new baby at every opportunity, so I was constantly in germ protection mode. My four-year-old had an allergic reaction to an immunisation shot and was on cortisone. My newborn baby seemed to cry most of time. I was hyper-vigilant, hyper-responsible and hyper-sleep-deprived.

To really drive home the point that I was doing too much, I got folliculitis and a painful case of mastitis. The thought of those days and nights breastfeeding an unsettled baby when I had a fever and excruciatingly sore boobs still unsettles me and is a powerful reminder of what not to do.

---

1   *The Gifts of Imperfection: Let Go of Who You Think You're Supposed to Be and Embrace Who You Are*, Brené Brown

While refusing to be seen as struggling and vulnerable, I was pushing myself too hard and my body was pushing back even harder.

When friends and well-wishers dropped in to visit the new baby, I made sure everything was in order, that the kids looked well cared for, the house was neat and everyone seemed content. I was focused on what people would think and my ultimate goal was to look as though I was in total control, regardless of the challenging circumstances. I wanted to raise the bar and make it look easy.

What would have helped me move from perfection to excellence was showing vulnerability and asking for help. I would have also benefited from giving myself permission to be less than perfect and showing myself some compassion and love.

> *"Many people dedicate their lives to actualising a concept of what they should be like, rather than actualising themselves. This difference between self-actualisation and self-image actualisation is very important. Most people live only their image."* Bruce Lee

How is perfectionism cultivated?

Well-educated, intelligent women would not wittingly choose to chase perfectionism. However, the Gender Code breeds perfectionist behaviours and we try to measure up all the time.

> *"I think it comes from our parents and then the school system, and it's just all throughout society. Boys go out, they fail, they're brash, they're arrogant and they scrap in the play yard. We're supposed to be very well presented, quiet, agreeable and perfect. We aspire to perfectionism, and I think that it's a very clever way of having constrained our development from a very long time ago."*

From childhood, women and girls are judged on packaging, presentation and 'agreeable' behaviour. When interacting with young girls, an adoring adult will almost always comment on the girl's appearance first. Wow, that's a pretty dress. I love your sparkly shoes. Your hair looks so beautiful. Look at your colourful nails... More often than not, the comment is also delivered with a smile and a dose of happy energy.

What does this say about our value system? That appearance and presentation are important. How does it make a girl feel? That she is worthy of love and belonging.

Thus agreeable behaviours are welcomed and rewarded and behaviours which present challenges to guardians are penalised. The 'good girl, bad girl' approach is a powerful way to control women. The exceptions are tomboys, who reinforce behaviour stereotyping.

A concerned mother, Karen, spoke about how she sees signs of perfectionist behaviour in her seven-year-old daughter. During homework she sometimes becomes hysterical when she makes a mistake in her maths. She says "You don't understand, I can't get something wrong." Because of everything Karen experiences as a woman, she is determined to start changing her daughter's attitude, to teach her that it's okay to not know the answers and be perfect. Karen finds herself constantly saying "What do we do if we get something wrong?" and her daughter will respond "We learn." Karen then asks "What's the benefit of if you never get anything wrong?" and her daughter replies "We never know how to fix things up."

"It is amazing? She is in Year 2 and she already feels that pressure. I don't know whether it's because Eve took a bite of that damn apple."

How does perfection influence the work environment?

The fallout of perfectionism in the workplace can be catastrophic. It results in poor leadership and organisational performance, and is detrimental to working relationships, productivity, engagement, culture and psychological safety.

Understandably, when you are highly productive and efficient and can see a solution clearly you prefer to do the job yourself. However, from a leadership perspective, when you go from being a doer to a director or a leader or helping other people perform, it is important to let go, because otherwise you start micromanaging everyone around you, and micromanagers are poor leaders.

"People will leave. No one wants to be micromanaged; they want to be coached. When I get stressed, I start to micromanage people, and my team will tell me I'm doing it. For a while it was pretty horrendous for them, I imagine."

In addition to business performance and culture, a perfectionist leader can have a detrimental effect not only on their own health, well-being and state of mind, but also cause burnout in others.

If a leader constantly seeks perfection, but does not know how that really looks or feels, how can she articulate it? How will anyone ever know if they are on the right track? This may cause a crushing lack of confidence before discovering that everyone at the same level feels the pressure.

"About ten years into my career, I had a terrible boss—absolutely dreadful because that person didn't delegate. Therefore you felt completely undermined and not trusted and clearly not good enough. I couldn't reach the expectation. And I learned through that. It was her perfectionism holding her back and perfectionism can lead to burnout of the people underneath you because you never actually make the grade of the leader.

"She didn't maintain her position and ended up leaving. But three of the direct reports had already left. Excellent, high calibre people.

"I learned some of my best lessons from some of my worst leaders. And I just made a promise to myself: I'll never treat anyone the way that I'm being made to feel right now."

How does perfection influence relationships?

When people are outside work and in relationships, the continual pursuit of perfection may affect them negatively and prevent them feeling safe to be who they are as they burn out, feeling they will never measure up and make the grade.

"My ex-husband and my current partner told me nothing's ever good enough. I recognise that in myself in a work sense, and I often temper that a lot because I put high expectations on people. I'm just not sure whether I recognise that in the relationship sense. If that was me talking to somebody at work, I'd be far more supportive and lenient than if it was in a relationship."

I wondered to what extent the perception of perfection of both the perfectionist and the person in a relationship with the perfectionist influences their behaviour and communication.

While we were married Fred constantly accused me of being a perfectionist. I always felt I was working to the excellence model, and that his accusations were due to my perception he was a Half-arsed Harry out of work but a corporate superstar in his chosen profession. When he compared the effort and attention he was willing to invest at home and in our relationship to the amount I invested, of course I seemed like a perfectionist.

Fred felt almost nothing he did was ever good enough in my eyes. Still not accepting the perfectionist tag, but wanting to understand more, I recently asked what he thought would have helped him not to feel that.

"At work with a perfectionist manager," he said *"you could map out a strategy about what happens if there's some sort of miscommunication."*

So I came up with a structure, strategy and firm agreements leveraging our strengths. There were no more moving goalposts, and he said *"Yeah, that might have helped."*

I expanded it a bit further to having a shared mission everyone buys into and then developed a strategy to get there. Using Fred's work perspective helped us to make sense of relationships.

Why ditch perfectionism?

"Research shows that perfectionism hampers success. In fact, it's often the path to depression, anxiety, addiction, and life paralysis."
Brené Brown[2]

Perfectionism costs us dearly. If you focus on tidying up all the loose ends, making sure everything is perfect and perfectly packaged, it may handicap you too.

It may seem easier to continue as you are, but there are compelling reasons to try a different approach. Moving away from perfection gives you an opportunity to move towards new ideas and experiences both at and outside work, and your leadership performance will improve your relationships and wellbeing.

---

2   Ibid.

"I think we absolutely need to kill perfectionism. I say this as a perfectionist myself, a recovering perfectionist. The key thing we really need to do is support women to accept and experiment."

How to ditch perfectionism?

Ditching it requires energy, attention and work. First a commitment to try a different approach and the confidence that you can implement it, then a slow-build approach rather than going cold turkey.

You can stop worrying so much about how people perceive you and realise that no one is actually paying you that much attention. So being perfect probably doesn't matter as much as you used to think it did. Thinking more about what you value and having a higher opinion of your own abilities helps you to focus less on how other people view you.

"It's a long journey. My tendency is for everything to be perfect all the time, doing everything for everyone. It's a constant internal battle. You've got to start to truly consciously decide how you're going to get back to a good equilibrium."

How to be comfortable with imperfection?

Most women I spoke to admitted they were seeking or recovering from perfectionism and shared useful ways to navigate through it.

Knowing when to ship it

It is important to develop a sense of when enough is enough and be okay with it.

"I do a lot of writing; it's like anything creative, you could keep adding layers to it and keep finessing and adding more voices, doing more. Is it enough? It really does reach a point where you're experienced with what you do too. You know that you keep the main points and it's ready to send. It's like that old saying about shipping it: you just have to ship it.

"I know when my ship it is. It's just efficiency. With time, you just have to. Enough is good enough."

The 80 per cent approach

It is important to accept that if someone else can perform tasks or take responsibility and accomplish 80 per cent of what you could, you can let them run with it and then focus on helping them. If they want help with the extra 20 per cent, then coach, don't do. It is important to allow team members and family members to do it their way.

This is also known as the 80/20 rule or the Pareto principle and is backed up by numbers and data. The concept is that it takes 20 per cent of the total required effort to achieve 80 per cent of a task. With the belief that 100 per cent perfection is not possible, it then requires 80 per cent of the total effort to achieve that remaining 20 per cent. While this is not universally true and more of a guideline than a law, the idea suggests that most of the tasks we perform and things in life are not distributed evenly. Consequently, striving for perfection results in inefficiencies and diminishing returns.[3]

> "I'm not a perfectionist. I'm not looking for perfection, I know of a probability saying that 80 per cent is good enough. Having those strategies works for me."

Fail fast and fail forward

Accepting that failure is part of life is important. Looking at everything you do as an experiment and a learning opportunity can reduce fear of failing.

> "It's okay to fail, but fail fast; perfection is really not worth the effort. I mean great if you've gotten something perfect. I think you can give yourself a little bit more preference to try things and tackle things with confidence."

Relieving the pressure

Do you follow the perfectionism model or is excellence your goal? How does the way you operate affect your relationships, performance and personal thinking? Is it causing you to feel increased pressure?

Would you like to ditch perfectionism and move toward other opportunities you had not previously thought possible?

---

3   *Equip*, Eddie Gandevia and Simon Breakspear, pg 30

Perfectionism pressure release

Here's a useful practice based on the insights shared. I use this personally and professionally with clients—and it works.

When you sense you may be crossing the line from excellence to perfection, ask yourself:

- Am I buying into this having to be perfect with a ribbon tied around it before I give it to someone? Will the ribbon add value or be an opportunity cost?

- Is it time to 'ship it'?

- Is this 80 per cent, and is the extra 20 per cent worth it?

- It's okay to fail and fail fast—I can be a scientist and experiment.

- Enough is good enough.

9 Productivity and caring pressures

"I've called this the 'competition bias': the reflexive way in which we value competition over care. But perhaps... this bias is better understood as a mystique—an ineffable something that we are drawn to and strive to imitate without fully understanding why." Anne-Marie Slaughter[1]

Are you competitively busy?

When you ask someone how they are, how often do they reply "Busy" with a sigh? And when people ask how you are, how often do you reply "Busy"? It is a way of bonding, showing we are all in this together, but it can be a sign of competitiveness and a way to ensure everyone knows how much you are doing.

It has become part of our daily narrative, but is our language around productivity contributing towards feelings of overwhelm and exhaustion?

Are you driven to be productive?

What is it about productivity that drives us? Before I became a parent measuring productivity was easy. I was used to allocating my time and energy to tangible units in terms of hours worked, tasks completed and outcomes achieved. I received regular feedback and could ascertain my

---

1 *Unfinished Business: Women Men Work Family*, Anne-Marie Slaughter, pg 120

effectiveness through positive reviews, my pay packet, bonuses and promotions.

I did not value investment in relationships and people as highly as productivity and work and would almost always choose a productive task over an opportunity to build a non-work relationship. It was not that I didn't value relationships, but I valued productivity more.

Working in the corporate world one week and being a parent the next was quite a shift in terms of environment. However, I brought my productivity approach to being a full-time carer to my baby son. I had a shower and set myself up for the day as early as possible—no sleep-ins. I timed how long my baby breastfed, recorded calories burned in the gym, kilometres walked with the stroller in the Pittsburgh snow, how long he slept, how many nappies I changed. It was incredibly frustrating to be unable to measure exactly how much breast milk he was consuming, which made me worry he was not getting enough. I considered weighing my boobs before and after a feed, but could not find the right piece of equipment back in 2006.

I needed a list of accomplishments by the end of the day to prove to myself that I was productive and not just staying home and minding the baby. Raising a child did not seem to be enough for me to feel worthy.

This pattern continued over several years until I eventually noticed I was so focused on tasks that gave me a sense of accomplishment and productivity that I was sacrificing rare opportunities to engage openly with my sons. I would tidy the house, weed the garden, prepare food, sort out toys—any measurable task rather than playing board games or relaxing with the boys. I invested time and energy in activities contributing to their learning, fitness, health and general wellbeing but just 'being' seemed to be wasting time.

My measures of success were based on outcomes and not the benefits and rewards inherent in the process of achieving the outcomes. I did not value my contribution to their flourishing and growth in the same way I valued productivity gains. I filled the days with tasks until I realised that limited the opportunities to really see and understand who my boys were, the whole reason I wanted to be with them rather than contribute to the paid workforce. Old productivity habits die hard.

I changed tack and started to look at how I prioritised and ascribed value. Productive activities where I received the highest measurable return won out each time. I also noticed the extent to which this played out on everyone around me. If Fred was not at work he was on his phone, computer or sleeping—not present and engaged with his family.

I finally realised that when we invest in relationships there is no measurable outcome to help us understand if we have done a good job. Parenting is a great way to learn this valuable lesson as it is a lifelong process where the outcome cannot be calculated in definable units. It's about who your children are, how they develop and your other relationships, and a constant challenge to strive for a healthy mixture.

Do you prioritise the tasks with more measurable outcomes?

Why is it hard to understand intangible feedback?

Investing in a process, person or mission without obvious, short-term rewards can be more about laying a foundation to build and nurture relationships. You rarely receive immediate feedback in tidy units of measurement. You have to tap into something intangible, using your perception and instincts. This requires listening to understand rather than to respond and solve, as well as awareness, reflection and curiosity. It takes more time and energy.

Part of the challenge is that it is really difficult to grasp the impact your contribution has and how people flourish when you care for them. Sometimes you can see how it works for other people but you don't know how much you are influencing them.

Trusting your instincts when there are no easily identifiable returns is difficult, but the returns can be exponential.

Can you take a leap of faith and trust yourself and the process? Believe that your support was and continues to be valuable, whether the person concerned ever realises it? Then you can shift your mindset. You can move from giving your energy and attention, with the objective of getting a return on your investment, to making a choice to give for the sake of giving without expecting a reward.

"I have to recognise that spending time with the kids on holidays, being with them and talking with them and playing board games with them or something—that's not wasted. Just because we haven't gone out and done anything doesn't mean that you haven't had a good day."

Do you believe competition beats caring?

In *Unfinished Business*, Anne-Marie Slaughter believes the challenge is around how we value competition. I prefer productivity, but she calls it *"the competitive mystique"*.

She sees this mystique as equally attractive to men and women because they feel that they are setting and achieving goals and beating others in the process, and says *"it is a mystique that has steadily grown as the world itself has become more competitive over the past few decades, largely through the twin forces of globalisation and technology."* It is easy to see that more and more people are relentlessly competing with each other.[2]

The socio-cultural system challenges analysis and change. Capitalism favours the rich and powerful and is a pathway to success.

One research participant pointed out that more people are awarded the Order of Australia, which is based on achievement and service, for basically doing what they are paid to do, and fewer for working in community service.

Only 30 per cent of the honours have been awarded to women, and both men and women are more likely to nominate a man for the award. In education, an industry dominated by women, 58 per cent of the nominees were men and in 28 of the 31 categories there were more male nominees in 2018.[3]

> *"Society rewards people with power and money. That's how success is measured."*

Fear of missing out—FOMO

A significant factor driving competition is fear of missing out, the perception that if someone else gets a piece of the pie, then there is less for the others. This may be real or imagined, but the feeling of scarcity is powerful and can result in reactive and negative behaviours and lead to depletion, burnout and health complications.

---

2   *Unfinished Business: Women Men Work Family*, Anne-Marie Slaughter, pg 120
3   https://mobile.abc.net.au/news/2019-06-07/women-lacking-queens-birthday-order-of-australia-awards-list/11187978?pfmredir=sm

What value do we place on care?

Care and care-giving are unquantifiable, despite the investment of energy, attention and time. Often care-giving is about being reliable: being there when it is important, supporting and focusing on other people's needs, whether finding a tie or a book or the car keys or listening with genuine attention. Care-giving includes, but is not limited to, coaching, problem-solving, encouraging, role modelling, character building, disciplining and holding boundaries in the midst of tears, tantrums and emotional discombobulation.[4]

While the work landscape is changing, there still seems to be a higher focus and value placed on competition and externally measured success. Why don't caring for others and contributing to human flourishing rate equally?

It is clear that our society does not value nurses, teachers, nannies, aged care workers or any profession that is fundamentally centred on helping people flourish rather than winning themselves. The relatively low remuneration of these roles substantiates this, and Anne-Marie Slaughter believes *"The most obvious, at least to most women, is that we are talking about men's traditional work versus women's traditional work, and we have traditionally valued men more than women."*[5]

Similar to the idea that you are more likely to ascribe a higher value to tasks with a measurable productivity outcome, the same rule applies to professions that involve competition more than care. In traditional men's work and competition roles it is easier to ascertain who won and how to compensate the winner: *"the deal, the lawsuit, the sales contract, the race to invent a new product. It is much harder, as teachers and education reformers both know, to measure learning outcomes."*[6]

Drawing parallels with hunting and gathering or breadwinning and care-giving, hunters have significantly been elevated and received positive attention over millennia. It is a performative act; what has been achieved and recognised by others is clear. Conversely, care-giving or gathering acts do not receive the same attention. Keeping people alive, passing on knowledge, cultivating survival skills, keeping things ticking

---

4   *Unfinished Business*, op. cit., pg 103

5   *Unfinished Business*, op. cit., pg 117

6   Ibid., pg 117

over are generally expected rather than appreciated. The skills in these acts are not recognised and there is no trophy moment.

Gathering requires perseverance, dedication, experimentation, patience, reliability, consistent care and attention. Knowing and believing this, perhaps the high value we place on competition and productivity and the comparatively low value on care are grounded in our desire to be seen more as hunters rather than gatherers.

Although the Gender Code dictates that the gathering is women's work, perhaps we have lost focus on how important it is to our survival.

This is backed up by numerous studies on the gender pay gap or analysis of wages and salaries across industries and professions. Caring roles are not valued in the workplace; the lowest paid jobs in society are the ones with care at the centre, are traditionally done by women and are referred to as 'pink collar' jobs. This theme translates seamlessly into communities and families, where the greatest caring role of all, parenting and in particular motherhood, is not even remunerated.

The value of motherhood

"What we value is ultimately up to us." Anne-Marie Slaughter[7]

The role a mother plays is typically considered to be influential however the unpaid work a mother does has a low value on the importance scale and is totally gendered.

> *"It's about the value placed on caring for children and about society's valuing of that and how masculinity is defined. Whether it's masculine to be a stay-at-home dad and what that means. The culture needs to shift dramatically around that and, again, people feeling safe to take time off work and not go back into the workforce having been penalised either in terms of their role or their ability to be promoted or financially."*

I did wonder though whether what drives people in caring roles is their contribution. Nursing people back to health, educating children—it's not about making money, so when you start putting financial expectations into nurturing roles it can cause a conflict of values.

---

7   Ibid., pg 118

And motherhood is viewed by society as the ultimate nurturing role. The question though is how much is gender training versus what someone is naturally good at and interested in.

Perhaps it is that women's work is not seen as a skill, but as a vocation—unpaid work—followed by someone who cares. Consequently, there is no economic value in caring in our capitalist society, and so women's work does not need to be paid.

> "Also the age-old assumption in society still prevails to a degree: if there is a male breadwinner, the wife can go and do the kindergarten teaching and the nursing and all that because she will, in fact, be supported by the man in the proper job."

How can we improve the way mothers are valued?

Rachael, having been a senior marketing manager for a financial services company, worked a combination of full-time and part-time while her children were young. The situation was not sustainable so she decided to stay at home with her four children. Rachael questions her choices at times, which is driven by how she is valued. She believes fundamentally in our society we don't pay childcare workers or teachers well. This pulls through the whole of our culture and, generally speaking, whatever is happening with kids is not seen as requiring a high degree of skill. So being at home performing the family tasks is not considered rocket science and is not really highly valued.

> "I think a cultural shift would be needed for what I do as a stay home mum to be seen as valuable. But right now, to make my days valuable, I'd have to go to work. I'd have to find some kind of way of making money for society and to monetarily contribute to my household. For me to seem valuable I would have to do something that was useful and purposeful for broader society. Then I would feel more valuable."

Fed up with the fixation on titles and using her wicked sense of humour, filling in forms Rachael has called herself Ass Kicker, Laundress, Nappy Changer, Unemployed and Bus Driver (the family has a minivan).

If we started to value early childhood education we would probably see an ongoing flow through to mums at home. If highly qualified childhood educators were respected it might increase the value placed on motherhood, but since motherhood takes place at home alone the community is not really engaged in the day-to-day operating rhythm.

What happens when you bring productivity and caring together?

"I'm a better leader, having been a mother.

"As my children grew I started to think, from a leadership perspective, that my role was not to come up with the answers. My job is not even to tell them what to do: it's to create the conditions under which other people succeed. And that's what you do as a parent. You can't tell your child what to do. You don't own your child, but you can create the conditions under which they succeed. And to me the same thing goes at work. You can create the conditions in which the people around you succeed."

Parenthood fundamentally changes you and this was articulated by every person I spoke to. Just as at work you move from being an individual contributor to a leader, you take on a leadership role in the family. Another human is relying on you not just to stay alive, but for emotional and intellectual nourishment.

While being focused on one or the other can be detrimental, what happens when you bring productivity and care or human flourishing together as a career, leadership and relationship asset? It is not career limiting at all.

"I think being a parent helped me just have a stronger sense of self and comfort. I'm a lot more at peace with who I am."

Parenting can sharpen your EQ skills

All but one of the people I interviewed agreed that their leadership style had changed for the better after becoming a mother, and everyone said that after becoming a parent they had developed and sharpened important skills. Most had developed a greater sense of empathy, understanding, critical thinking, acceptance and perspective, and improved organisational skills, adaptability, flexibility and prioritisation—and realised the importance of people over processes.

They also felt they became more emotionally intelligent and creatively resourceful in terms of finding solutions to manage all of their responsibilities.

> *"Leadership comes very naturally once you're a parent, because it's so similar. It's really about focusing on them. I think as a parent you become very other people centred (OPC). As a leader as well, you become completely OPC. It's all about them and the people who I connect with to really be in the best shape possible. So, my job is to understand if there are any roadblocks, how can I help in removing those roadblocks? And, what else do they need to have or feel to really be at their best?"*

Neuroscientist Sarah McKay provides scientific evidence too that *"Parenting requires us to repeatedly deploy cognitive skills such as planning, organisation, working memory, flexibility, attention and decision-making. We practise and refine empathy, emotional regulation and resilience. All the evidence from non-human animals suggests that motherhood bestows a cognitive advantage."*[8]

Parenthood involves continuous learning over a lifetime: *"at each stage of our children's development we're faced with new challenges, decisions to make, dilemmas to solve and new emotional storms to navigate. Rather like a brain-training game, parenting pushes us to upskill with each new level."*[9]

Who would have thought that parenting and motherhood could actually make you more intelligent? It is time to bust the 'Baby Brain' myth.

The strengths and attributes of being a leader and a parent are evident in the workplace—even if they are undervalued in society, emotionally intelligent leaders can identify the benefits when women bring these skills to the workplace. Add single parenting and a mortgage to a woman's list of responsibilities, and efficiency and productivity levels increase even further. These are the people who get things done and are more empathetic.

Leaders who have people queuing up to be a part of their team, who have people constantly asking to be mentored and whose principals

---

8   *The Women's Brain Book: The Neuroscience of Health, Hormones and Happiness,* Dr Sarah McKay, pg 215

9   Ibid., pg 216

offer to sponsor them and catapult their careers care about people. They understand that they have future generations in their care.

They are adaptive leaders.

Prioritise and build independence

You learn a lot through being a mother and raising children. You have the opportunity to see your role as a mother as creating independent adults who are good citizens, and you can bring that same type of thinking to work.

> "Parenting makes you a better person because you've just got to get on with it. Some days are hell and some days are good, and you put one foot in front of the other and do the best you can at everything and hope that everyone comes through okay. It's hard balancing and you have to get really good at prioritisation."

Sharpen acceptance, empathy and critical thinking

A common benefit of productivity and human flourishing is that they can give you a better sense of tolerance, empathy and joining in. The insight helps you become a better leader and allows you to be able to quickly discern between a critical issue and a small issue. Your daily life is about meeting different needs and being able to dial up different degrees of leadership or management as required. At home and in the workplace.

> "Pre-kids, I was much more dogmatic. Then expressing your nurturing and growing traits with your children means you develop these skills and you bring these into the workforce. You're a better leader because you are constantly thinking about how do you grow and improve and empower your team to achieve, not just yourself. I think you have a real sense of being part of something bigger and I think that motherhood really helps with that."

Higher business performance and flexibility

> "I certainly became a better leader and business owner. I have been able to create an environment now with my business where much more flexibility and consideration is given to those that need it.

"It has given me a massive appreciation of particularly the need for understanding and flexibility for people at work. Not necessarily families, it could be anybody—people have lives outside of work and have needs."

The world needs more people who care

Do you need more convincing that skills developed and sharpened as a result of parenting are valuable? According to the World Economic Forum *Future of Jobs Report 2018*, the skills needed currently and for the next five years are aligned with the skills developed as a parent:

1. Analytical thinking and innovation

2. Complex problem-solving

3. Critical thinking and analysis

4. Active learning and learning strategies

5. Creativity, originality and initiative

6. Emotional intelligence

7. Reasoning, problem-solving and ideation

8. Leadership and social influence.

People with these skills are well positioned to thrive now and into the Fourth Industrial Revolution. This flips traditional collective thinking, the accepted code and the traditional order.

How do you value your contribution?

Could you entertain the thought that everything you do right now to contribute to human flourishing is important and is enough? The seemingly menial tasks you complete day in, day out, the people you support in all your roles—coaching, training, counselling and listening—all of it is important. If you realise how important you are, can you dial down the busyness, release some pressure and take your focus off productivity?

Productivity and caring pressure release

Notice the human flourishing tasks

Do you ever have mornings, days or weeks when it feels as though you are not getting anything done? I know I do and it is frustrating.

Perhaps it is because you are trying to focus on achieving productive, measurable tasks when you are mainly doing caring and human flourishing tasks. It can feel like you are spinning your wheels and not moving in the direction you want to.

To relieve this pressure, think about what you are doing and acknowledge that, however menial, it is important work and needs to be done — but you are not necessarily the person who has to do it all of the time.

Can you then recognise and appreciate what you are contributing?

It may seem like just an extra thing, but if you keep a list of all of the caring tasks which are not on your productivity list, you may be surprised.

I have created a model to illustrate this which is in the Appendix on page 308.

10 Have it all pressure

"It's that classic thing that women can have it all. I think that definition of having it all really comes back to how hard you are on yourself. You've been a working woman for so long and then your whole life changes; the way in which you perceive productivity changes too."

Why do we need to Mind the Gap?

Unmet expectations can be a relationship and passion killer. The huge gap between what you expect from yourself and what you can realistically deliver, and what you expect from others and what they can realistically deliver may result in frustration, disappointment, conflict and disconnection—leading to isolation and loneliness.

What is causing this though? Aspiring to the model of success without knowing what it really looks and feels like? Wanting more out of life? Knowing how hard you have worked, but are still dissatisfied?

Do you harbour fears of not being seen, not being fulfilled and not living up to potential, and feeling dissatisfied, unproductive, incompetent, constricted and contorted? Driving the fears is the universal need to be acknowledged and feel worthy of love.

Do you feel the pressure to have it all?

Do you put pressure on yourself and expect high returns, focusing on parenting, work and the interplay between the two? For several decades women have been driven to have it all (another pressure placed on us externally and driven internally). Some people believe it is not possible to have it all without personal or professional costs, while others believe it is possible, but just not all at once.

Why do we want to contribute to the world by engaging in meaningful work whether paid or unpaid and, at the same time, care for others? Do working and parenting give us a greater sense of wellbeing and fulfilment?

Are contributing, developing confidence outside the home and caring roles seen as an indulgence when the societal expectation and Gender Code dictate that women should suffer in the service of others and support their significant male? Is 'having it all' the ultimate violation of the Gender Code and why women work so hard to feel as though the success/suffering equation is worth it?

It is time to ditch the either/or thinking and change the conversation from *can* women 'have it all' to *what* is the 'all' that each person uniquely wants. Then explore how that looks and feels and how it can be achieved. The third, alternative, world is waiting to be created.

First, let's dive deeper into what is behind the 'having it all' illusion.

What is the lifelong model you have built?

> *"The hardest part for me was more the illusion of what motherhood would be and the fact that it was pretty boring and relentless. I always say it was never the boys that were the most difficult part of parenting; it was me becoming a mum, and my expectations of what it would be like versus the reality. A lot of that was the fact that I was no longer this person who had this job and was autonomous."*

To understand where you are at right now, it is important to review how you have created your personal identity. Have you built a model founded on a super-duper career? Or decided that the only way to exist is to have children and forgo your career? Or do you strive to do both? Or something else?

96

If you are feeling fulfilled, then excellent. However, if there is an expectation gap between where you are and where you would like to be, it may be difficult to change long-held views and decades of training and create something different.

Liz's perspective

Liz, the chief operating officer of an international bank, admitted that she could not do her best at work and be the parent she wanted to be. So she chose not to have children, focusing most of her energy on her career. She believed that if she had children she would feel as though she were failing at both.

> *"I firmly believe that you can't have it all. I absolutely could not do this job and have a family and not feel like I was failing on both fronts."*

Liz, an incredibly high achiever, appreciates that when people have children they need to prioritise their family, and that there will always be another opportunity in their careers to take on the next role and progress.

It was clear that she treated her colleagues as family and nurtured them, providing a safe environment, stability and care. *"I chose not to have children; now I have 300 of them in my department. I make that joke probably once a month. I am the matriarch."*

Liz didn't like the model she had growing up, and wanted to create a financial and emotional stability and care model with her own family, and also with her work family. This provides tremendous drive and purpose.

She is respected and valued, and the key to her success is not just her intelligence, work ethic and professional performance, but also her focus on helping her team to flourish.

My own perspective

Based on my own value system over a decade ago, I also believed I couldn't contribute my best at work and be the best parent; however I chose to have children, be a stay-home parent and not return to paid employment. A primary focus on parenting was more important to me than my career at the time. This theme of not being able to parent and have a career at a high level is common.

Kate's perspective

Kate is an executive in People and Culture for a mjaor corporate, and has a young daughter. She has maintained her high-pressure role but feels incredibly conflicted. Could she be considered successful after becoming a parent, as she was not doing as much at work as before, because her life had changed?

> *"Maybe I'm the worst problem in all of the people involved in my concern for whether I'm doing enough. If I felt like [I were] doing enough internally, then perhaps it would be fine. The story that I'm telling myself is that it is a problem. It's more my own perception; deep down I know that I'm not doing enough at work and I'm not doing enough at home. Because I can't possibly do it all."*

This is what women struggle with.

Like many other women, Kate felt she was failing in each area when she was in the other. She believed she couldn't do it all because being the ideal mother was not compatible with her perception of career success.

> *"If you asked me what makes a great executive in People and Culture, I would paint the picture of what I used to be in terms of the hours needed and how I constantly innovated and changed things. If you asked me what a perfect mother would look like, it would be one that's got a nine 'til three job. I can drop off the kids, pick them up, do some chores, and be really calm. For me, that's the perfect mum and I haven't transitioned.*

> *"How can I fit into those two roles of still doing a great job, but not feeling guilty that I am not pushing and innovating as much as in my earlier career? I feel like this still two years after becoming a mum."*

With many career and businesswomen there is a tension between the expectations of *wanting* to do it all, an *obligation* to do it all and the perception that *it is not actually possible* to do it all. The expectations we set for ourselves personally and professionally can be at complete odds. But that is another myth which you may be telling yourself without even realising it.

You may be trying to achieve something that is ultimately elusive—an imaginary world comprised of the best bits of your parenting and professional worlds. But rather than trying to bring the two worlds together, dedicating energy and attention to balancing and blending, a third approach is possible.

Let's rethink expectations

If you ditch the idea of having it all and accept we don't need to aspire to that, but that each of us is unique and will respond differently and everyone needs to make their own choices, then you can feel comfortable with what works best for your family and situation.

> *"I think over time you can hope that people are seeing enough to understand there is a spectrum of success, because it comes back to what they're defining as success. You can define success as number one, you are achieving your career goals. Or you can define it as number one your children are healthy, happy and achieving whatever it is you want them to achieve.*

> *"I've tried full-time work; I've tried part-time work. I've tried not working. I fundamentally got to the conclusion, there's no nirvana. Everything comes with compromise and consequences and you just have to choose the one that has the least number of problems for you."*

What if you also accept and embrace that what you have right now and what you experience every day is actually having it all? Could you consider another view of the dynamics at play? That most reasons for how you operate and the model you are building are driven by the rules of the Gender Code, your lifetime training and the constant messaging?

Can you question the Gender Code, start a different training programme and create your own messages that work for you rather than against you?

Have it all pressure release

Decide where you sit on your spectrum of success and fulfilment right now.

What are your top priorities?

Do you have an either/or approach and you are trying to straddle two worlds or mash them together?

Accepting this is an inside-out solution, what do you need to tell yourself to adjust your expectations?

You can skip ahead to chapter 17, 'C is for Core', for a workable solution to having it all.

11 Pressure to work harder

"As professional women, because we put so much hard work into getting to where we are, especially in a male-dominated industry, we're always trying to prove ourselves and our worth, to work harder than everyone else, to be that successful woman, because it seems like it's a harder thing to achieve than to be a successful man."

Do you need to work harder to be equal?

A frequent theme was women's perception that they need to work harder than men just to be equal.

Do you feel this? If so, what could be driving it?

Where does the idea you need to work harder come from? It is a result of gender or training: a combination of the messages you have received, who delivered them and how often, what has resonated most, what you subconsciously choose to believe and to what extent you have locked it into your behaviours and beliefs.

Many factors contribute to the pressure to work harder exerted by the Gender Code and fed by personal expectations. These include but are not limited to eight major challenges for women: working in male-dominated industries, becoming the main earner in the family, having high personal expectations, perceptions of professional confidence, the expression of opinions, who is awarded credit for achievement and how, the fact that mistakes are judged harshly, taking longer to be forgotten, and the question of commitment after becoming a parent.

1. Playing by the rules in male-dominated systems

It is tough working and carving out a career in male-dominated industries and workplaces. This was my home base during my finance career working for corporations in engineering services. I believed that my performance, work ethic and professionalism should determine how I was perceived and treated.

Early in my career I observed those ahead of me, both men and women, and emulated their behaviours of working long hours, being dedicated to the job and the company, looking for opportunities to progress and being constantly available.

My early and mid-career workplaces had a strong drinking culture, where the extent to which you could push yourself in pubs and clubs after work was an indication of your toughness and calibre. One senior leader had a policy of conducting work functions Monday through to Thursday evenings in the belief that it is better to recover from a hangover at work rather than at home over the weekend. Sharing stories of the night before was also a way to build working relationships.

I was a wannabe member of the boys' club without knowing it.

When I reflect on that time, I maintain that the competitive, 100 per cent results-focused part of me was in the driver's seat — the competitive qualities typically associated with the gendered male way of operating. For most of my life I had thought that gender differences are based on outlook and that we determine the extent to which we are discriminated against. I believed in the power of the individual to shape their own destiny. I disliked gender quotas, a question I was asked at a job interview at a big four accounting firm, and was convinced merit was more important. I felt I had worked hard to be where I was and achieve what I had, and that taking personal responsibility was the key to success.

I blindly thought I wanted to work harder than the men and be as productive as possible, in competition with everyone. Sometimes you need to see and feel other people's suffering to recognise your own and do something about it.

Everything changed as I researched this book. I saw how gender biases have operated in my own family, workplaces, local community groups, educational institutions and sporting clubs throughout my life. And how I have been innocently perpetuating the patriarchy. I came to understand that merit is actually defined by the people in charge, whose biases within the pyramid system create, consciously and unconsciously, inequality and gender-related pressure.

Amanda, who works in banking, thinks it is more about her than the male colleagues.

"It's probably more definitely about my perception, are they freer than me? Because a lot of the men I've worked with over the years, their partners never worked so I was always different. I've only ever worked full-time. I've never worked part-time. So I've just always felt different. And its male work, male-dominated always."

As a stockbroker working in a male-dominated industry, Teagan feels the full force of the Gender Code. She attends a conference annually and at the most recent one she attended there were 10 women in a sea of 200 plus.

Although small in number, Teagan says these are very powerful, strong-willed women, and the men in the group equate them to a man. She feels as though she needs to be man-like to be okay in that environment.

"You can't be the perception of what a woman is and be successful in a male-dominated industry. It's changing, I think, with all of the talk of equality. But equal pay isn't really going to bring about change in someone's mindset. It's interesting how they'll then say to you 'Oh, she's all right. She can deal with that, because she takes it like a man.'"

2. Are you the highest family earner?

With more women in higher paid roles, there is an increase in the financial contribution of the female member of a partnership to the family income pot. This is a double-edged sword as it also means a greater degree of responsibility.

Belinda, the director of an accounting firm, said that being the main income earner gives her more responsibility, so she feels she has to work even harder. There is no pressure from her partner—the expectation is hers, and it impacts her career choices and how she operates.

"100 per cent it's things that I've put on myself."

She believes she has to work harder than her male colleagues to be the main earner. Her partner's parents are quite traditional and make comments, but it works for them.

"I feel like I do, but I don't know whether I do or not. That's a really hard question, I think. You feel like you're always trying to justify yourself, but whether that's all in my head or not I don't know. But maybe if that's what you feel, then that's what it is."

Whatever you believe is true for you.

3. Women have higher expectations

No wonder women have higher expectations than their male counterparts in terms of their performance, when the system dictates we need to operate in the preferred male way, but does not train us in how.

4. Let's talk about confidence

"I think men have more confidence than women, which is really hard on a woman. Because you feel like you can't be confident, you feel the discrimination and they make you feel lucky to have your position, and you feel like you should pull out the stops."

Lack of confidence is one of the most frequent explanations for discrepancies in competitiveness and achievement between women and men, although this umbrella explanation needs deconstructing to see why women perceive a need to work harder than men.

Is the confidence gap fact or fiction?

The confidence gap has been used to explain why women don't pursue promotion and earn less.

Studies highlight how confidence in pre-adolescent and teenage girls can dip markedly compared to boys of the same age, although self-esteem in boys at this developmental stage is now being examined more closely and some controversial research suggests that there is no gap in confidence between genders.

A study conducted by the University of Minnesota involving almost 100,000 participants found that the confidence gap shrinks considerably by the age of 23. Other research shows that this may be more to do with men over-rating their abilities and self-promoting.

So in general women may not necessarily lack confidence, but men are overconfident. The constant comparison handicaps women. Males tend to be more confident in the workplace as they have been trained to achieve and succeed within a structure created to suit their preferred way of operating. There is no perceived deficit and less pressure to bridge any gaps.

Women have typically not received the same level of training and may be less confident operating within a structure not designed to ensure they achieve and succeed. This may contribute to their drive to make up for the lack of gender training by working harder.

While there are a few exceptions in terms of physical differences, in sexuality and aggression we are more similar than different, however women and men have been brain-trained differently.

5. Is your voice heard?

Not being acknowledged or valued is not only frustrating, but can lead to disengagement. Or you may become more determined to ensure you are heard, and work harder in the process.

Having worked in her company for three months, Tracey, a chief financial officer, tackled a problem with the chair of the board, who said he didn't have confidence that she knew what she was doing because she said 'um' too often in meetings.

Tracey decided it was an important issue to address and wanted specific feedback from the chairperson one-on-one outside the meetings, so she organised a coffee meeting with him planning to go straight to the point and build up their relationship. He was surprisingly open to her questions and her feeling that the board was chauvinistic, and admitted his treatment of her was driven by experience with another female director who had *waffled and talked too much*", which had infuriated him. Although she had been considered talented and a high-level contributor, the chairperson could not see, hear or value her due to her way of speaking.

"The chairman is an engineer and he wants things in a very short, succinct format. He's 70 and has limited patience."

This is how male training results in men pulling the problem inside, processing it internally, finding a solution and then sharing it externally. Contrastingly, female training results in women sharing the problem externally, processing externally and sharing externally, building relationships with people in the process.

Tracey has had several coffee meetings with the chairperson now and, as a result of her creative approach, he is a great deal more receptive to her communication style and values her contribution more highly.

Less obvious factors such as accepted practice may push women to work harder. They should be examined as they are why some women are unable to progress in the workplace, which explains why women perceive a gap in productivity expectations that they need to work harder to bridge.

6. Do you get kudos?

In her article 'Women Need More Money. Being More Confident Won't Help Them Get It', Sarah Green Carmichael suggests that, generally speaking, women receive less credit for their work, particularly when they work with men.[1] Based on a current study in the USA, it found women have started to ask for pay rises as often as men, but are less likely to receive them or receive a smaller increase.

7. Are you judged more harshly?

Mistakes made by women both professionally and personally are usually judged more severely and take longer to be forgotten. Also, when women do not act in accordance with gender stereotypes, they are judged more harshly. Penalties for women violating the gender stereotype are greater and can affect being hired, performance reviews and evaluations and leadership opportunities.

---

1 'Women Need More Money. Being More Confident Won't Help Them Get It',
   Sarah Green Carmichael, Barrons.com, 13 February 2019

Research conducted by Assistant Professor of Economics Martin Abel from Middlebury College, USA, found that criticism from a female leader led to lower job satisfaction and engagement with a company, as compared to criticism by a male leader. There is a higher expectation that people will receive criticism from male leaders and an expectation they will receive higher levels of praise from female leaders.[2]

If the people you lead have subconscious expectations of your management style and you violate the gender stereotype, they feel unsafe and may react negatively, making you feel that you are being judged more harshly and need to work harder and get training and/or coaching and/or strategies to 'be better' and progress in your career.

Do you play a part in perpetuating the Gender Code? Do you have high expectations and judge your female leaders, daughters, mother, friends and other women in your life more harshly when they violate the gender stereotype?

8. Is your commitment questioned?

Women who are also parents are questioned consistently in terms of their commitment to their paid work, which contributes to the drive to work harder.

> "And it's the comment you get like, 'Oh, you're only part-time?' Or, and I get told all the time you know, 'You're a part-time director?' I'm actually not. I'm the director, and I just happen to work part-time.

> "I'm not a part-time parent. I'm a parent.

> "I get them all. One time we were at a seminar and someone senior said 'You don't need to be listening to half of this. You only work half the time.'

> "I thought 'That says so much more about you than it does about me.'"

This view is based on gendered expectations and not the reality of the individual's contribution. Anecdotal evidence and research on academics reveal that women are more productive after motherhood.

---

2 'Do Workers Discriminate against Female Bosses?', Martin Abel, IZA Institute of Labor Economics, Discussion Paper Series, IZA PD No. 12611, September 2019

An experienced senior male executive I interviewed believes that a woman having a child is one of the cheapest time efficiency training methods possible. When he wants something done, he gives it to a woman with children. Another said that the highest level contributor in terms of getting things done is a single woman with children and a mortgage.

> *"They are masters at getting shit done. When I give her a job, I know I can 100 per cent rely on her."*

Work harder pressure release

While it is unfair that women should be under pressure to work harder and still not be necessarily considered equal or above male counterparts, there can be upsides.

If you have spent most of your life looking for ways to go above and beyond, seeking opportunities, applying yourself to tasks and projects, then this is an incredible skills database. I have witnessed the efforts of and spoken with women who have not only worked really hard but also been incredibly creative, going outside 'the system' to get things done. You may be doing the same right now. If not, it is possible to become creatively resourceful!

When you know that you have this, you can draw on it whenever you need to achieve something.

The Gender Code dictates that you need to work harder to be considered on equal footing. You can use it as a limitation or as fuel.

12 Mental and emotional load pressure

Being a parent is a labour of love and a gift. All of that giving with what seems like little thanks and all of the needs and requests of multiple stakeholders fired at you constantly and sometimes simultaneously can be overwhelming.

Cries of exasperation from mothers include "I don't want to be a servant" and "If I died tomorrow the place would not function."

Can you relate to this?

Do you take on the mental load?

Women predominantly carry the mental load of managing work and family with list-making, planning and organising the lives of dependants, and some carry the financial load as well.

This may lead to being hyper-responsible—coordinating everyone and everything to give yourself a sense of control. Add a few pets and it is organised chaos at best, but sometimes you feel you can't share the mental load even if the support is there, which depletes your energy.

Why do it and what does it cost? Living this way can be a barrier to success and fulfilment, health and wellbeing. Do you need to feel indispensable or are you just trying to make everyone happy?

Be a hard-arse mum

One person's hard-arse mum may be another's view of building capacity. A senior executive in a not-for-profit organisation told me about carrying the mental load and being hyper-responsible, but frustrated that her children and husband did not contribute to the same extent she did at home. I noted Kathy performed more tasks for her children in terms of personal organisation than I was prepared to for mine when I was a stay-home parent.

Kathy had never wanted to be a housewife or stay-at-home mum. She was aware that I had been one for a number of years, so she quizzed me on my methods of operating and then told me a story illustrating her frustrations.

Rushed and under pressure, Kathy screeched into her work carpark one school morning and found her son's clarinet in the car. Options ran through her head, and the one that won was to take it to school for him. The knock-on effect meant she was late for all her meetings that day, she struggled to focus and she was exhausted by mid-afternoon.

Why did she put herself under that pressure, I asked? She replied *"What else could I have done? I didn't want to be a hard-arse mum."* She asked me what a stay-at-home mum would do.

Acknowledging my own hyper-responsibility and the solutions I implemented for improvement while conducting the research, I replied "I guess I would have been a hard-arse mum. Or rather, created an opportunity for my son to learn and grow while demonstrating my priorities are important too. I would not have dropped the clarinet off at school."

Kathy was shocked.

I have had several experiences of my sons leaving musical instruments, swimming bags, homework and goodies for friends in the car or at home and always chose not to turn around and drop the forgotten item off. I knew they could handle the disappointment and frustration, and I was able to live with knowing I could mitigate the situation and that it was a foundation for working with bigger problems in the future.

One morning I watched as my eldest got out of the car in his school uniform, complete with tie and blazer, but without his sport uniform on Sports Day. I wanted him to take responsibility for remembering key information and to reduce my responsibilities. I wondered how the day would play out, given sport and PE are his favourite subjects, and I was curious about the effect it would have.

He jumped into the car that afternoon and his body language did not give away anything. I asked him how school had been and had he played any sport. He replied "Yes." Not forthcoming and no mention of his uniform. I pressed him "So how did you get on?" He was unfazed: "I just took my tie off."

A sigh of relief from me that he did not have to deal with teasing—or didn't deem it worthy of note—and was not at all upset. In fact, I was slightly miffed as I had wanted him to learn a lesson, but he was confident and secure enough to deal with the situation.

Kathy just wanted to make sure her son was happy—that everyone in her life was happy. Her perception of being happy was that the people she loved did not feel disappointed, frustrated, sad or judgmental and she was driving herself into the ground and feeling depleted in the process.

Kathy is representative of the vast majority of parents and it is okay. I shared with her that it was not my goal or wish as a parent to make my children happy. Once again she was shocked.

After years of trying to engineer Utopia for my children, I eventually realised post-China that it was holding them and me back. All three of my children have a different view of happiness or fulfilment. It is out of my sphere of control. What I can do is create the optimal conditions and environment for them to flourish. And that is good enough.

Now my aim as a parent is to guide my children and help them flourish and live a good, moral, meaningful life and fulfil their unique potential as human beings. By building resilience, caring for others, becoming independent, building self-awareness and their self-knowledge database, using their strengths and being who they uniquely are, they get to decide what happiness looks and feels like for them. They also get to decide if they even want to pursue it.

Why do we feel the need to make others happy? Why do we struggle to be a hard-arse mum and release some of the load?

Do you carry the emotional load?

It turns out that once again, the messages contained in the Gender Code and the lifetime of training are driving it all.

Arlie Hochschild first wrote about emotional labour in her book, *The Managed Heart*. She brings attention to the issue of mothers doing most of the mental and physical caring with the intention of making sure everyone is happy.[1]

Emotional labour is when someone introduces or masks emotions to provide comfort or keep people happy. This was first identified as customer service, but is particularly appropriate for women's roles.

Gemma Hartley, the author of *Fed Up: Navigating and Redefining Emotional Labour for Good*, says that while the upside is caring and helping other people, the costs in depletion, burnout and resentment are considerable.[2]

While the caring aspects of emotional labour and supporting others are valuable and may lead to human flourishing, only about half of the population is trained to perform the work, which is completely out of balance and distributed along gender lines.

Women are trained by society in accordance with the cultural code. Our vocation is to care for others, keep everyone comfortable, be emotionally intelligent, show empathy, be nurturing. The constant messaging is that women are naturally inclined to carry out this work, and some are even raised to believe tending to other people's needs is a godly path.

Women's indoctrination encourages the belief that they are superior to men at emotional labour tasks and naturally inclined to care and nurture, but while that may be good for the ego and male-bashing sessions it is not so good for mental and physical wellbeing, especially since recent studies conclude that there is no evidence for this: it comes from internal bias and goes unquestioned.

Many males able to captain ships, run corporations and create engineering masterpieces seem incapable of picking up after themselves, let alone ensuring everyone is on task, because they have not received the training and don't value it very highly.

---

1   *The Managed Heart: Commercialization of Human Feeling*, Arlie Russell Hochschild

2   'Is the "work" you're doing emotionally draining you?', ABC Radio National *Life Matters*, 11 March 2019

The traditional Gender Code requires men to suppress emotions, place less value on caring for others, use focus and drive to further their own accomplishments so as to succeed, and be reliable breadwinners. This means that they miss out on opportunities for richer relationships and leads to their world being smaller. When emotional labour is balanced, everyone wins.

What are the benefits of emotional labour?

So how does emotional labour, an energy drain for many people, translate to contributing to human flourishing? How can we feel positive emotions about what we do to care for, support and serve others?

The first step is changing your mindset to acceptance and choice rather than obligation and duty, which just redistributes the load. When daily tasks are performed in a centred, purposeful way, they feel worthwhile and become an energy source—no longer sacrifices but choices.

How can you balance emotional labour?

Do you feel there is a bit of work to be done in your family to balance out the emotional labour? It is possible to achieve when everyone is on board with the idea.

Awareness and understanding are the first steps—and if that works you can reorient—though harmonising emotional labour with your partner may be fraught, and full of clunky, messy conversations reflecting on culture, conditioning and understanding. However, they should lead to a deeper practical understanding of each other's point of view and way of life.

In chapter 19 there is a guide on how to build true partnerships. One element is to view the important family administration tasks as a 'big bucket of family jobs'. Then when there is the belief that everyone is capable of performing the majority of the jobs, it becomes a process of building capacity in others rather than distributing according to the Gender Code.

Mental and emotional load pressure release

Stop taking all the responsibilities

The Gender Code is telling you that women need to take the lion's share of the responsibilities. You now know that this is neither natural nor instinctive, but based on nurture and neuroplasticity.

Build strength in others. Can you help partners, children, family members and work colleagues to start their own training programme, knowing it will create opportunities for a richer, more connected life?

13 Guilt and judgment pressure

"The mother guilt we have from the time they're babies to the time they're grown-ups—I think you always have mother guilt when you work. Have I spent enough time with them or done the right things? That, I think, was a challenge. Learning to be able to let go of work. That was one thing. It's taken me years, I think, to be able to really master that one a little bit better and to be able to find that balance."

The main pressure for most women who are parents is guilt. It ties in nicely with judgment and working hard to have it all and seeking the illusionary idea of balance. Perception of judgment, your own and others, fuels guilt. So before we launch into guilt, it is important to put judgment under the microscope.

Is judgment useful?

The desire to control our lives is strong in most of us and it is okay. This requires us to constantly make decisions about everything in our lives—from small things like what to have for breakfast to bigger things like career choices. Making decisions all day is exhausting—and it depletes willpower—which is why it is so much more difficult to resist chocolate and wine at night when you just want to unwind or reward yourself.

But using your judgment makes things easier. When you stick labels on boxes you can drop people, behaviours and experiences into them, which uses up less energy. Your brain likes this approach as it tends to want to operate efficiently based on well-worn convenient neural pathways. This is helpful when you need to put parts of your day on autopilot to achieve a daily rhythm. However, if you only read the labels on the boxes then you teach, interact with and treat people according to the description on the box and you may be ignoring treasures inside.

Poor judgment and categorising may focus on what is different and can be separated or compartmentalised rather than what is common and can be integrated. Assumptions prevent connection, which may cost you.

What makes you judgmental?

"There are... variables that predict when we judge and whom we judge. Typically, we pick someone doing worse than we're doing in an area we're most susceptible to, shame: Look at him. I may suck, but he sucks worse." Brené Brown[1]

Brené Brown explains this is why parenting is a 'judgment minefield'. As parents, we make mistakes constantly and it may be a relief to see someone else struggling even more, if only temporarily. It may provide some sort of comfort in the short term, but it will not solve your challenges if you are in judgment mode.

Can you think of what makes you judgmental? Do you find yourself making unkind comments about other people's appearances and personal presentation? You may express it outwardly to others or keep in locked in your head. Perhaps the achievements of others are difficult for you to accept. Maybe it is the behaviour of other people's children. Whatever it may be that activates your judgmental feelings, there is a high probability it is something you struggle with personally.

There may be hurdles, detractors or derailers and negative self-talk, but ultimately judgment usually comes from dissatisfaction with yourself which you then project onto others.

---

1   *Dare to Lead*, Brené Brown, pg 228

Do you want to dial down the judgment?

"The good news is that we don't judge in areas where we feel a strong sense of self-worth and grounded confidence, so the more of that we build, the more we let go of judgment." Brené Brown[2]

It turns out that it all comes down to your sense of worth and confidence, which clear the way to redefine your present and future.

Violet's story

Violet is now a CEO of a not-for-profit. Twenty-five years ago she was a hard-working career woman in her early 30s when she had her first son. On one occasion, she took the baby to a women's organisation meeting where she served on the committee and he projectile vomited. This was not viewed with compassion by those at the meeting yet to experience motherhood.

Violet excused herself and tried to change him, but felt her only option was escape. When she got to her car she couldn't collapse the pram, her son started crying and Violet was so distressed that she asked a man walking past for help. He saw she was upset, walked over and helped her.

When Violet got home, she started to think *"I'm so stupid. Why do I have to worry about these things? I'm just going to be myself and it doesn't matter what they think. It's not important."*

The experience was positive, because Violet gave herself permission to be herself and not judge by other people's rules. When many of those women eventually decided to focus on their families, she realised that she had judged herself too harshly. *"Maybe that was just me—it wasn't them, it was probably more me."*

She examined her negative self-talk and her perceived judgment by others and realised that she was struggling with insecurity brought about by moving from career woman only to career woman and parent.

"That's the message. It was a hard lesson for me. I think there are things you've got to live through to understand what motivates you. For me, for a while, it was important what people thought, and then later I thought, actually, it's not. It's about how I feel or what's

---

2 Ibid., pg 145 and 146

important for me to be true to myself. That I don't have to be perfect and I don't have to be able to do everything. So once I was okay with that, then it was good."

When you can ignore external messages and build up your confidence, you can ask what this really has to do with you. Understanding this helps you to look to others to inspire you, rather than envy what they seem to have acquired over their lifetime. Building this muscle and using it is the antidote to judgment. It also helps with guilt.

Do you have mother guilt?

"With mother guilt, I think that mothers, working mothers probably put it upon themselves. I have to be a great mother and I have to be a great worker. So we probably put that expectation on ourselves."

Some researchers and experts believe guilt can be a healthy emotion: your conscience talking, helping you to pay attention to your behaviour and choices and motivating you to do better. Possibly, if used for growth and improvement, but I am not convinced that the way we view guilt is a positive motivator. Most often guilt is used negatively, as a way to reduce self-worth and confidence, and provide an obstacle to fulfilment and progression.

The term 'mother guilt' appeared regularly in the research interviews, and guilt plays a crucial role in building your identity. Women are conflicted by wanting to be able to achieve objectives at work, but also not wanting to feel that they let the family down.

"You work twice as hard at home as well just to make sure the family is okay.

"Being engaged at home with my family, I probably apply myself better at work, but also I suppose it takes that guilt away of actually being a working mum."

The feelings of guilt impact all areas of your life and when things become unstuck at home, it is hard to achieve balance. If home is your priority and things are not right, it is hard to be focused on everything you need to be focused on at work without feeling guilty about home.

Men can feel it too

Guilt about working and parenting is not only felt by women. While it plays out differently according to gender stereotypes, fathers suffer too.

A male perspective is that people can substitute care-giving opportunities and experiences for money, but then feel guilty about missing time with the important people in their lives.

> *"People take themselves out of the home life by working 12 hours a day, going out on a Friday night, taking off on a Saturday. Then the kids may say 'I never see you' and the wife or the partner whinges. People feel guilty, so they spend money. You feel like you need to substitute that failure or sense of lack of attention by spending money."*

Mark says that although societal messages and expectations tell people that by spending money they will feel better, the reality is a downward spiral of feeling worse: more guilt, more debt, more work to pay off the debt, and less time for loved ones.

The guilt experienced by Mark seems closely tied to the pressure to be the breadwinner, which fits the gender stereotypes, but now there is more pressure to be an engaged parent too. Women are typically socialised or gender trained to be carers and now they feel pressure to be a breadwinner too. Guilt from the two perspectives manifests differently, but in accordance with the Gender Code.

Is there more to mothers' guilt that we need to know about?

I believe there is a greater depth to mothers' guilt that we do not really talk about and it needs to be explored. Perhaps it is other emotions we feel: nervousness, excitement, exhaustion, depletion, disappointment, fulfilment and uncertainty. Women with pressure at work who are parents are constantly feeling these and other mixtures of emotions, so why dump them all in the mother guilt bucket? Women are constantly having to compromise, so it is no wonder there are difficult feelings to deal with.

> *"Wherever you focus, the other part of your life is lacking, so it's this constant state of guilt—where I've put all of these hours into my work day, so my house isn't clean, or I haven't remembered that this kid has this thing on, or something like that."*

There may be a chance you are feeling resentful. This can be one of the most detrimental challenges a woman can face as it drains energy, destroys clarity and, as a result, is a huge barrier. Persistent resentment destroys relationships—the relationship with yourself and with others—and so it is crucial to identify and eliminate it.

Next time you feel you may be having an attack of guilt, ask yourself if it could be other feelings you are experiencing, knowing that it is okay to feel them.

How can you dial down the guilt?

Guilt may be a necessary part of a full, rewarding and purposeful life, but it doesn't need to be so overwhelming.

Women who feel that their contribution matters—as a stay-at-home mother, working full-time in a demanding role or working part-time—suffer less guilt. When they are satisfied with their contribution and feel valued, they are confident. They are also able to work on mindfully being where they are—wherever they are—embracing it and ascribing value to the experience at the time.

> "When I go overseas for work, the stay-at-homes ask 'Do you feel guilty, do you feel bad?' They share my pain. I miss my daughters of course. If I watch a movie, and it has anything to do with kids, I cry on the plane. But then, we just call all the time and we FaceTime, and we do little things that make it work. For me, I just think 'Find a solution.' It's doable."

Karen's story and her term 'stay-at-homes,' which she delivered in the most non-judgmental way, makes me laugh as it resonates with my own experiences. When I was a stay-at-home I felt no guilt about not working. I was exactly where I was meant to be. When I started to build my business I did not value it as much as being a stay-home parent, so there was conflict. When I ascribed a higher value to my work and felt valued working, I did not suffer regular guilt or conflict as my children had received the best parts of me over the years and they continue to do so. There are moments of guilt and they hurt, but I don't feed them with energy and make up stories in my head about it so they don't become barriers.

Do you feel shame pressure?

"We live in a world where most people still subscribe to the belief that shame is a good tool for keeping people in line. Not only is this wrong, but it's dangerous." Brené Brown

What is the difference between shame and guilt?

Thanks to the solid work of Brené Brown, over the past decade we have become a great deal more familiar with shame. It is tempting to place shame and guilt under the one umbrella and often people use the two interchangeably, but she says that how people experience guilt and shame is different and there are distinctions *"in terms of biology, behaviour and self-talk, and they lead to radically different outcomes."*[3]

Most clinicians, researchers and experts in the field agree that guilt is experienced as "I *did* something bad", whereas shame is experienced as "I *am* bad."[4]

One is a focus on behaviour ("I made a mistake") and the other is a focus on self ("I am a mistake"), so the language is important:

"I can't believe I forgot to pick up my child from the event. I was so engrossed in my project/work/task/conversation. I will pay more attention next time or ask someone else to do it."

versus

"I can't believe I forgot to pick up my child from the event. I was so engrossed in my project/work/task/conversation. I am such a bad parent. I am crap at this 'doing it all' business."

Exploring shame is personal and outside the scope of this book; however, understanding how judgment, guilt and shame are playing out in your life is an important step to understanding the pressure points you may be experiencing. Then you can release them.

---

3 *Dare to Lead*, op. cit., pg 128
4 Ibid.

Guilt and judgment pressure release

Is it mother guilt or something else?

You may experience guilt persistently or intermittently. Can you describe your state more deeply? The language you use with yourself and with others is important and shapes your moment by moment experiences.

If you prefer a list of words:

https://www.cnvc.org/sites/default/files/feelings_inventory_0.pdf

If you prefer pictures, emoji charts can be effective.

The challenge is to avoid the default term of 'mother guilt'. Using it feeds it.

Focus on the present

When you are able to be present in each moment and to think and believe that you are giving your best, there is no room left for guilt, even if you are failing to get through a gargantuan list of tasks. People know if you are emotionally present for them or only physically present and concentrating on something else — it is just a choice you make. Should you think about work while you cook dinner if your child wants your attention?

14 Time pressure

"An hour sitting with a pretty girl on a park bench passes like a minute, but a minute sitting on a hot stove seems like an hour."
Albert Einstein

Time was cited by research participants as a huge challenge. Scheduling and managing work, home and community in a complex environment that is evolving and changing rapidly can overwhelm you. But are perceptions of time just another myth? We all have 24 hours a day and we have to use them better.

How do you perceive time?

Time poverty is a problem of perception and of distribution. When did time become so important?

"Time poor", "I don't have time", "I have run out of time", "I wish I had more time", "There are only so many hours in the day"—those phrases create a sense of scarcity. "Cash rich and time poor" makes both into a resource, and having an equal amount of time should be a leveller, so how can there be more or less?

One explanation can be traced back to when the clock was first used to synchronise labour in the 18th century. Since then time has been understood in relation to money. With hours quantified financially, people become more concerned about using them profitably—saving time and wasting time. As economies and incomes grow, time becomes more valuable, and as the value of time increases, so too does the perception of scarcity, becoming more how people see time rather than how much time they have.[1] So we ascribe a higher value to our time, but what about the tasks themselves and the decisions as to how to use time?

Are you using time wisely?

There is pressure to use financially quantified hours wisely and be productive as a higher value is ascribed to actual or perceived income producing activities. If you are not productive, the precious resource of time is being used inefficiently and your level of contribution is diminished.

Time poverty pressure contributes to trying to be everything to everyone and feeling nothing is ever good enough. So you don't feel you are doing enough since caring for others without financial rewards is not considered time as well spent as time dedicated to the pursuit of a salary. We assume full-time carers' time is not as valuable or important as office workers' or any paid workers' time and that carers can be more flexible and adaptable.

This perception reinforces the myths around parenting too, although focusing on benefits rather than rewards should reduce performance pressure. We discussed this in chapter 9, 'Productivity and caring pressures'.

How does time fly so fast?

As my children grow up, I have more conversations about how time flies. Many people talk about how quickly their own children are growing up, and how much they wish they could slow time down. Some feel out of control and others worry they have missed out on important milestones.

Do you ever feel this way? One minute it is the end of January and the start of the school year and it seems like the next thing you know, you have to manage Christmas, the end of the school year and summer holidays. Does it seem like each year is elapsing at warp speed?

I have found that time seems to pass at different rates over the years and it is all down to feeling valued and being present. When I am feeling

---

1 'In search of lost time: Why is everyone so busy?' *The Economist*, 20 December 2014

present, there is less temptation and a lower tendency to jam more tasks into the day and consequently more opportunities to reflect.

Over the years of being a parent, I have shared most of my eldest son's experiences, frustrations, challenges and milestones with my parenting L plates on. We have forged paths together: new schools, communities, sporting clubs, friendships and countries. At times he has completely blown me away, and I have both loved and been challenged by every stage of his human flourishing, but I never feel I would like to revisit any time — especially the discombobulated toddler stage — nor is there any regret or wishing I had done things differently. I did the best I could with the resources available to me at the time. That is good enough.

However, when I shifted my focus to paid work, time seemed to speed up all of a sudden. The school terms whizzed past and I felt I was not keeping up. I felt the increased stress of trying to meet everyone's needs in addition to my own. I was struggling big time.

What helped me was reflecting on my eldest's tenth birthday several years earlier. Time seemed to go by at an appropriate rate back then and I wondered why things had changed so much — surely more than the change from non-paid to paid work.

I started to think differently. By accepting that wherever I am is exactly where I need to be and it was okay to use my energy for working and parenting. This mindset shift reduced performance pressures. Then I valued each task and activity I was dedicating effort and attention to, whether it was a human flourishing task, a business task or an investment in my own wellbeing.

The final part of the process was to be present in each moment. Whether at work or at home or wherever you are, being present creates the right conditions for better outcomes for everyone.

This approach helped reduce the feeling of being out of control and wasting time. It may seem counterintuitive, but being present creates space. Being in the moment — the acts of sharing, connecting and enjoying — nourish the soul. Conversely, being overwhelmed, disengaged and down can be excruciating and soul-destroying.

It is a continuously evolving work in process. I have not eliminated feelings of being overwhelmed, but I have dialled them down and have a procedure in place during the tough moments when I am on the verge of being reactive.

Do you use time as an excuse?

This is an area of fascination I have explored for many years and it was a particular focus when I became a parent. The go-to response when we cannot or will not do something on another person's terms is often "I don't have time." However when you think more deeply about it, this is actually code for "It is not a priority right now for me."

Why are we not more honest about time and the pressures we feel? It is rather obvious that most people do not want to let others know where they sit on the priority ladder as that can be difficult to digest for people who are not near the top rung. It can cause discomfort for all involved, regardless of how true it is.

However, when you are honest about your priorities, at least to yourself, it is possible to learn more about who, what, where, how and why you ascribe value to what you do. Which will help you release the pressure.

Being time poor is another myth we have innocently bought into to explain productivity expectation gaps. Rather than fighting for time and attaching expectations and hope, focus on what each experience provides.

Time pressure release

Expand time

The Einstein quote gives a clue about how to expand time—it is more about how you feel and how you flow. You don't actually need more time—you need more depth of experience in the time you have.

The solution is to be present.

Look at your language

Could you be using "I don't have time" as an excuse for "This is not a priority"?

Try this experiment:

1. Make a note of how often you use time as a reason or explanation for why you can't do something

2. Try not to use time as an excuse for a day, a week, a month.

What do you find out?

part four
HOW TO WRITE AND EXECUTE YOUR OWN CODE

15 Where to next?

Questioning, interpreting and understanding the Gender Code and how it influences your own personal code, I looked at how to release the pressures it creates. While it is helpful to have a deeper awareness, how do you navigate your way to feeling you are doing and being enough?

A conversation with my son showed me.

The first Code conversation

It is 4:09 pm on Thursday, March 14th, 2019. My middle son and I are surrounded by surfboards, surf accessories and surfers. There is a huge widescreen TV blaring in the background telecasting the latest world championship surf competitions. The alluring scent of coffee beans wafts through the air with the accompanying sound of grinding beans as the barista prepares my long black.

Leo and I are in our favourite local surf shop/café while my youngest is enjoying himself close by in drama class. It is a perfect opportunity to spend one-on-one time with Leo. No brotherly competition for my attention and energy, no need to elevate or play the sibling family role. Just Leo and me.

I started to ask about his day, how his friends are and if there was anything he wanted to discuss. He did not seem interested in pouring his heart out to me, having a deep and meaningful discussion or even sharing his joys, disappointments, fears and challenges as I had hoped.

I thought it was the perfect environment for him to express himself as he had centre stage. However as is typically the case and incredibly perplexing and frustrating to me, when all three boys are together and the adult to kid ratio is 1:3, they are full of ideas, thoughts, challenges, questions, stories, and compete with each other to be heard. Conversely, when the ratio is a balanced 1:1, they become less chatty and I need to extract goodies from them.

It seemed this time Leo was more focused on his smoothie and surfing than sharing, so I started talking about my work.

I told him about working towards breaking the Gender Code and how its rules had been embedded into our culture for millennia, determining how we think, feel and behave.

He digested it, paused and asked *"Mum, is your Gender Code anything like the coding we do in CIY (Code It Yourself) club?"*

I felt a rush of excitement and all sorts of light bulbs started popping.

"Hold that thought," I replied, sensing we were about to have an important conversation I wanted to capture.

I had my dictaphone handy as I was in the midst of conducting interviews for the research project. I whipped it out, pressed record and asked Leo about his experiences with coding, why he loved it and why it was important for him to participate in the after-school classes, which he had been doing for three years.

He replied *"I am usually the worker person and my big brother is usually the person who bosses me around, but in coding whatever you are coding does not boss you around. You get to do whatever you want with it. I am in charge, so I can do anything I want when I make my own code."*

I had to pause. The connection between deconstructing and revealing the Gender Code and Leo's love of coding created fireworks.

What is coding?

"Coding is just like telling something to do what you instruct it to do."

Types of coding

"There are different ways to code, using either Python or JavaScript—different types of coding with different types of symbols.

"Using Python or JavaScript you can make up anything. Not anything—you can't tell it to bring you ice-cream or something. You have to give the coordinates. You code it for the things you want to do."

Understand and read

As the coder, you have to understand how coding works and be able to read code.

"Before I knew how to code, if I saw a bunch of coding or something like a robot with loads of coding, I would be really confused.

"Now I can read code, if it pops up in something, somewhere, then I know what to do or what to say, because I know what it means.

"If you have a problem and there is a code to help you fix the problem, if you don't know how to read the code then you can't understand."

Question and choose

"I can make a choice to do what it is trying to say to do. Or not.

"If you are coding and it tells you what to do and you copy it and it makes sense, you do it. But if it doesn't make sense, doesn't have the right thing or something is missing, you have to fix it. You have to fix it and add the right things for what it needs."

Learn to create your code

"Sometimes you will have a plan.

"Once you know the basic stuff and you think it is right, then you try it. If it does what you want then you will know what to do next time."

Execute, experiment and apply

"When you think it is as good as it gets, you remember what you can do and then you can try new things. If it works, you remember for next time and you can use it again.

"Not all code has been created yet, so you can try new things that haven't been created yet and create it. When you try a new thing and it actually works then you can use it again. It will mean something different because no one has seen it before and they haven't used it.

"Then you can add on if you want something else."

Future

"In the future there will be robots. You will want to do things so you can use your own robot to help you. If you know how to code you can tell your robot what to do straight away. But if you don't know how to code then you will have to pay someone to do it. That will take more time and money."

I felt all the dots connect as things fell into place. Inspiration and connection can come from anywhere and anything. Every conversation counts.

This revealed to me that there are all sorts of codes in place and the Gender Code is one of a multitude. Code and coding is a fundamental part of our lives, in nature, music, families, workplaces, community groups, teams, friendships. Parts of the code are written and explicit, and some parts are unwritten and implicit.

As Leo said, when you understand how coding works, you can read the code. You can then see if it makes sense and make choices about which parts of the code resonate with you and which parts to dump. When you learn how to code yourself and create your own unique code, you are in charge. When you experiment with what you have created you can create new opportunities, which may evolve into something you had not thought possible.

Completely floored by the revelatory nature of our conversation, I gave Leo the biggest, warmest hug. I sensed he could feel how I saw his brilliance and that it had helped me. It still lights me up to think about it.

This provided the foundation for a framework to deconstruct collective thinking and look at an alternative.

- *Understand and read* — What is your code?

- *Question and choose* — Ask if the code still makes sense. Do you want to continue to follow, tweak, delete and/or create?

- *Learn to create* — Write your own code, execute it and experiment.

How you can take charge and control

If you would like to continue with your current code then that is perfectly okay, but it is important to make an informed choice. It does not have to be all or nothing, and although it may seem radical on the inside, the shift can be a matter of reorientation rather than transformation.

You can seize opportunities in our increasingly complex and continuously evolving world to write new codes. Become even more of an asset in your profession by being a sustainable agent of change and contributing to restructuring a more mobile and responsive society. Keep parts of the code, delete others and create new parts. Build a different, more fulfilling reality.

16 What you need to know before writing and executing your new code

Choosing something different is a bold move. Rewiring is not for the faint-hearted. You may experience denial, anger, frustration, sadness, and then ultimately acceptance and growth, because becoming a code breaker and violator inevitably causes judgment and guilt or shame. You may worry about being selfish by putting yourself first or that this new way of operating is not for the greater good, but I assure you that it is absolutely crucial for the health and wellbeing of all involved.

Violating the code and becoming 'other'

Whether you violate the Gender Code, marriage code, parenting code, work code, family code or friendship group code, when you write your own code and live on your own terms, you may be perceived as 'other'.

When you no longer fit in, people who play by the rules find it difficult to relate to you in your new context, but you have to understand that they are doing their best with the resources available to them.

In the absence of data, storytelling plays a powerful role as we create stories to explain our world and the people in it. These stories range from innocuous to fanciful, isolating code violators and elevating those playing by generally accepted rules.

Sense of self

If you accept that personal fears and insecure thinking drive negative behaviours, building a strong sense of personal security and self is the antidote.

When you are strong in yourself and able to stand firm, prove you are bulletproof and strong. You still suffer, but not for long as you are resilient, able to go beyond what you previously thought possible and push boundaries.

How do you build a strong sense of personal security?

It is an inside-out job. Rather than focusing on building confidence with external resources, it is more valuable to build capacity based on your internal resources.

What you have right now is good enough, ready to be brought to the surface. To write your own code, you can use what you already have and be who you are. It is not a case of acquiring more, training more, planning more or believing you need to be more.

Think of yourself as a well: there is a great deal below the surface.

How do you use what you already have?

The ideal approach is to work on self-awareness and build your self-knowledge database. While it is beneficial to work with an experienced person one-on-one or with others in groups and workshops, for you, this next section of the book will help. I have developed a guide to help you design your own solutions without any pressure or competition. This advice has worked for the people I have interviewed over the past two years and for me too.

Thinking in circles

Circles are inclusive, moving and creating an upward spiral. The sphere shape gives the sense of being able to hold and support everything within.

This inspired me to develop the acronym CIRCLE.

C = Core

I = It is

R = Release

C = Conversations

L = Leverage

E = Energy

Using this six-part guide, you can:

- Build self-awareness and self-knowledge

- Understand what is most important to you and what is at your core

- Find ways to be yourself in all your roles and relationships, and to release pressure

- Gain insight and connection rather than disconnection in conversations

- Leverage your strengths to build confidence

- Harness your energy to sustain and support you and all the important people in your life.

Are you ready?

17 C is for Core

The first part of the CIRCLE is Core, and it is foundational. Core is all about helping you to understand what drives you by using other people's experiences. This clarity allows you to be your wholehearted self in everything you do. Core comprises two sections:

1. Be clear about what is important to you

2. Be your wholehearted self in everything you do.

1. Be clear about what is important to you

> *"The most compelling source of purpose is spiritual: the energy derived from connecting to deeply held values and purpose beyond self-interest... We become fully engaged only when we care deeply, when we feel that what we are doing really matters. Purpose is what lights us up, floats our boats, and feeds our souls."* Jim Loehr and Tony Schwartz[1]

People who are able to deal with judgment and guilt stay centred and focused during tough times and live on their own terms with a strong connection to what is most important to them. They instinctively and purposefully use this as a place to come from rather than a destination to get to.

---

1   *The Power of Full Engagement: Managing Energy, Not Time, Is the Key to High Performance and Personal Renewal*, Jim Loehr and Tony Schwartz, pg 131

They work out what is most important and then make decisions. They don't fit what is important to them in and around what they think they should do or what other people expect, nor do they spend excess energy on the decision-making process or bring emotional baggage to new opportunities.

How to have it all

"I am just going to do what is important to me. My major achievement, I believe, is the fact that I've had senior roles for most of my career and I've also been everything that I wanted to be, and been there for my sons."

Rowena has a very pragmatic approach to keeping things in perspective and giving her best in all her roles and responsibilities. She knows what is most important to her and she does it — to the point where her coach encouraged her to write a book about her best practices and the result is *Live, Work, Shine: How to Use Time for What Matters*.

Rowena attributes the fact that she has not achieved chief executive officer level to putting her family first, but she is content with her choices. It is more important that her boys see the mix and know her. Rowena is also involved in community groups associated with her boys' school and been the treasurer of the school P&F.

"I guess it's the different elements all mixed together. I wasn't just doing the domestic or just doing the community or just doing work, but I was doing all of those."

While it is not always a smooth, predictable path and there will be times when one role will require more than the others, staying focused on what is important is key. When your family is growing and your children are young and your support network is not robust, choices are limited.

"You can't leave your children at school; you can't leave them at childcare. There are going to be times when you're not in balance to where you want to be. As long as you're not out of balance for too long, because that out of balance will become your new balance."

Having that sense of clarity is the starting point and the compass.

How do you know what is most important?

What is important to you and what are your personal values? Understanding and truly connecting are vital for building your reservoir of self-knowledge.

From coaching clients over the years, I've learned that they usually know what they don't want, but not necessarily what they do want and value. Gaining clarity often shines a light on what drains your energy and attention.

You do not have to adhere to your values at the expense of personal and professional growth. You need to find the sweet spot where your purpose becomes the foundation for a fulfilling life.

Purpose can provide an anchor, and stability during tough times, and drive a substantial level of effort. Challenged by inevitable personal and professional storms, you need a strong sense of purpose to hold your ground.

Get to know your values and purpose

To understand your values and purpose, it is critical to build self-knowledge and a strong sense of self.

Society has not focused on understanding personal core values in the past, but this is changing rapidly, particularly in terms of purpose-driven organisations aiming to improve commercial performance. Progressive organisations understand the importance of aligning their values and purpose with those of their people to positively impact culture.

For some research participants, clarity followed a major event such as divorce or death, a health scare, becoming a parent or a change in family circumstances. For others it has been more organic and led to a tipping point; still others were driven by an employer offering internal and external programmes.

All challenging processes identifying values and what is most important to you require self-reflection, soul-searching and self-awareness. To achieve the best outcomes, it is important to be honest about your values, first with yourself and then with the people in your life.

Where are you now?

If you were discussing your values and you nominated health and family, what would your credit card statement reveal? Where do you spend your money? What tasks do you ascribe value to and who and/or what do you allocate time to? If you eat out regularly with colleagues and stakeholders and buy a lot of alcohol, then perhaps you should reassess.

> *"If you told me health versus work, I'm going to take health every time. If you told me marriage versus work—and I've had this discussion recently with a boss of mine in Hong Kong—I'm going to pick the marriage. It doesn't matter how much you sweeten this deal, I'm always going to pick the marriage. Whereas work's great, ambition's great, they're not going to look after you when you're old."*

Devoting energy to work through what is important and what your values and purpose are is a luxury, but it can be a powerful solution to catapult your career and your relationships forward.

How to transform from cortisol to clarity

Picture the quintessential high achieving banker, who came from London to Sydney during the GFC—aggressive, assertive and ambitious. She seldom spends time or effort on non-work activities without improved, measurable outcomes. She works hard, produces, repeats.

Her company, a well-known bank, sends her on a female leadership training programme, which she doubts will help her much, but feels something she cannot put her finger on is not quite right. She and a group of female colleagues commit to being a part of the experiment for a three-month period.

Until this point, she has never really thought about what was most important to her, but during the training programme she does exercises around her core values.

The effects of the training programme hit her like a truck, and there is a sudden decrease in adrenaline. She recognises she has been constantly hyped and is running purely on adrenaline and cortisol. The full knowledge of their addictive nature is disturbing.

Before understanding herself better, she was highly functional and had high energy, but now she questions whether she has the energy and really cares enough to actually make changes in the way she operates.

It is clear that she is almost at the point of burnout, and she is not comfortable with that.

It is a timely intervention and she commits to the process, motivating herself through curiosity and the will to experiment. As she notices changes, she commits to practices and invests in behaviour change.

She is amazed that when she starts to prioritise the things that she identifies as core values and puts them into action, her performance at work improves. She is a more effective and productive person to work with, more herself, which means she can build a better network. She is now not just bringing the machine to the office, she is really connecting with people.

As she moves through the transformation, she gains momentum by understanding how to use her energy in a more productive and focused way and she learns to pick her battles.

As she shares her experiences within her organisation and in leadership forums, her new vulnerability results in people following her example and being more honest and open.

She credits her experiences during and after the experiment with propelling her, careerwise. Sharing her transformation results in greater visibility and she is now a passionate advocate for the real benefits of being clear on values and investing in core values of wellbeing and self-care. Since she is socially awkward and introverted, when she gets up on the stage and starts talking about what she is passionate about, people buy into it.

"If you've met me before and it was just me and my spreadsheets and I was like 'Yep, what do you want?' It's much harder to see how someone like that could be a leader."

She has built connections by listening to other people's stories, in particular about how some of the first initiatives she introduced to improve health and wellbeing have transformed their lives. People have lost 20–30 kilos, have changed jobs, have left banking—and the common theme is that people she has influenced have taken a thorough look at their own core value system and lives and started to weigh up and question their priorities. "This is good, but this is not great. This isn't the best version of me and I can do better."

The unintended consequences of working through the process of understanding core values have changed everything personally and professionally.

Question yourself about clarity

While some people use external programmes to explore and identify what is important to them, for others it can be a slower realisation based on self-reflection and questioning, a step-by-step process of moving towards clarity within yourself, connectedness and understanding your purpose.

It is important to take stock of self-awareness and gain self-knowledge, not in a flippant "Oh yes, I am an extrovert" manner, but truly understanding and accepting what makes you insecure. What makes you unhappy? What baggage are you carrying around and what are you really afraid of?

Anne found that when you start to analyse yourself, what you fear and who you are, you don't necessarily need to talk to anyone, because you are limited by how you want them to view you, subject to performance pressure and trying not to show signs of vulnerability. However you can be honest with yourself.

> "I found when I started to ask that question, I realised I'm scared of running out of money. I'm scared of looking incompetent. And so people say 'Really? So am I. But I didn't think we could actually say that.' But then this is social conditioning around what's acceptable and what's not."

Understanding your fears can provide insight into what is important and what you value, so that instead of trying to run away from what you fear and don't want, you can use what is most important to you to get what you do want.

Work on your values

There are many other pathways to identify values.

Allison, chief financial officer and Telstra Business Woman of the Year finalist, worked very hard at her favourite competitive sport of field hockey and played for Australia, so from the age of 14, when she started to make state teams, she was taught about time efficiency and goal-setting.

After an injury which stopped her from playing hockey, Allison started travelling. She kept journals detailing her adventures in 86 countries and years later, as she tried to work out where she was heading personally and professionally, she reread them. She realised she needed to tap back into her adventurous spirit and wanted to find out more about what was important to her, so she took an online mental strength programme. While she probably knew what she valued most all along, she hadn't formalised a structure, and the course helped her to define and connect with what was important.

Allison is clear on her values and uses them as a compass to make decisions every day. She now lists her values in her diary and in the front of every new book she buys.

1. Health—because if you don't put your own mask on you can't look after anyone else
2. Family
3. Independence—Allison does not like being somewhere from nine to five and needs work that's flexible
4. Continual improvement
5. Fun—friends and socialising.

"So that's what I try to live out in a balanced week."

Can you identify your top five values and use them?

Live your values every day

Having your values and what is important at the centre can help you moment by moment, every day.

When you find yourself facing a decision and wondering what to do if several options are attractive for different reasons, you can defer to your top five values.

For Allison, the conversation goes, *"Right, values are 'I better go to the gym first before I do anything.' If I can't decide, I run through that list and think 'Okay, which one's first?' Now that doesn't always win. Sometimes I go out for wine with my friends instead of going to the gym. Because sometimes socialising, even though it's fifth, is more fun than the gym. But that's the process. I'm still acknowledging it while it's checking off in my head."*

Making a conscious choice about where to direct your energy based on your values is crucial—similar to an internal compass. Even though Allison has committed to her values, she still experiences emotional reactions such as guilt that need to be pragmatically addressed.

"There's always guilt. There's always mother guilt. But I just work out how to deal with it. And there's always that fear, 'What if I don't take action?' But I say 'Fear is a waste of my energy, either do it or stop thinking about it.' Don't deliberate. Yes or no? And then get it out of my head. I have a motto 'Just do it and magic happens.' I try to be quite decisive. Sometimes it's wrong and sometimes it's right. But it's better to decide than spend hours thinking about what I'm going to do."

Although sometimes it is necessary to deliberate about more serious discussions, for habit-building, day-to-day decisions and the hard ones it is important to tap into your values and use your best assets and strengths.

Despite playing hockey for Australia, Allison does not like exercising, so she creates a structure to ensure she follows through and she uses her top five values to help.

"I have a friend whom I meet to go for a run early in the morning and we call it 'coffee on legs'. She and I meet three times a week. And then I have another friend that I meet on Tuesdays. And then I have a friend on Friday that I go for a walk with. I actually find that if I don't arrange to meet someone, I go back to sleep or I sit on the couch. So I know that's my weakness, so then I create things around my weakness to force me to live to my values."

Values in action at work

"A value is a way of being or believing what we hold most important.

"Living into our values means that we do more than profess our values, we practise them. We walk our talk — we are clear about what we believe and what we hold important, and we take care that our intentions, words, thoughts, and behaviours align with those beliefs." Brené Brown[2]

People who are clear about their values and purpose develop a stronger sense of self and personal identity. This self-confidence is an incredible

---

2   *Dare to Lead*, Brené Brown, pg 186

asset personally and professionally, leading to career progression and richer relationships.

> *"I'm not afraid to speak up and I've done it at board meetings where I've called someone out for making a joke about someone being on maternity leave — and that was the president. I do it respectfully, but I'm not going to stand there and laugh along with them. You've got to decide what you value and then you stick with it."*

In the work arena it can be seen as a career limiting move to stick to your values when it causes uneasy feelings for people in senior roles with influence. A beneficial solution is to practise being self-aware and develop a sense of "I'm not desperate to work here."

If you are "not desperate to work here", you can let go of the illusion of scarcity — "There are no other job options for me" and be open to "There are so many opportunities for me and this job is just one of them". This forms a solid platform to launch and be who you really are.

Value alignment helps with this. When your personal values and the company values are aligned, and the culture is supportive, progression is more likely, although a change in leadership may change company values and cause disconnection and disengagement.

While it is important to operate with integrity and not give up who you are for a job, it is equally important to be respectful, compassionate and sensible and to listen to people and acknowledge their views, dealing with points of contention and disagreement.

One inspiring person I spoke to believes that focusing on what drives her has allowed a point of differentiation. In the work arena people (mostly men) have felt that in order to differentiate themselves they must compete to tear down the competition.

> *"I tend to stand by my own achievements and my own value adds and I try not to exhibit those negative elements of the competitive behaviour because my main competition is myself. That has been one of the strongest positives in my career and my career progression."*

Using your values can be a pathway to career success. Focusing on what drives you rather than on competing with others is more sustainable everywhere.

What do you value now you are a parent?

A predictable time for re-evaluating values and purpose is when someone becomes a parent. This prompts you to question what is most important to you, what you have wanted and what you do not want in the future.

Kylie was in banking when she had her first child, and after six months' parental leave she could see what she might become in five years.

"I could see how I would change, just around the edges. Being a parent has helped me understand that actually I didn't want to do that, and I didn't want to be that person. I needed to make a choice rather than just stay in the system of banking. It can be very common. You stick around because you stick around."

Being a parent helped Kylie clarify what she stood for and her own purpose, values and beliefs. She realised she was more comfortable just being who she was, which helped her recognise that it was time to leave the banking world, although she still felt good about her work environment.

"When I was going on parental leave, I was so vulnerable about leaving work. I was so worried about all these things, and as soon as my daughter arrived I didn't give two hoots, so it strips you back to the core of who you are or who you aren't, and that can be quite confronting or actually that can be quite comforting, and probably a combination of the two."

Whether you are planning to become a parent or struggling to be one and continue working, it is essential to be clear about what is important. The first step is finding the rhythm that works for you and your family and how to add to it without compromising.

If you care about dropping your kids off at school twice a week, stand firm and don't compromise. Or if you would like more flexibility or to restructure your work week, find that rhythm first and protect it, then work out the rest, even day by day. There are so many mixed messages trying to be everything to everyone, but stop and take a deep breath and ask what is actually important to you.

Why it is important to forge a unique path

What works for one person may not suit other people's environment. Routines adopted purely on the perception of accomplishment can lead to feelings of inadequacy, underperformance and disconnection.

Identifying and taking action based on what is important is an inside-out approach. It's an individual decision in terms of career and family responsibilities.

"You cannot think about what you want to do careerwise unless you're really clear. It's not to answer it all, because the flip is true as well if you're so entrenched in your beliefs and purpose and values. What I thought I stood for when I was 22 versus what I do now at 43 is quite different. You've got to be open to continually learning and challenging that as well. But you've got to have some sort of path."

What does work mean to you?

"My work is something that I'm really passionate about. It's not just a job for me. It's part of who I am. Working is important to me, as is being a mum. And I think I'm a better mum because I work."

There are opportunities you can create for yourself to choose meaningful work, or make meaning out of your work. When work is important to you and aligns with your values and who you are, you take yourself, your family, those you lead and your life in general to another level. Reflecting on why work is crucially important to you allows you to connect more deeply, or decide to make a change. Is work something you are passionate about or something that is bearable and pays the bills? Or something else?

What is important to most women I spoke to are other people. While roles and responsibilities differ, maintaining strong relationships is what drives them.

"My family knows my work is really important to me, and they've been on that road with me as well. So they don't mind sharing me, because they can see that the work's important. And I think if they didn't see that, it would be different."

How do you help everyone understand what is important to you?

Involving your family in the highs and lows personally and professionally is critical to helping them understand what is important to you. At
the same time, it reinforces your values and purpose.

Lisa talked about the life-changing opportunities her family has had
living abroad for a few months at a time in different parts of the world,
assimilating into different communities. As she works predominantly in
early childhood and education, she knows most of her children's teachers
professionally and trained some of them, so her children have been welcomed and included as part of their families.

Lisa makes her family aware of the benefits and positive experiences
they have received due to her work.

What do you know about yourself?

Deeply held values provide inspiration and meaning to engage with life,
becoming a powerful source of energy. Guilt can motivate you to do better, but if you are doing your best and living your values there should be
no room for guilt.

But are you living your values or merely talking about them? Are they
actual or an ideal? Where do you spend your time and money? What
does your credit card statement tell you?

Identifying key values and committing to live by them creates a
cogent motivator for change. By pausing, reflecting and asking "Am
I serving my values?" you can hold up a mirror to yourself and keep on
track, making the right decisions. Your internal compass will weather the
storms created by your environment—step into your personal power
and create life on your own terms.

What is at your core?

I used to think health and wellbeing were at the core for me, but after
digging deeper I discovered that they are the second inner layer. What
is most important is human flourishing and growth, and those are at the
innermost core and guide me moment by moment.

If you are uncertain or would like to refresh, have a think about what
is at your core.

1. Think about the five things that are most important to you.

2. Out of those five, which would you fight for? The answer may surprise you. It may be career, partner, children, home—there is no right or wrong.

3. What are the one or two things that you will not compromise on and you would fight to protect?

4. Then dig deeper. What is it about those things that is important to you? Do they reflect your values? Are they what get you up in the morning? Do they give you meaning, purpose and energy?

5. Put those things at the centre of every decision you make. And work out from there.

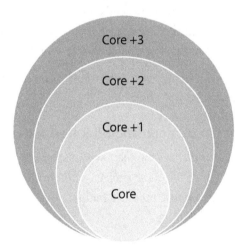

2. Be your wholehearted self in everything you do

"Integrity is when what you do is the same as what you say; and when what you say is the same as what you think." Mahatma Gandhi

Do you wear masks?

Do you sometimes wear different masks for different roles? Or a façade at work? How often do you stop and think about it?

It is the opposite of showing who you are, being vulnerable and showing vulnerability. Understanding what is important to you and knowing who you are brings you closer to being who you are. The person you know in your heart you are meant to be. Then you can be your unique self in all your roles.

If this is new to you, it may sound risky, so why is it important to try?

Driven by the fear of not being accepted and loved, and striving to be someone you are not because it is expected is the most detrimental pressure and stress you can experience. It not only thwarts your potential, but it can drain your energy, making the quest for internal balance even harder.

Living wholeheartedly and being uniquely human demonstrate integrity and generate trust. Being who you are and standing firm, flexing as needed rather than contorting or shrinking, will provide more of a flow as well as opportunities to step into a new world able to support and sustain your career, your own needs and everyone else's.

When you are open and accountable it promotes connection, so that people are more likely to trust you and your leadership.

"People are more forgiving when you show vulnerability and take responsibility. It can be very disarming."

Why is it important to be your wholehearted self at work?

"When all team members bring their whole selves to work and they share their foibles, if people have problems others know and they will back them up and support them; it builds connections and people trust you. Trust is a big thing."

Trust is absolutely a big thing. Trust can be eroded in a split second. Building trust and psychological safety requires your energy and attention. It is a slow build of micro moments and activities which make people feel they belong and their contribution is valued.

Leadership becomes a lot more personal as you become more open. Research participants who have achieved their sense of success are comfortable being themselves. They choose not to be predictable and use their business acumen, putting their stakeholders first and trusting their intuition.

When you are in touch with who you are, it frees you to accept other people and be less judgmental, which results in more harmonious work environments with less conflict and increased organisational flow.

154

The improved culture, ideas and higher performance boost commercial and business results, and enhance all your relationships.

How to be your whole self in the workforce

"The thing is, I always tell anyone new that my litmus test of how they're fitting is how long it takes them to take the piss out of me. So basically they all know that I'm an easy target and I'm happy to be."

The intention is to be 100 per cent human, show vulnerability and to be seen for who you truly are, which helps you to see others as they are, warts and all.

Have a laugh

By encouraging humour and banter, barriers are more likely to be broken down.

Pam has created an environment where her people feel safe commenting on her height or poor handwriting, because she feels it makes communication easier, and if they are confident enough to tease her then they are more willing to talk to her about what really matters.

"I want the opportunity to say 'Look, I'm really sorry and I'm really appreciative you came and spoke to me about it and how can we fix this?' So they know that they can do that and they know they can be upset with me and tell me."

Understand

It is important to create an environment of understanding and to empathise if someone is having a bad day. When it is okay for your team to talk about their children and their problems, their partners and their illnesses, they are more likely to come and talk to you. There is a greater chance they will feel seen, heard and acknowledged if they don't have to leave the fight with their partner at the door or not be able to say they are feeling unwell. This workplace environment also encourages team members to support each other.

"That's the focus for me. I'm not interested in hierarchy or being in charge. The value of me being where I am is that I can support the team. And protect them, basically, from the assholes."

Have a conversation

When you are honest and open and encourage conversations, you are more likely to know what is really going on in your team. If your groups are divided along subcultural lines, it is especially important to make an effort to speak to team members.

If you have time between meetings, pull up a chair next to a colleague and ask what is happening. People have lives, so go and talk to them and make sure they're okay. Emphasise that they just need to ask for whatever support they need.

Having a conversation about what is going on at work, what is getting in someone's way and what their biggest frustrations are builds trust. It is important to reconfirm that team members have the support they need and if there is a problem it can be fixed. And to learn what obstacles they face at work.

If you think about traditional forms of leadership, they are all about managing and leading—managing workloads, managing time and managing expectations. But the 'removing obstacles' approach provides a different angle. When you start with the belief that your people are capable and ask, how do we bring that out? Then you can focus on what needs to be done to remove the obstacles and support them.

Leave loudly

Leading by example and bringing your whole self to work and beyond may be aspirational rather than implementational, and it may be difficult to convince everyone that other areas of your life are important too if you are spending most of your energy and attention at work.

Kim first heard the term 'Leaders Leaving Loudly.' at a conference where a senior executive said he and his partner held high-level roles in multinational US corporations, but they both wanted to be responsible for caring for their first child.

When he wanted to leave the office at 3 pm, he would let everyone know he was going and would be offline for a couple of hours. He thought this would encourage people to prioritise other important activities as accepted practice.

Impressed by this example, Kim started to use the approach with her team.

On evenings when Kim has Pilates or personal training, she lets her team know early in the day that she will have to leave at 5 pm. On her way out she announces *"All right. I've got PT tonight. Have a nice night. Don't stay too long."* Kim is unapologetic. Equally, if there is a problem at work, something goes astray and her team is working back to finish important tasks, then she cancels and stays to support them. But these moments are rare, because she usually says *"Close your computer and go home. We can do it in the morning."*

Kim leaves loudly to the point where her team is also quite happy to leave. She encourages them to do what is important to them and their families and they feel comfortable saying why they would like to prioritise family and personal activities as they feel she will support them.

"Why would I discourage it? So for me, I think 'Do it and don't be apologetic.' In fact, be proud of the fact that you're involved equally in raising your daughter."

They support her personal commitments to the point where if she is caught up in an email they ask "Don't you have PT tonight?"

"Honestly the best way to encourage loyalty is to be loyal. I think for me to just embrace the fact that people bring their whole self to work means that when the proverbial hits the fan, I know they've got my back."

Connect like a human

When you put all your challenges and situations in context, you get positive impact. Understanding that everyone is inextricably linked as well as being an integral part of nature is a super-connection.

According to Karen, *"We're just human beings really. You can walk out, and you could die, so really at the end of the day we both have the same destiny, right? Let's not kid ourselves."*

Karen often gets positive feedback about her unusual ability to connect with people, and I have identified the three key elements driving this.

1. See all people as people and do not fear anyone more senior.

   "I just think, 'Okay, you're just very intelligent, and I'd love to get into that mindset and learn from that.'"

157

2. Be a little bit vulnerable. If you show that you are vulnerable, you hurt and things are tough, then that helps people connect with you.

   "You have got to let a little bit of yourself out—not to open up and tell them everything about your life, but enough for someone to think 'Okay, I don't want to make it hard for someone to read me.'"

3. Understand other people's perspectives and stories and what makes them feel vulnerable.

   "When you talk to people, you realise that they've all got a story when they were a kid. Look at them and just think of that little boy when he was at school. He probably got picked on and probably never got to date that pretty little girl, and it's still on his shoulder."

The strategic upsides to being yourself

Being your whole self and essentially human is crucial as you progress, and understanding people and being able to connect with them is important to achieving outcomes and realising strategic benefits.

When you have to be strategic to achieve an outcome, you take into account that you are dealing with human beings.

"If you want to get something done, there are people that won't want to play, and there are other people that do want to play. And, for those that don't want to play, there's always an angle you can apply to get them interested in playing."

If you can understand people and what motivates them, and that it's not 'one size fits all', then that's a leadership and career asset that differentiates you from the pack.

What can get in the way of being human?

"At my workplace we're not making watches; we're not making anything. It's all about service. And so it really is about relationships. So if you can't connect then you can't really do much here."

For some people it is a real challenge to bring their humanness to all areas of life. It can take a lot of letting go and a leap in the dark for people who feel safer adhering to their established code.

Traditionally in the work arena, people have thought that being a certain way, or presenting yourself in a professional, polished way and putting a guard up would build relationships with stakeholders. But do you really believe that it leads to connection? Do you really think that that invites people to call you back? What makes you connect with someone that calls you back to say "Hey, let's have lunch next week again" is if they've enjoyed the time with you.

Being their whole self is a challenging concept for some people, and they feel tension from society about whether that is actually accepted, but there are some good reasons why your workplace has such a big role to play.

"People would say, 'Why are you having a voice on marriage equality?' Well, for exactly that reason. This is our workforce, right? These are our people. If they can't feel at home at work, then we're in a lot of trouble."

Self-parenting

While it is important for you to be human at work, to achieve connection and trust and high outcomes, it works equally well at home with your family.

Regardless of how you see yourself and where you sit on the career and parenting spectrum, you can fall into the trap of being the stalwart and acting tough for the benefit of others, but making yourself bullet-proof does not actually help anyone, let alone yourself.

As a parent, you want to protect your kids and, counterintuitive as it sounds, the most effective way is to share your own vulnerabilities with your children. You may appear successful, but on the inside it is not always that way and it is really important that you talk to your children.

High achieving parents may be set on a pedestal. It is important for the family to feel they have some ownership of the Wonder Woman and be able to say "Really, you don't know what she's like at home!"

Lisa's choice to include her children in her work was initially a neces-sity, but has led to a deeper connection between them all.

"I share my vulnerabilities with my children, because I want to have that closeness and to empower them to know that they know me better than anybody else. When they hear other people saying things,

they've got this secret little giggle because they know how hard that was for me. They know that I couldn't find the shoes that I wanted to wear that day, and all those sorts of things. I think you need that vulnerability at home as well."

Part of Lisa's research involves giving public addresses that usually consist of a one-hour keynote presentation. This puts a great deal of pressure on her, so she often talks to her three boys about her ideas and what she is thinking of saying. Since her work is education based and concerns early childhood literacy and social justice, her children are interested in what she is thinking and provide feedback.

Several years ago, when her husband was away, Lisa took her three primary-school-aged boys to a keynote presentation after business hours. When Lisa was introduced, her 10-year-old sitting in the front row said "They don't know you're our mum!"

Lisa laughed and admitted that it is embarrassing when she is introduced with a long list of qualifications, books she has authored and contributions she has made to education, but the 10-year-old said "I'm going to make your introductions from now on." He has now created a short iMovie introduction for her.

"I don't watch it before the audience watches it, and that's part of the trust I have in him and he knows that as well. But he will introduce me and the topic from the perspective of me as he knows me… and it's hysterical."

It is an incredible way to demonstrate integrity in her work in education too. Lisa is living what she is teaching and creating and the upward spiral of sharing, teaching and learning.

"And so that's why he can have the relationship where he's like a research colleague of mine, because my family has become part of my work family as well. And so, because my son has such a presence in my work, in his little creations I often get the boys to test out different things for me and create me examples. But they feel that it's their journey as well."

The way Lisa chooses to show up as a mother, personally and professionally, helps her to blur the lines between her responsibilities. She has transitioned into a new world and achieved a real sense of flow rather than compartmentalising and containing.

> *"I don't know if I ever really labelled it. It's just who I am. I think because my work is something that I'm so passionate about, it's such a big part of me. It's not a career, it's who I am."*

Let's reconfigure the juggling act

> *"Work-life balance? There isn't a balance, there is just one life."*

When you are your whole self in all of your roles, you are in a better position to focus on balance within yourself. It is an inside-out job.

To help with this, the work-life balance myth and the juggling act where you try to keep all the balls in the air need a rethink and a reconfiguration. People have innocently bought into them and that makes everything harder. A more attainable objective is to create something different which results in a steadier flow to your life.

By being your whole self and writing a new code, you can reconfigure the juggling act and step into a new world, but:

1. There are many competing elements: balls, plates, roles and responsibilities.

2. All the elements need to be kept in motion.

3. It is a performance requiring constant attention.

4. You are responsible for 1, 2 and 3.

There is more focus on how the elements and your roles and responsibilities are different and distinct—and difficult to manage when you only have two hands. Add busyness and confusion, and it is a recipe for a continuous downward spiral.

Can you look at the positive patterns?

If you focus on similarities rather than differences, you move from separation to consolidation, identifying patterns and commonalities.

Finding meaning, purpose and importance (MPI) in each ball you are juggling mitigates the juggling act. It is a powerful mindset shift.

For example, if growth is a core value for you, although you may feel you are juggling your career, personal and professional development opportunities, community projects, your children's education and extra-curricular pursuits, you are actually driven by one MPI: growth. Your core values may be health, wellbeing, courage, compassion, achievement, financial stability, connection, contribution, parenting, resourcefulness, truth, self-expression.

Knowing this relieves pressure and alters the definition of working and caring. Rather than looking at the balls as unrelated roles and responsibilities and feeling a sense of obligation, you are choosing based on what is most important to you. These are choices, not sacrifices.

Imagine the MPI as a piece of Velcro on each ball. Stick the balls to one another until they are one big ball—your life and all your roles and responsibilities—which you can now hold firmly in one hand. You can even pass it to someone else or put it down for a while.

No more juggling, no need to keep everything in motion.

You have transitioned from separation to consolidation. And you can step into a new world.

Find your rhythm

If that is too much of a challenge, accept that your life is more about rhythms.

A state politician told me that she is relentlessly questioned on how she manages the work-life balance. Tired of answering this same gendered question many women are asked, she explains that her life is more about rhythms: sometimes it's hip-hop and sometimes a waltz is more appropriate—Irish dancing, a bit of tap and flamenco may all be required, and clicking into that rhythm is vital.

This really resonates with me—dancing is a lower pressure alternative to juggling, but still a skill that requires practice and muscle building and where you can create your own dance and be your own choreographer. Dancing provides pleasure and flow.

Can you be yourself?

Being yourself throughout your life is key to creating a flow.

You may already operate this way, reaping the rewards, or not acknowledging the benefits, but you can see what is possible.

18 I is for It is

The next part of CIRCLE is I for It is. By this I mean that it is what it is and acceptance is the key. You can stop blindly putting up with things, and realise that you can control your thoughts, behaviour and outcomes. The power of your thoughts can help you navigate many challenges and allow new opportunities and constant evolution as you transition into different life stages. It has two sections:

1. Accept it's an inside-out job
2. Accept the transitions.

1. Accept it's an inside-out job

"We are what we think. All that we are arises with our thoughts. With our thoughts, we make our world." Buddha (c. 563–c. 483 BC)

Your own thinking and beliefs are the key to being who you are and creating and executing your own code.

Sometimes it is more of a case of letting go of old thought patterns and mindsets—the unhelpful parts of your code—and being open to what is right in front of you rather than implementing new strategies.

Accept what is happening and move on. Then you are better able to access calm thoughts, tap into your instincts, make positive decisions, and create your own measures for success, purpose and fulfilment. Everything you do is valuable and you can achieve anything.

What is psychological weather?

"If you are distressed by anything external, the pain is not due to the thing itself, but to your estimate of it; and this you have the power to revoke at any moment." Marcus Aurelius (121–180 AD)

When you are feeling overwhelmed and out of control, you want to take action, any action. You may avoid difficult conversations and run away, or shout, lash out or rant on social media. This is called 'psychological weather'. When things become difficult, you experience a thought storm.

Thought storms vary. Some consist of dark clouds, a few peals of thunder, some lightning and perhaps wind. Others may feel like a full-force hurricane with record-breaking wind speeds and objects flying through the air, destroying everything in their path.

In my own thought storms, I usually picture myself on a decent-sized fishing boat trying to navigate through treacherous wind and rain and huge 10-metre swells. My worst nightmare is to be pitched against the elements, on or in the vast and powerful ocean. I love swimming when I can see the shoreline, but it scares me to think of being cast adrift on the high seas.

When life seems tumultuous and out of control my thinking becomes muddled, and self-doubt and negative self-talk scream. This is not the time to make important decisions.

Storms seem intense and create deep emotional tags, but they are rare although they use a great deal of energy and oxygen. Similar to environmental storms, thought storms are temporary and once they have passed there is calm. You have weathered the storm, and have an opportunity to reflect on good weather, to recognise that you have built up the strength and resilience to survive.

Most liberating of all is understanding that you do not need to reach for a better feeling or provide analysis or judge yourself harshly. The storm will pass and calm will follow. You may even be able to stop seeing the thought storm as a negative experience.

Navigate your psychological weather

"The truth is, everything will be okay as soon as you are okay with everything. And that's the only time everything will be okay." Michael Alan Singer[1]

If you can accept that your thinking is the key to life on your own terms, can you also accept that your feelings are a reaction to your thoughts? Your feelings and emotions monitor your thoughts, so can you take full responsibility for your emotional state knowing it is an inside-out approach rather than outside-in?

You can navigate psychological weather by choosing how you respond and the following may help:

1. Awareness—being aware of your mood and state

2. Acceptance—where you are is absolutely okay, and if you are in a storm you will eventually transition to the next state

3. Trust—having faith and trust that if you are in a storm it will pass

4. Be—all that is required of you is to just be, knowing that everything is okay

5. Truth—understanding that your thoughts are objects and require energy, and dedicating effort and attention to your thoughts may drain your energy

6. Breathe—take long, deep breaths

7. Notice—watch your thoughts as objects and create a distance from them.

Make choices and question your autopilot

"When I get triggered, I'm actually not choosing how I respond. I'm letting my automatic pilot take over and react in probably not an optimal way."

An effective way to navigate thought storms is understanding how you react rather than respond. When the autopilot kicks in and you operate

---

1   *The Untethered Soul*, Michael Alan Singer, pg 152

in default, the act of pausing and understanding what actually happened is important. As Peggy sees it, the meaning you attach to things prescribes how you will react:

"That's just the muscle that you train. When I started this, it was always after the fact that I could see 'I was triggered because this is what happened; this is the meaning I attached to what happened and that's how I then reacted.' Over time, you practise it every day, all the time. And now, not always, but most of the time, I can actually feel when I get triggered. And I can choose how I respond. That's the emotional mastery that you want to get to."

Your quality of life will improve if you can first of all understand what emotional mastery is and practice it. It prevents automatic pilot from taking charge of your wellbeing, reactions, happiness and sense of inner peace.

There will always be opportunities to practice Peggy's concept of emotional mastery. When something happens to upset you and cause a thought storm you may stay under a dark cloud for weeks, but if you get better at emotional mastery the thought storm becomes shorter.

"After my first child I had some anxiety, not diagnosed; I pushed on. After my second one I was diagnosed with post-natal depression and I had some counselling. I was thinking 'Why do I take antidepressants?' I had never taken them before. 'Or do I go down the path of really working on this?' I decided not to take them; I went down the path of really working on it. I did a course a long time ago that got it all going for me.

"I think you really go and learn most when you are going through some kind of trauma or challenge. So, if I reflect back on my life, the times I've had the most opportunity to grow, and I did grow the most, were always when I had some drama going on. It's not easy to go through but I know each time I will learn. The dark clouds clear much quicker. So you think after training this muscle of emotional mastery that when you still are in a really challenging situation where there's a cloud or something, you can say 'I know it's going to pass, I know I'm going to grow from this.'

"Since that post-natal experience, I haven't been depressed, because I also know if you go down there's only one way up and that's you. You have to get yourself out of there again. I don't really go down there any more, I intercept it really quickly. I still think, 'Well, everybody still has challenges in life.' I think I've trained myself really well to feel when something's going on and to get out of it myself."

Go beyond thinking and thoughts

"Your perceptions and feelings do not happen to you; they are created within you. They are your thoughts in action, brought to life in your consciousness. It is impossible to experience something without your thinking being involved. You won't see a beautiful sunset if your mind is not focused on it… Without thought, a particular sense, impression, feeling, image or idea cannot be a part of your experience."[2]

Knowing how your thinking determines your reality, you can understand that the way you navigate life is an inside-out job, which strengthens your ability to move through psychological weather, harnessing the power of your thoughts to write and execute your own code and live life on your own terms.

2. Accept the transitions

"Facing the most difficult truths in our lives is challenging but also liberating. When we have nothing left to hide, we no longer fear exposure. Vast energy is freed up to fully engage in our lives. We celebrate our strengths and continue to build them. When we make a misstep, we take responsibility for it and reset our course." Jim Loehr and Tony Schwartz[3]

When I trawl through the research and reflect on the conversations, what stands out as key to building a strong sense of self, feeling fulfilled and thriving is acceptance. People who acknowledge, accept and take responsibility consistently seem to be able to achieve great outcomes and

---

2 *The Power of Full Engagement: Managing Energy, Not Time, Is the Key to High Performance and Personal Renewal*, Jim Loehr and Tony Schwartz, pg 163,164

3 Ibid., pg 163, 164

make a huge positive impact on others. They are also in a better position to write and execute their own code.

Do you accept or resist?

Resisting change and personal evolution may result being stuck and not transitioning to a new phase, a barrier to a fuller, richer life. When you accept your life and transition phases, a pathway opens to myriad personal and professional opportunities.

Being focused on career comes with a list of expectations, and when you become a parent another list of expectations is created externally and driven internally. Then when you are determined to achieve highly and meet the expectations there is tension on both lists.

You can create a different life by accepting you have transitioned to a new stage. You can dump the old expectations, question the new ones and reorientate on your own terms, creating a new world you had not thought possible and focusing on what you can control. You are the product of a process and not the outcome.

Who am I and why is it important to know?

This is a huge question, exciting, daunting and everything in-between. Venturing down the existential route, you may ask why you are here. The way you perceive your inner and outer worlds helps you to build your identity.

You are born with your unique wonders. As a baby you are open, curious and experimental, and if you are lucky enough to be nurtured in an environment with a focus on human flourishing and encouraged, what is natural or inherent forms the basis for your identity and sense of self. From this base, you can build confidence and mastery.

But if your wonders start to emerge and they are not appreciated or encouraged, you start to think you are wrong. If you see other people rewarded, you lose the sense of belonging, and start to listen to messages in your external world, tempted to build an identity and sense of self that is praised on the outside, but conflicts with how you feel on the inside.

Since external messages can be fickle and at times cruel, you may build an identity on quicksand rather than a stable foundation based on who you truly are. Consequently your core identity is subject to change, but you are not in charge.

"There's probably so many mixed messages for women, and I'll call women out particularly, but it could equally be true for other cohorts: what you should be, that you should go in and ask for a pay raise, and you should do this, and you should do that. If that's not inherently your style, then I wouldn't recommend that."

There are many transition phases in life when your sense of identity is tested and open to question. The most challenging for most women are becoming a parent and transitioning from an individual contributor to a leader. These often coincide and complement each other.

The mother of all transitions

"It was a huge time of change, but I think the biggest change was around the fact that I was no longer working rather than I had become a mum. It was more the change and the loss of identity than the formation of a new identity that for me was the hardest thing."

Forming a new identity can be tough. Moving from career focus to caring focus is huge and it determines how you feel about yourself and value your contribution. You are suddenly under a microscope; whether you put yourself there or it feels like other people have put you there and are analysing you, you may be sensitive to judgment, guilt and shame.

As a new mother, you feel the push/pull of being a parent. It is a time of huge change when you question yourself and create unrealistic expectations. You may wonder, 'Why do I not love this new baby/parenting gig? I thought being a mother would make me feel fulfilled and complete. I thought I would want to put my baby first all the time, but what about me?' You may feel there is something wrong with you and you are unable to measure up to the motherhood ideal.

Adding to the melting pot of challenges are the changes in your hormones, your body and, as a result, to your mind when you are pregnant and then when your child is born.

This transition phase has been called 'matrescence' by Dana Raphael, the American medical anthropologist.

"Childbirth brings about a series of very dramatic changes in the new mother's physical being, in her emotional life, in her status within the group, even in her own female identity. I distinguish this period

169

of transition from others by terming it matrescence to emphasise the mother and to focus on her new life style." Dana Raphael[4]

Can the idea of matrescence dial down the mother guilt?

Why is nobody talking about this? It makes so much sense and may provide relief for new mothers and experienced ones too—and could be another key to relieving the mother guilt pressure.

Contrasting and comparing with another phase of disorientation and reorientation, adolescence, a great deal of attention is devoted to helping teenagers navigate this stage. Countless resources are available, and there is also a level of acceptance that their hormones will be unpredictable, and things will be tough for a while as their bodies change and their brains rewire. Transitioning through adolescence takes years and there is little pressure on teenagers to get it over and done with. It is generally accepted that there will be an adult on the other side.

In 'matrescence', dramatic hormonal, brain and body processes are taking place. There is a level of acceptance and confirmation bias around changes during pregnancy, however once the baby is born, you are expected to hit the ground running, bounce back to 'normal' and be the centre of the baby's world. And shrink the baby belly while doing it. The problem is, things will never be normal again.

The work of Dana Raphael and reproductive psychiatrist Alexandra Sacks is inspiring. Alexandra says that *"when a baby is born, so is a mother"*[5] and that they are both unsteady in their own way.

"This is profound but hard, so it makes it human."[6] Alexandra Sacks

In her TED Talk, *A New Way to Think About the Transition to Motherhood,*[7] Alexandra nails why women experience intense after-birth emotions and talks about the push/pull phenomenon.

4   *The Tender Gift: Breastfeeding*, Dana Raphael, https://www.matrescence.com/
5   *A New Way to Think About the Transition to Motherhood*, Alexandra Sacks, TED Talk, May 2018
6   Ibid.
7   Ibid.

What is the pull about?

Since new baby humans are dependent and need a great deal of help to survive and thrive, nature provides assistance in the form of the hormone oxytocin. It is released around childbirth through skin to skin touch, so not only birth mothers experience it. This hormone helps your brain to focus on your baby, ensuring it is at the centre of your world.

What is the push about?

While your brain is helping you focus, your mind is pushing away. You remember the rest of your identity and there is an emotional tug of war. You remember other relationships and interests, work, spirituality and seek engagement on an intellectual level. You also remember that you have physical needs to sleep, eat, exercise and have sex and intimacy.

Therefore there is a huge amount of tension.

If you do not understand and accept this transition after childbirth, it can have an enduring effect on you as a parent.

Understanding that mixed feelings about motherhood are normal helps reduce any shame or guilt. Confiding in friends, other mothers, partners and trusted professionals and understanding your transition provides a solid foundation for moving through matrescence.

"When you preserve a separate part of your identity, you are also leaving room for your child to develop their own." Alexandra Sacks[8]

Work at your own pace across the continuum

Understanding matrescence is foundational; acknowledging that your world is changing and an 'I just want to get my life back' attitude is unhelpful and unrealistic.

What is positive is to reflect on what is most important to you, to accept where you are and where you are coming from, and ask yourself what you expect. Then direct your energy and attention towards getting there.

To feel fulfilled rather than in pursuit of an ideal balance equation, it is important to accept that you are likely to contend with a dynamic mix. It is possible to move across the range, but crucial to accept where you

8   Ibid.

are and that things may feel uncomfortable at times. Ultimately, you are in charge of where you stay and for how long.

You may accept demanding roles that mean you put in long hours. Projects may require long days and late nights, but you decide if it is temporary or a new pattern.

When your children are young, they may not like after-school care, so you may decide to be flexible and find other options. You may work for yourself, collaborate with colleagues or start a new business, and at the time it may seem to take forever. Accepting the stage you are at careerwise and familywise helps you flex across the career and family continuum and create new worlds along the way.

How do you know when to shift?

"It got to the point where I had to do something different because it was not fair to anyone, including myself. So when you can see it's longer term, then something has to give. Or you're not going to be the best of yourself for anyone, really."

When you are in the thick of challenging times the path forward may not be obvious. With the benefit of hindsight most people I spoke with realised they just responded to changes in their personal or professional environment or a gradual evolution that seemed to make sense at the time.

Upon reflection, some women would tweak their choices, but said they were able to learn, improve and apply their own best practices.

Some said that they would have taken more time off with their first baby, but they felt the career and financial pressure to return to work. Naomi said that taking a longer period of leave after her second child was beneficial both for career and family. Negotiating to work part-time or flexible hours for 6 to 12 months also helped with the transitions.

"My daughter, my first child, is very well grounded and she's going to uni next year. I don't think she has suffered. Your children are going to be with you for the rest of your life. It's probably important to have that time with them to start with. And if you've got a good company they will still respect you when you come back."

Use the reverse career plan approach

Most women I spoke to did not follow a predetermined path. More often than not they looked for opportunities and created meaningful connections along the way.

Mandy presented a reverse-planning approach and suggested reflecting on what you would want the last phase of your career to look like. She emphasised that it is important to ask questions to work through this: do you spare no effort until you burn out and deplete all your internal resources? Do you want to change what you are currently doing? Your skills and capabilities can be used to create roles and businesses you have not considered.

Mandy went from a high-pressure banking role to being a consultant. She was able to pick and choose the clients, hours, days and work she wanted. Then she went back into a high-level banking role when her children were older and more independent. Mandy chose a non-linear path and was able to build her career capacity, fulfil her caring responsibilities and offer the skills she had developed as a consultant to her final employer.

Rather than thinking short-term, when you use a different mindset and think long-term or reverse-plan, each phase you go through can be part of your bigger mission.

Eventually the women I spoke with overwhelmingly chose acceptance rather than resistance. They recognised that transitions are easier and it is possible to move more fluidly between career, family and personal wellbeing and personal projects when energy is not wasted on fighting changes.

Keep the fire alight

The significance of maintaining connections to continuous professional development was often mentioned. I can attest to the importance of this from my own experiences. Taking time out of the workforce can result in damaged professional confidence, ranging from a dip to a nose dive.

Women with teenagers admit it was difficult, when their children were young, to work and maintain their professional skills and be the parent they wanted to be. Many were exhausted, but knew it was important to keep the career fire burning. They accepted that there are times to fuel the fire and times to reduce the intensity, but the most important objective is to keep that fire alight.

This approach opens up possibilities. Your professional life will progress and you are more likely to build solid relationships with your children as they leave their teens.

The big changes from individual contributor to manager to leader

> *"As you mature, you can be generous with your time and your ideas. You can be generous by being patient. I had to work a lot on being patient and to be generous with my patience, because I'm very impatient. And then that gives someone the space to speak up and do things."*

Overwhelmingly, people realised their approach to working and leading required adapting and adjusting. Most understood that as their work became more complex, they needed to rely on more people and processes and to hold them accountable. Managing through relationships alone was not sufficient.

Most people experienced an epiphany of sorts, realising that they were managing specialists aligned to their own expertise. When they acknowledged they could not engage in the detail any more, rather than trusting proven people they trusted people until they were proved untrustworthy. Pam explained that she has gone from retentive control freak to supporting her team.

> *"It started with mindset and that I'm not here to get my people to work. I'm here to support my people when they work. It's a really minor change of context, but it changes the way that I approach everything I do. That's that plasticity element, that powerful position or role."*

Leadership pathway story

This illustrates how expectations, choices, behaviour and mindset affect outcomes and growth.

Natasha is determined to succeed and constantly pushes boundaries. She used to lead from the front, bursting out of the trenches bringing everyone along with her, but had unrealistically high expectations before her first child. Maternity leave gave her a deeper perspective.

"I probably didn't have a lot of empathy before children. I really felt when I came back as a mum versus as not a mum my demeanour, my whole attitude, did change. I was quite amazed at that. I think I didn't appreciate before what mums went through. So then I softened slowly over time. And I led from alongside."

Natasha's style changed to being there holding her team members' hands, but working together. Then her company decided to sell the business and the due diligence process dragged out from months to years. Natasha was swamped with work and responsibilities and found she couldn't lead by holding her team members' hands any more.

Natasha had a mentor at the time who warned her that she was going to kill herself operating at that pace and cautioned her to slow down to go faster.

"I had to slow down. And the only way I could slow down was to stop being alongside. I just had to tell my staff to go sort out their problems because 90 per cent they'll get it right. And that 10 per cent they don't, I'll have to just deal with it and fix it, rather than wanting to see everything before."

Using her values and understanding her side-by-side approach was not sustainable, so her leadership style evolved to lead from behind. It was difficult initially, but she found that by equipping her team, setting them up for success and removing obstacles, she was able to help them build capacity. She realised the power was not in the leader but in the team, and harnessing it drove positive business and personal outcomes.

"And so then I came up with this leading from behind, which actually was the most powerful when I look back, the most powerful role. Because my staff didn't need me. They elevated themselves to go and solve their own problems."

Further developing the idea of evolving leadership, as children grow mothers adapt their parenting. This can mirror their experiences in the workplace as they adapt their leadership styles as their teams grow.

What can get in the way?

"You want to be liked, but I think as you go through in leadership roles you end up losing that need to be liked. Actually, you are here to do a great job and you're here to do the best by them and look after them."

Your desire to be worthy of love and belonging and be liked by everyone can be an obstacle to going through leadership stages. Most women I spoke with agree that moving past their own personal motivations to be seen to please everyone is actually of benefit. Being clear you have an important role in a business, there are organisational goals and that everyone you connect with in the workplace has a part to play helps you to rise above the need for social media likes.

People I spoke with accept they need to be prepared to provide context and then reach business and personal outcomes. Team members need to feel cared for, and have opportunities to celebrate wins and some fun along the way, which all contribute to a positive, psychologically safe workplace.

However, ultimately, as a leader you have to perform—and will not be liked all the time because you have to make tough decisions. If you are fair and articulate, then it is probable you will be respected.

Being respected is more powerful than being liked.

This is equally important when you are a parent and in relationships.

What can you now accept?

You are now in a better position to decide what you accept and what you resist. You can view transitions related to parenting, work, personal identity and leadership through a different lens, and having a greater awareness and understanding will help build your sense of self.

19 R is for Release

The R in the CIRCLE is for Release and is all about helping you release the pressures related to feeling you are not doing a good enough job. Compassion plays a major role in helping you find ways of release and there are support structures you can access. Release has three sections:

1. Let go — know you are doing and being enough

2. Be your own best friend

3. Access support and solid structure.

1. Let go — know you are doing and being enough

"But to women who continually up the ante on themselves, believing that if they just got up earlier or used their time better or tried harder they would somehow be able to make it all work, I say, stop. Let it go."
Anne-Marie Slaughter[1]

So far this book has explored the expectations and myths encoded in almost every aspect of life, the expectation code around gender and motherhood which permeates families, workplaces and society as a whole as well as what you have bought into and the barriers that may be creating for you. Knowing your external environment, you can change your internal environment and shift your mindset and perspective using an inside-out approach.

---

1   *Unfinished Business: Women Men Work Family*, Anne-Marie Slaughter, pg 162

Acknowledging the pressure you have placed on yourself to be best at everything—mother, leader, daughter, partner, community member, soccer coach, friend and mentor—can provide relief. So many women lead very different lives, but feel just like you. And it is absolutely okay.

To release the pressure, there are a few conversations to have with yourself about reducing the planning, organising, logistics, chores and activities and ditching the emotional judgment, guilt and shame.

Write your own code.

Do you want to let go?

Participants in my research were often unaware of the detrimental effect they had on people while trying to be hyper-responsible for everyone and everything. Their families, direct reports, colleagues and children were often disempowered and some participants experienced epiphany moments brought on by a close shave, health scare or marriage break-up, while others said that straight-talking, trustworthy friends provided a turning point. When faced with "You are not helping your son. You are actually hindering his development," it is difficult not to look in the mirror. For others it has been an evolving process of letting go.

Could you be disempowering others and limiting their opportunities? Do you see people you know doing that? Sometimes it is easier to identify in others. But it is helpful to ask if this applies to you too.

It is important to feel needed

Is there more to it than breaking the pattern of behaviour?

> *"Being needed is a universal desire and the traditional coin in which mothers have been compensated."* Anne-Marie Slaughter[2]

In addition to the gendered brain training, another reason why women struggle to let go may be due to wanting to feel needed. If you understand that trade-offs are important in order to contribute in the paid workforce and progress to leadership roles, and if you are prepared for your partner to be equal care-giver in the same way you may choose to be an equal competitor or breadwinner, then you have to be honest about your deepest needs and desires.

---

2   Ibid., pg 158

"It is one thing to let go of the housekeeping. Quite another to relinquish being the centre of your children's universe." Anne-Marie Slaughter[3]

Part of the challenge may be ego.

What are the upsides of letting go?

Taking everything on creates a level of dependency in relationships. It is crucial for you and everyone you are in relationship with to reduce some or the entire load and release the pressure.

But what if everything falls apart? Yes, but what if dumping the load, rewriting the code and busting personal expectation myths results in your feeling lighter, freer and more creative?

There is nothing more frustrating, when you are overwhelmed, eyeball-deep and about to explode, than having someone say "Just let go!" They may mean well, but you actually hear "You are not doing a good job" or "You are not managing well", or "You might as well give up" or "You are ridiculous thinking you can manage everything", or "You are not good enough at this parenting and working gig. You really can't have it all."

I admit I used to sit firmly in the "Why should I let go?" camp. I didn't trust anyone else to do as good a job and I was unwilling to delegate important tasks to others. Over the course of the research project, I identified some attractive reasons to trust other people that provided a motivator to experiment:

- Relieves the pressure of being responsible for everyone and everything—hyper-responsible—creates opportunities to do things you love, such as investing in wellbeing and developing your skills as a 'hunter' or carer

- Opportunities for connection by reaching out for support

- Opportunities to be heard and take action

- Builds capacity, confidence and trust in others to be self-sufficient, independent and contribute

---

3   Ibid., pg 158

- Opportunities to collaborate with people and processes with innovation and creativity

- The opportunity to live without that one hand tied behind your back and to step fully into who you are.

How do you show your love and care for others?

Anne was brought up according to the gender and culture code to believe that her primary purpose was to look after everyone. She finally realised that this is not the case, and we are here to take care of the people we love.

"There is a big difference between having to do everything for everyone and taking care of them."

Doing everything may involve tasks and activities which you resent, but taking care of the people you love is an opportunity to use your strengths and be who you are. You may choose how you care for others and it may be by preparing food, having conversations and listening to their points of view or helping them solve problems. It is different for everyone.

The way my mum shows she cares for people she loves is doing a stellar job of the clothes washing and shopping for clothes and hard-to-find items. For other mothers it may be cooking a favourite meal, helping with homework, writing personal notes of encouragement, taking people on fun experiences, turning up to all sporting events, exploring new ideas, reading stories...

How do you show your love and care for others right now? If you are not happy with this way, how would you *like* to show your love and care?

You can choose how you care for others and help them to understand what is important to you.

Asking questions is helpful:

"Why is it natural for me to get up and get the girls' lunches? Why isn't that natural for my husband? We talk about equality. But equality is not going to come until you start to create equity first."

Anne's determination to build equity and equality helped her share with her husband. She insisted that he be responsible for more family tasks and that the children also take on more responsibilities.

She questioned everything she and her family did and what it was necessary for her to do herself. She also examined the language she used and made some changes.

> "My husband's a very bad cook. He doesn't try to cook any more. It would turn out so bad, and no one ate it. So I thought, 'What you're going to do is, on those days when I'm not going to cook, we're actually going to do takeaway.'

> "I also changed every time my kids would get up and say 'Mum, what's for lunch?' I started saying 'Ask your dad.' Stop asking me for lunch because it just keeps coming back to me again."

Do you want to give beyond the family?

> "I have learned that I don't have to give everything I have to my family. I can give a large portion to it, but I want to keep a little bit of it for others who are not my family. It could be anyone. It could be the homeless person I see at Central Station who doesn't have anything and I drop him a $2 coin."

The amount of energy you can draw on in a day is finite; however the energy created by love is infinite and an incredible fuel source. It is important to maintain the love energy. Doing things for others motivated by obligation and guilt is draining. When you do too much for other people you can feel depleted as your energy is exhausted.

If you are dedicating the best of yourself to your family, work and closest friends who keep raising the bar in terms of their expectations of you and what you can provide for them, then of course you will be exhausted, especially if you do not feel appreciated or respected and the conditions you operate under no longer make sense to you. Your exhaustion may also be caused by your high expectations of being loved in return.

Another strong motivator to let go of your expectations.

> "I thought, 'Aactually they can make their own lunches today. They can take themselves to school. They can take whatever — Uber — because I'm going to spend some time today going and giving. I'm going to spend two days at a Thriving Workplace wellbeing event. I'm not

going to charge anyone for it. I'm going to give all that information today, and I'm going to help someone.'

"For the two days that I'm staying there, the family can take care of itself. It gives me energy to love others."

Find out what is most important to your important people

"I always worked, and then I stopped working. I was really involved with the girls' lives. And when I went back to work I realised I couldn't do it all. So it was partly my reassessment of, actually, what's really important to them?"

A change in circumstances may provide the catalyst for evaluating what is important and letting go of unfeasible expectations. When Jessica realised that a lot of tasks were habits and not important to her or her daughters, she stopped doing the less important ones. When her world did not fall apart, she simplified her life.

Jessica believed that everyone making their beds every morning was really important. But she started to question, is it actually really important? She used to be an absolute stickler, but now she thinks "Well, if you don't make your bed just shut your bedroom door. As long as I don't have to see it I'm all good." Jessica has found it quite freeing.

Keen to experiment, I tried Jessica's 'just shut the door' approach with general mess too. It required some exposure therapy, acceptance and dialling down of expectations after years of practice. It was surprisingly successful and I agree that it is really freeing. It has become an internal mantra when my physical environment feels disorderly. I ask if it actually is important and, if not, then I metaphorically 'just shut the door'.

How to work out what is important to others

How do you identify what is important to you and your family and what is at the core?

Regular conversations are crucial. Asking what is important to them. That changes, so you need to have these talks regularly.

Jo recently re-entered the paid workforce as a senior economist for a big four accounting firm. While she was not working, she was very involved in her elder daughter's school activities but, no longer having scope for the same level of involvement, she told her daughters that her priorities had shifted, but she could support them in other ways.

The night before Jo was to give a speech with Penny Wong, Federal Shadow Minister for Foreign Affairs, her elder daughter mentioned that her class was learning about trade. Jo said "I know a little bit about trade" and her daughter was impressed and asked Jo to speak to her class.

"So she generated that idea and she went to her teacher and said "My mum knows a lot about trade. Can she come in?" And I did that, and she loved it. She sat up the front doing the slides for me. So I think it's sometimes about quality not quantity."

However when Jo went from working four days a week to full-time, things did not work as well. To find a new sense of rhythm, she asked her daughters:

1. What are your pain points?

2. Tell me what is hard for you.

Having quality conversations with your children and people you love, stating the problem and asking for their perspective can dial down the pressure.

Jo's elder daughter was fine, but the younger one really hated Jo leaving early in the morning and having to get to the train station by herself. So two or three times a week Jo started work later and drove her daughter to the train station.

"Which sounds really obvious, but it's only obvious if you take the time to step back—rather than me saying 'Oh, I'm doing all this stuff for you,' actually sitting back and saying 'So what is important to you? If you could change one thing, what would that be?'"

Every child has a different perspective, so the conversations really count. Some children might want their mum to cook dinner or go to a basketball game or read to them at night. Partners might want a night out, a night in bed, full attention during a conversation, or just a walk together. The many possible permutations and combinations have to be part of the process.

"In my industry, early mornings is where we're the busiest. So coming in a bit later actually is not simple. But what's interesting about that is I always used to say to people 'I'm so proud of my kids. I leave home and they're still in bed. My little one gets up and gets dressed and has breakfast and walks to the train station and she's always on time and I'm so proud of her.' And yet that was her biggest pain point.

"It's interesting that what we think is important to our children may not actually be the reality of it."

This was a complete epiphany and a powerful reason to have potentially difficult conversations and ask questions rather than assume! You may be flogging yourself to be what you think everyone wants, when the reality from their perspective is quite different.

You may want to create a childhood based on parenting books and blogs and your own childhood experiences, but how often do you stop to ask the important people in your life what they would like?

When your children are mature enough to understand what is important to them, you can use your experience, curiosity and instincts in thoughtful, constructive conversation. Then when they are in their early twenties they won't say "I know you did school canteen, came to all of my sport, worked full-time, coached my soccer team, made healthy meals, gave me a cuddle every night, served on a not-for-profit board, helped me with my homework, drove me to friends' houses, organised fun birthday parties and came on outdoor adventures. But I just wish you had given me a lift to the train station two or three times a week."

Maybe if there are only a few things that are important, you can let go and cross a few things off your to-do list.

I discovered that the most important thing for my two younger children was nightly cuddles. My eldest didn't have any particular area of importance, but this precious information reduced my workload substantially.

What you can and what you can't control

"Sometimes life is overwhelming on every facet of your life at the same time. The first thing I try to do is work out what can I control versus what I can't control. So, the old saying, you should only really stress about the bits that you can control."

Holding conversations about what is important so you can change the way you operate is valuable, however there are difficult situations where it is hard to let go with clarity and integrity.

Women living with higher degrees of fulfilment adjust their mindset around what is within their control and what is not.

While they still dedicate effort and attention to all challenges, they understand that to release pressure it is essential to identify what you can control and what you can't and follow up with two further steps:

1. Is there anything easy that can almost immediately release some pressure?

2. Of the things you can control, which are most important for significant people — children, boss and direct reports — that will reduce the most pressure?

Picking off the easy wins can make a huge difference.

You may feel overwhelmed by the week ahead, but sometimes it is as simple as paying a carer or asking for help and one text, phone call or email can often solve how your kids can get to sports and be fed, and where they will sleep.

Work on being patient

"Ultimately, there has to be that sense of 'We'll get through the day.' And at some point too, an ability to not take responsibility for certain things that are beyond your control, and recognise that, even if they're really shit, it's not necessarily of your causing or of your fixing."

Working towards permanently letting go of control is a long game and patience is required. This is a more dispassionate approach, where you need faith. You do as much as you can when people are facing difficulties, but at some point, however painful, in order to stay sane, you have to let them find their own path.

Sally is the managing director of a community-based, feminist health and wellbeing centre for women. Over the course of her career she has learned the importance of patience and having faith in the process.

"Over my time in the work that I do, I recognise when you're working with people or with communities rhythms are different, and sometimes

you just have to let it go before it will come of its own accord in a way that perhaps you hadn't seen.

"You have still got to drive it, but in a way that is less exacting, and having faith in the process as well — having faith in the people and the process. It's about how you do it, and how you do it will determine where you get and that's the critical thing. It's not the goal that you should be ultimately driven by. You need to have integrity in the process, and you will ultimately get the result that you want, even if it's not exactly what you thought it might be."

Crucial to letting go is having faith in yourself and trusting the people and processes. It is actually not about you, but if you can guide the process and support the people, you can create an enabling environment.

So letting go and understanding it is not about you sets up conditions where others can flourish. While you may understand this in the work environment, do you apply it elsewhere?

"And then all of my children started to grow up and I started to see. I started to think about, from a leadership perspective, that my job is not to come up with the answers. My job is not to do the work for other people. My job is not even to tell them what to do. My job is to create the conditions under which other people succeed. And that's what you do as a parent. You can't tell your child what to do. You don't own your child. But you can create the conditions under which they succeed. And to me the same thing goes at work. You can create the conditions around which the people around you succeed."

This quote above from Anne is so meaningful and universally applicable that I have used it twice!

Let go at work and build psychological safety

"You have to constantly triage everything that comes your way, if you're inundated all the time. 'This is what I'm going to deal with first thing tomorrow morning; this is what I'm going to deal with throughout the course of the next day or the next week.' Hence the zero inboxing, because stuff gets put into buckets of import."

Letting go of the load at work can be a huge challenge initially, but once you accept that building capacity in others will strengthen your team and influence you can do it. One of the biggest mindset shifts is conquering the fear of failure or impostor phenomenon. Believing that if you don't deal with everything by the end of every day you are not doing your job and will be found out does not help anyone.

It may take a while to get used to the fact that not doing everything every single day is okay and that it is more about learning and identifying what is critical. Who your critical stakeholders and the most vulnerable people are—and this is exactly the same as your important people outside work. You need to prioritise these people, the ones who need and demand your help and the problems that require your help.

This way you build capacity in other people, and bring them to the stage where they can deal with work and daily life challenges themselves rather than bringing everything to you to solve.

> "A lot of that was building the psychological safety for them around if they try and it doesn't go well, that's fine. They are in a safe environment in which they can fail and come to me and say 'We tried to do this; it didn't work. Now we really do need your help.'"

Establishing psychological safety is a slow process that can take up to about 12 months to instil in your team at work and is entirely dependent on leadership and workplace culture. People tend not to believe it is acceptable to make a mistake until they see for themselves or they see you being honest about your own mistakes.

Retrain your brain to let go

> "I think one of the barriers, and this is one of my downfalls, is being sometimes so routine-driven. Sometimes my husband gets a bit worried that if he does a grocery shop he's going to buy the wrong sauce and I'll say 'Oh, I don't buy that sauce.' I need to take a step back and say there's sauce in the house so that's a good thing. I do need to remind myself to be like that though."

When you have been operating a certain way for a long time, your brain reinforces behaviour patterns for perceptions and experiences. We develop neurological and behavioural shortcuts to find a smooth path.

Neurologically, it is easier and more efficient to continue this way; however you can rewire, reprogramme and reorientate to create a new route.

Can you use exposure therapy?

Trying a slow-build approach or exposure therapy is an effective way to start rewiring.

It is easier and a lower energy option short-term to complete tasks yourself—more efficient and there is more confidence that outcomes will be positive—but long-term you create an expectation that you will tend to the others' every need and increase your workload.

Building capacity in others is hard work in the short and medium terms and involves coaching, motivating, monitoring, reviewing, editing, giving feedback and requesting rework. It can be soul-destroying when you don't see why other people cannot ascribe the same value and apply themselves to the task. However, like any training regime aimed at achieving mastery, the results of practice, discipline, pushing boundaries, reflecting, tweaking and being coached can be exponential.

Experiment with letting go

Deciding that I needed to do things differently based on all I was learning through the research project, I started to experiment. In discussions with my family and support crew, I agreed to stay open to a different method of performing tasks and the order of tasks, provided it did not result in energy leakage, inconvenience or reduce my values.

I started accepting shortcuts with meals, but not convenience in the form of processed foods as that flies in the face of my value of health and wellbeing. I can now accept different processes and procedures with household operations if they do not cost me energy in the form of rework which does not align with goals around organisation and order.

One of the most life-changing practices I created involves asking myself some important questions:

1. Is my primary goal to have a sense of order and to ensure my environment fits my definition of orderly?

2. If so, is it helpful or handicapping?

3. Am I trying to build capacity in others by giving them responsibility in contributing to the shared mission of running a family?

4. Is this helpful or unrealistic to expect?

This approach can be applied in all personal and professional relationships.

Let go when you want to explode

Faced with challenging environmental situations, it can be tough to release without exploding.

You are feeling exhausted after a day of dealing with a constant barrage of people and problems. You try to shake it off, but the frustration and disappointment are front and centre and all you can think about are the emails and projects you need to churn through after the kids are in bed.

You've kept it together all day and avoided taking things out on the others at work, and all you want is to walk through your front door and feel a sense of peace and calm. You fantasise the house will be tidy, the kids organised and content, dinner cooked, lunches made for the next day and all the important but boring family flourishing tasks done.

Instead, as you turn the key, you can hear the dulcet tones of your kids arguing. Dinner aromas are absent and you are a millimetre away from tripping over a skateboard in the entrance. You are greeted by your worst nightmare: your home resembles the aftermath of a sand storm and every couch cushion is dislodged. Clothes have been expertly 'walked out of' and abandoned, and Lego pieces and food scraps are everywhere.

A barrage of disappointments and explanations of crimes and misdemeanours committed by siblings greet you. You are reminded of what is wrong in their world and there are more people and problems for you to solve.

What can you do to access your inner calm?

1. Take deep breaths and focus on what is strong in this situation and not what is wrong—strength spotting

2. Remember your way may not be the best way. It is certainly not the only way. It is the way you have been doing it—compassion and acceptance of others

3. Stay open to a new way—beginner's mind

4. Ask questions rather than make assumptions—curiosity

5. Leave

6. If you need to, yell a bit at an inanimate object.

Looking at people's strengths takes the focus off what is out of place and is an opportunity to regain order. By telling yourself that your way is not necessarily the best or the only way, you are being compassionate and using an open mind rather than a closed one.

Being curious and asking questions allows you to understand and reflect rather than react.

Leaving—either physically or emotionally—helps you to look at what you have just walked into. That's it. It is temporary and it is happening right now. It is just a form of chaos and does not mean you are failing.

You may still need to yell—I know I do sometimes—which is okay. If you feel badly after downloading, apologise. You are building a muscle to stretch out the time between crappy crescendo events and reactive behaviour choices—great solutions to model to everyone you are in a relationship with, particularly your children.

Can you now let go?

"Sometimes there are simple things that you can do to make a change which is going to have the biggest impact. We really do all have a choice, and for the majority we've just got to have the discipline to create the habits to actually just do what is required. I think we sit in the comfort zone of 'Well it's too hard for me to change so I'll just put up with what I'm not necessarily content with.'

"If we all really think about it, if we want change we can actually make it happen."

You have made the choice to be where you are right now. Once you let go of the expectations you have bought into and commit to the process, the fun begins. Taking into account what is important to you, your clarity and sense of self, you can tell yourself to let go.

A great sage once said *"Train yourself to let go of everything you fear to lose."* It was Yoda—*Star Wars: Episode III, Revenge of the Sith.*

2. Be your own best friend

"I don't beat myself up about it. It's the same as giving the kids baked beans for dinner. As long as it doesn't turn into a habit. You can't be on the ball or 100 per cent all the time. You do need to go easy on yourself."

Once you are clear about what is important, then you know who you are, can accept your transitions and practise letting go, and will be able to practise compassion, self-love and kindness, and work towards becoming your own best friend.

Even if you are pretty good at self-compassion and self-acceptance, when you are overwhelmed and stressed it is easy to use your default systems and the Inner Mean Girl can start speaking more loudly. Also, those comparison and scarcity gremlins can jump onto your shoulder and cause quite a bit of damage to your psychological wellbeing.

What do the experts say?

Dr Kristin Neff, a self-compassion evangelist, has dedicated 10 years of research to studying the mental health benefits of language. She has developed interventions based on her research and experiences to teach people to be more self-compassionate in their daily lives. She has also devised the Self-Compassion Scale (SCS).[4]

Kristin speaks about it *"not as a way of judging ourselves positively, but rather relating to ourselves kindly, embracing ourselves as we are, flaws and all."*[5]

---

4 *The Space Between Self-Esteem and Self-Compassion: Kristin Neff at TEDxCentennialParkWomen*, 6 February 2013, https://www.youtube.com/watch?v=IvtZBUSplr4

5 *Kristin Neff: The Three Components of Self-Compassion*, 16 October 2014, https://www.youtube.com/watch?v=11U0h0DPu7k

She has identified three key components to self-compassion:

1. **Self-kindness vs. self-judgment**

   Self-compassion entails being warm and understanding toward ourselves when we suffer, fail or feel inadequate, rather than ignoring our pain or flagellating ourselves with self-criticism.

2. **Common humanity vs. isolation**

   Frustration at not having things exactly as we want is often accompanied by an irrational but pervasive sense of isolation — as if 'I' were the only person suffering or making mistakes.

3. **Mindfulness vs. over-identification**

   Self-compassion requires taking a balanced approach to our negative emotions so that feelings are neither suppressed nor exaggerated.[6]

Studies have shown that being self-compassionate is good for well-being, and people practicing self-compassion report lower rates of stress, anxiety and depression and higher levels of happiness, fulfilment and engagement.

If we agree that self-love and self-compassion are the cornerstones of self-belief and self-efficacy, the window to connectedness and the antidote to painful self-judgment, why do they seem so difficult to manage?

Give yourself permission

It turns out that one of the biggest challenges to releasing pressure and being your own best friend is the refusal to give yourself permission. This can be categorised as permission to:

- Invest in your own wellbeing, aware it is not at anyone else's expense

- Take time out and do the things you love

- Be nice to yourself and gain energy

- Make choices, small or large, which you think will impact others unfavourably

---

6   Self-Compassion.org, https://self-compassion.org/the-three-elements-of-self-compassion-2/

- Fail

- Lower your self-imposed standards, knowing you will still be loved

- Ask for what you need and want, create your own adventures and live life on your own terms

- Recognise your strengths

- Celebrate your excellence and successes.

Does this ring true for you? There may only one that applies to you, perhaps only some, but maybe even all of them.

This is important to know

When it seems as though you are living and fighting with one hand tied behind your back, restricted and contorted while trying to squeeze into a model that you know does not quite make sense any more, consider whether the measures of success you are chasing are restricting you from stepping fully into who you are.

You may not believe you can give yourself permission to untie the hand and use it to become more yourself. But, when you do, you can build a stronger sense of self as you create and execute your own code, and dial down feelings of judgment, guilt, comparison and expectation gaps. Then you can deal with difficult situations and gradual changes.

Invest in your wellbeing

Women who feel they are doing and being enough more often than not prioritised their own wellbeing, which is a huge act of self-compassion with a positive impact.

Approximately 80 per cent of the people I spoke with placed great value on health and wellbeing. Prioritising and investing in wellbeing has been shown in study after study to maximise performance, increase fulfilment and improve connection. Most people are aware that after a good night's sleep, exercise, a nutrient-dense meal and having some time to recover, play or meditate, you invariably feel better, contributing to the energy source that moves you through the day with purpose and ease.

There are four core components to staying on track which may seem obvious but are not easy to consistently commit to:

The Core Four

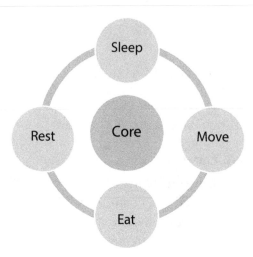

- **Sleep**—when you link your values to use it as a primary fuel source and you feel life has meaning, you usually sleep better.

- **Movement**—when you connect movement to your value of health or a value that prioritises your health and wellbeing, have a healthy sleep routine and feel rested each day, you have more energy to commit to movement which produces endorphins and positive feelings.

- **Nutrition**—when you connect to your values, sleep, include movement and feel positive about yourself and your body, you make healthier food choices, which help reinforce your values.

- **Rest and recovery**—when you have nailed purpose, sleep, movement and nutrition, and are in a positive frame of mind, you are more likely to invest in fun, play, rest and recovery, and when you go through the day investing in movement, nutrition, rest and recovery and have a sense of meaningful contribution, you sleep more soundly.

And so the cycle continues.

Most people experience challenges with one or more of the Core Four, which is okay. Obviously a regular challenge with all of them is not, and leads to reduced performance and poor health outcomes. For me the main challenge is sleep.

I console myself with the thought that I invest in movement and nutrition and sometimes in rest, recovery and play, which do contribute to a solid night's sleep regardless of the actual hours. Once my head hits the pillow I usually do not wake up until my alarm sounds around 5:15 am, but it is hard to get to bed early.

The thought of enjoying the quiet time when the kids are in bed and all the chores are completed provides a fuel source to push through the dinner and bedtime shenanigans. I am sure I am not alone in this. I cherish being able to enjoy doing what I want without interruption, having time purely for myself even if it is only 20 minutes, and this prevents me from going to sleep earlier. What helps sometimes is substituting the 20 minutes to myself with 20 minutes of sleep. Which is essentially time to myself—I am just not awake to enjoy it.

Go easy on yourself

Self-care also extends to going easy on yourself if things are not flowing well. Perhaps sleep in rather than exercise—investing in sleep is good for wellbeing. Perhaps you ate that piece of chocolate cake at morning tea—it is just a piece of chocolate cake and does not mean anything, but move on without heaviness or negative self-talk.

When the Core Four are working well, there is a greater chance you will experience a sense of thriving and firing on all cylinders and be able to deal with tough situations. When you are feeling overwhelmed, pause and ask yourself, how am I sleeping? What about my movement? My nutrition? And rest, recovery and play?

What is Peggy's Pyramid?

While the Core Four foundational components are grounding, investing in wellbeing has even deeper layers, and maintaining priorities for mind, body and spirit is crucial for thinking, being and performing.

Peggy, a senior vice president, mother of two and all round high achiever, believes her strong focus on being connected to herself is a major contributor to her success. To build and maintain that connection she does what she calls the basic things about taking care of herself, body, mind and soul, and calls them Peggy's Pyramid.

Peggy's Pyramid

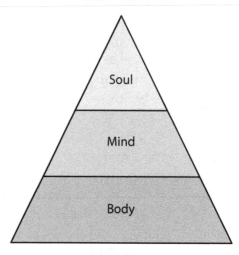

- **The basic layer is body and the physical.**
  Peggy believes she cannot progress to the next level of needs if the basic needs are not met. She makes sure she sleeps well and treats her body with respect, eating all the necessary nutrients. She still loves dark chocolate and has some when she feels like it.

- **The second layer is the mind.**
  Peggy concentrates on emptying her mind. Before going into meetings, she focuses on becoming fully present and emptying her mind of clutter. Meditation is her key and every morning she performs her rituals, meditates and takes time for herself. In her meditation, she focuses on gratitude and on connecting to her higher self, to her intuition and how she really is.

- **The last layer of the pyramid is the soul.**
  This is Peggy's purpose, and she believes the only way for her to stay connected to herself is to keep in mind why she is here and what she is here to do. Peggy tries to lead a life that is inspirational for others, to help them dream big and be authentic, and feels this allows her to tap into her intuition.

Peggy prioritises her wellbeing activities despite or because of her demanding role in a multinational corporation. She studies, works on interesting projects, is a flying solo parent of two small children, and has a very full life.

"My pyramid, that is the thing that helps me most. That's the basic, that's the minimum in my life. I take care of myself.

"I have that chat with my children multiple times. They know, so I explain to them that for me to be the best parent I can be, it's important that I take care of myself. They were here this morning as I was meditating. They either have their breakfast or they sit there on the iPad or they read a book and I'm outside meditating."

You can't give anything to anyone if you're empty. Peggy suffered from post-natal depression and her experience has taught her that she feels like a lousy mum, a lousy friend and lousy at work if she does not take care of herself.

Her children and team recognise how important it is for her and support her self-care activities. For Peggy, taking care of herself is the start of everything and not what you work towards.

It also dials down the guilt.

"In the beginning it's a bit tricky because you do feel a bit guilty. But the kids see the difference. They know that sometimes I put on music that really brings me inner peace, I love listening to Ludovico Einaudi. And the kids know when I put that on — they sometimes say 'Mum, it's time for inner peace.' They know.

"Also, when I'm running or working out or meditating, I know that I will be a much better mum afterwards. So, it's like you have to put something in before you can take something out. If you take a watering can, you have to put water in the can before you can give water to your garden."

Peggy feels the difference when she operates according to Peggy's Pyramid, and also sees how it contributes to the greater good and a sustained performance.

Can you take time out and do the things you love?

"I do need time, and my daughters are very respectful of it. I think they know and that it is actually beneficial for them too."

While it may be an incredible challenge when you have competing priorities, giving yourself permission to create space to do things you love, enjoy your own company, connect with others and just be delivers personal benefits.

A healthy dose of self-compassion can form part of your enjoyable activities.

"It's a bit like a Fitbit. I don't need something that chains me, and tells me I'm never good enough. In an ideal world I'd love to do four exercise things a week. But I think 'Look, if you've done two, that's great, and if you get to four, wow! This week was an awesome week.' So being a little bit flexible about how you think about it, I think is important. This has evolved."

Taking the opportunity to go on outdoor adventures and connect with nature is a good way to recharge and fill your emotional well. Going offline for a while and disconnecting from family responsibilities, technology and competing demands is an act of self-compassion. That may be difficult to commit to initially, but there are benefits during and afterwards.

Taking a break can be an effective way to fill your emotional well, which may be overflowing when you come back due to a combination of not rushing all the time, distancing yourself from daily responsibilities and spending time with people you love.

You can be creative with taking time out and doing what you love. Bianca, a mother of two small children and finance expert running her own business, takes her kids along to her mums' training group, so she feels they are all doing push-ups together.

"So it's me time, but it's still playtime. So, do I have anything that's just me time? Probably not enough, but I'm conscious that I had probably a good 38 years of that, so I'm okay with it at the moment."

Bianca's perspective really stands out, as rather than viewing the personal training group as a chore where she has to drag along her children, she views it as me time and playtime. She accepts that due to her parenting responsibilities and the ages of her children, she needs to concentrate on self-compassion and kindness.

> "My mum was like that: play was big. I still remember my mum baking cakes for all my dolls. I still remember going with mum and being so proud of her exercising and I was on the sidelines as a little girl, thinking I was doing it. I was involved as a kid and my memories of that are happy. I believe my kids are happy when we share that as well. I think that's just the way I've been brought up."

Can you be nice to yourself?

> "I think beating up yourself is so resource intensive that you have got to forgive yourself and move on. Just get on with it."

If you need any more reasons to extend compassion to yourself, then avoiding the energy drain of negative self-talk is one. Accepting yourself and embracing your flaws can be an energy source.

> "I used to really beat myself up, but now I've learned from experience that you've just got to get over yourself. I've come to the realisation that if our bodies or our dieting were a tank of fuel that you couldn't refill until overnight, you would choose how to spend that fuel. How do you want to actually divert that energy to get the best out of the day? The best out of yourself?"

The fuel tank analogy resonates with many women.

Are you going to go cross-country, which will use up a lot of energy, or will you take the backroads? It does not mean you cannot do everything, but you need a lot more energy to do the things that don't come naturally.

Choose purposefully

Some people believe guilt can be helpful but, like most people I spoke with, I don't find it a motivator to change and prefer to rely on reflection and honest feedback to self-assess. Understanding what is important to you, living your values and allowing yourself self-compassion combats parent guilt.

Karen is the CFO of a major financial institution. Her background is Lebanese, so she could fall into the trap of feeling guiltier than most working mums, because most of the friends she grew up with choose not to work. But when her first baby was born, and she came back to work after five months, she didn't feel guilty, because she never felt she was choosing between her career and her children.

> *"I was expecting a stronger sense of guilt, and I thought 'It's fine. I'm not doing anything wrong.' And I'd always get 'Do you feel guilty?' and then think 'Why don't I feel guilty?'*

> *"I firmly and strongly believe that if I have moments where I think I'm not spending enough time with the kids, I must be a bad mum—I shouldn't be working. But it just wouldn't work, and I don't want them to see that either. Everyone's different, and as long as I feel that they're getting enough of me and I'm getting enough of them, and they're not feeling that they're not a part of my choice in what I want to be involved in, then it's fine. So, when I have this work-life balance thing that I'm trying to balance, I think for me they co-exist."*

If more women had a similar perspective, the mother guilt confirmation bias could be ditched and tremendous opportunities would open up for women everywhere.

The work-life balance myth would be discredited and all areas seen to co-exist.

Karen's key points:

1. You feel as though your children and people who are important to you are getting enough of you.

2. You feel you are getting enough of your children and people who are important to you.

3. Your children and people who are important to you do not feel they are bystanders.

You can choose how you define 'enough', and with self-knowledge, curiosity and confidence your intuition will guide you.

Fail fast and move on

Feelings associated with failure can linger and drain your energy reserves. Giving yourself permission to fail occasionally, and knowing you have an opportunity to learn from the experience, may release the pressure and be a gateway to growth.

> *"It does come from your own learning, how you're raised as a child, your role models, what you're exposed to in life. I've always had a mentality of fail fast, so if I made a mistake or did something wrong, I didn't really reflect on it as a huge failure."*

Merewyn believes the trick is to identify the failure quickly, and then move on.

> *"I don't think there's really anything wrong with failure. I really do think that it's okay to make mistakes. Sometimes it's actually important to make mistakes, as long as you fail fast and you move through that quickly and don't get stuck in the stage of internal paralysis."*

Another helpful way to reframe failure is to view your behaviour and choices as a series of experiments which are contributing to building a meaningful, flourishing life. If you think like a scientist rather than an analyst, there is no pass or fail moment with your experiments, which become more of a review and interpretation of the result: learning from it, making some adjustments and conducting a new experiment. You can build confidence in yourself knowing each experiment is an opportunity rather than a potential failure.

Perception is everything.

Some practical steps to self-compassion

You may find yourself experiencing a huge expectation gap and playing a familiar story in your head. This exercise I have developed has helped me and my clients immeasurably during challenging times:

- **Story:** I can't do this (code for feel like I am successful) as I don't have any support. I am running this show on my own. I have to do everything myself. I have always had to rely on myself. No one else is dedicated enough, consistent enough or disciplined enough to help me. I have to take the entire responsibility for everyone and everything. Everyone else ends up being unreliable.

- **Outcome:** You may reach a point where you are fed up and completely spent from trying too hard to make things happen. You create barriers for yourself, and a shift is needed whether you realise it or not at the time. Your problem is not your environment or the people in it, but the fact that you may be outsourcing blame and disappointment and not understanding or taking responsibility for the part you play.

- **Way out:** Develop compassion—for others and for yourself.

Compassion enables you to build compassionate habits. Compassionate habits replace negative habits of judgment, criticism, shame and blame which result in anxiety, anger and frustration. Being compassionate is therefore not a matter of giving in or giving up, but having the intention to minimise negative habits and the resulting negative emotions.

Compassion for others

What if you look at people through a different lens? Everyone has their own strengths, character and qualities. Perhaps you hope to encapsulate all the values and behaviours you believe are missing in yourself. Do you want a mini-me? You could be placing too much pressure on the important people in your life to be everything you want them to be.

Humans all want to be content and free of suffering—we just have different ways of going about it. So if you accept everyone has a shared mission with a different strategy and their intention is not to make things difficult for you, it is easier to take them as they are rather than who you want them to be.

The only element you can control is your own perception of your environment and the people in it, so can you change tack? Ask what you can realistically rely on others for, logistically, mentally, emotionally, physically, spiritually, having seen their strengths, attributes, values and behaviours, and understanding that there are gaps. And it is okay. Is it really possible for one or two people to tick all the boxes? You may be embodying and projecting your own dissatisfaction and self-criticism and Inner Mean Girl onto others.

Compassion for yourself

Analyse and review the individual parts that make you who you are.

Loving all your individual parts

- **Step 1.** Identify the roles you play and who you are when you perform them. Reflect on the things you love doing, things you just need to get done and are neutral about, and things you don't really want to do. Have fun with the names and titles:

- **Step 2.** Looking at all of these titles, you may feel a surge of satisfaction. No wonder there are challenges: there are a lot of roles and responsibilities.

- **Step 3.** Reflect on how you fulfil these roles each day and why. Which part of you needs to be in control and when? Use the analogy of flying a plane.

In the mornings, in order to get everyone to school on time, you may choose drill sergeant to be captain, connector as co-pilot and meticulous planner to keep an eye on the jump seat.

Once the kids are at school, you could say to drill sergeant and meticulous planner, "You two are relieved from duty. Leave the cockpit and have a rest in business class. Actually, this morning was particularly hectic and we have a full schedule after school till bedtime, so enjoy a recovery in first class."

You could then choose creative problem-solver and connector to work as a team during the day with risk-taker in the jump seat. The permutations and combinations are many and varied, and I don't advocate spending much energy on the process, but this exercise is to help you create awareness and understanding with humour.

Wherever you are right now is completely okay. Whomever you put in charge of flying the plane is the right choice, because it is the choice you made. They are all parts of you and they are all okay.

Can you be more compassionate?

Can you speak to yourself more kindly, as if you were your own best friend? Can you also give yourself permission, believing it will benefit everyone you are in relationship with, including yourself?

These are the most important conversations you will ever have with yourself, and a huge step towards creating and executing your unique code and living on your own terms.

3. Access support and solid structure

"Forging deep and meaningful relationships professionally and personally will nurture you and carry you. They're strength. They're your sounding board, where you reflect and learn. When you're feeling unsure or insecure, you need a kind voice, and relationships are what life is all about."

Whom can you trust?

When deconstructing the Gender Code, we explored the importance of the tribe and working together. When children are born and while they are breastfeeding, the mother is the significant carer. After that all family and village members are capable of caring for the youngest members of the tribe.

When working collaboratively and effectively, better outcomes are possible. Responsibilities are distributed, the opportunities for relationship building, care-giving and breadwinning are shared, and parents are able to practise their skills as hunters and gatherers.

I never thought about this until my AC (after China and post-marriage) life and during this research project. Building support networks and relationships has been nourishing and beneficial, and allowed me to plug back into the world. It also cleared a path for me to meet my current partner.

Who is in your corner, and whom do you want in your corner? How can you redistribute parenting activities more evenly, advance your professional career and do what you love?

What does support look and feel like?

Most women are resourceful, able to create opportunities for connection and set others up for success.

A step towards the success equation is creating true partnerships, opportunities to work together toward a shared mission, maintain a healthy operating rhythm, deal with hurdles and move forward side by side. All the while putting yourself first.

The main areas of support you may be able to access are partners, family, paid carers and a support team, and community members and the village.

Partners

Build a true partnership

True partnerships in the home are the first step towards gender equality.

The idea of a partnership was a consistent theme throughout the research. Breaking free of the Gender Code and viewing raising a family as a project in which everyone plays a part is an opportunity to embark on a partnership.

A true partnership looks and feels different for everyone, and whatever you believe is the best version is true for you. The benefits of having a partner in your corner working towards a shared mission cannot be underestimated.

> "To be honest, I never thought I'd be in a leadership position. But I've taken opportunities because of my husband. He is the one that supports me when I go home, and he says 'Of course you can do it, you'll be all right.' If it wasn't for him in the background saying 'You can do it; I know you can,' maybe I wouldn't have taken the challenge of moving into the leadership role."

The most profound partnership elements are less about household chores and caring for children than living with someone who truly wants you to flourish and succeed, someone with no personal agenda, conditions or preconceived idea of who you should be. Someone having your back is a great help in progressing personally and professionally.

Does your partner *have* your back or do they *hold* you back?[7]

Steps to build a true partnership

I have identified seven crucial elements to work through as a guide to build up your capacity for true partnerships:

1. Understand your context

2. Ensure your core values are understood, aligned and appreciated

3. Develop and agree on a mission together

4. Develop and agree on a strategy together

5. Identify and agree on partnership portfolios

6. Communicate clearly and consistently

7. Reflect, review and reassess.

1. Understand your individual context

> "The context is so different. I started to realise that actually my context, each one's context, is unique. When people start to say what's normal about what my husband does and doesn't do and what's abnormal, it's pertaining to their context and their context is not my context. It is unique to them. I need to understand my context and what's making me feel this way."

Everyone's context or family situation is unique, and the starting point is to understand your own. It is important to view your context in terms of your own, your partner's, your whole family's all integrating to create your total context. This reduces the opportunity for comparison, cherry-picking and scarcity thinking. Your context is not relevant to anyone else, and theirs is not relevant to you.

---

7   Adapted from Gus Worland, co-founder of Gotcha4Life

You can gain a deeper understanding of your partnership's context by asking if there are family or friends to lean on, if anyone in the family has special needs you and your partner should manage, what the work hours, travel and commitments are.

2. *Ensure your values are understood, aligned and/or appreciated*

"If you're with someone for your whole life, or even 10 years or 20 years or whatever it is, people make compromises, and you need to be comfortable with those compromises. Otherwise you end up resenting the other person."

Interviewing women in various stages of relationships, from married with strong partnerships to divorced and re-partnered or in-between, provided insights into what is needed for long-term relationship building. The theme that emerges is the importance of sharing similar values or at least understanding why each partner has these values and accepting them.

All the conversations, agreements and shared mission and strategy planning in the world are ineffective if you and your partner do not understand each other's values.

"It's not that I would rather be at work than with my husband, but this is why I'm passionate about what I do, or this is why it is important to me. I think it goes all the way down to that why, because for years he just assumed I was very ambitious, but when you start going down to the fact that I have a really deep core value of financial security and of stability, and of control, he then starts to understand it a lot more."

When people in relationships understand that their wife or partner is working to provide for their family with the intention of always being in a position where they have options rather than what they may have experienced in the past, it provides context for their deep core value of financial security and stability.

There is less room for judging and making assumptions that you may be super-ambitious and focused on getting to the top of the patriarchal pyramid and neglecting others in the process. Clear communication of your values and what is important to each of you is essential, and then opportunities for connection increase.

Stay aligned

Some participants said that they married young and were fortunate to have grown in the same way as their partners. Most agree they experience challenges in their partnerships. Men and women with a strong sense of personal security can usually appreciate and support their partners better. Key are a sense of humour and respect, and understanding the other's perspective.

Violet said that her husband of over 25 years is humble, comfortable in his own skin and does not worry about who is the main breadwinner.

> *"He knows his strengths and he runs his own business and he does it well. We share a lot. At home he does a lot of cooking because I get home too late. We know what works for us. He doesn't have an issue about the shopping."*

Violet's husband feels proud of the work she does as CEO of a not-for-profit organisation. They share the same values and he understands and ascribes a high value to the work she does in creating a better world. He is proud of her.

> *"When I won the Telstra Award he was very emotional, because it was about recognition not of me but about the things that are important to us in life. About a better world, a fair world, people who are vulnerable and being recognised. Having our two children in common, we're proud of them. They're young adults. We invest in that. It's a lot too, investing in the children."*

True partnerships are not only about sharing each other's values, but believing in them and living them even when it becomes uncomfortable or painful. In relationships and workplaces where values are not aligned life is hard work: value statements rather than values in action.

3. Develop and agree on a mission together

Similar to any major project, building and maintaining a true partnership means developing and buying into an overarching mission. Some people scoff at the thought of using a mission strategy approach to a partnership, while others agree it is important to invest the energy and attention.

Organisations and workplaces invest billions worldwide each year on mission and strategy initiatives. Space and attention are dedicated to fundamentals as there is so much at stake in terms of running a thriving business and its impact on culture and employees' lives. Your partner and family are even more important.

You must consider your current context, partnership values, what is important to you both and where you see your relationship heading. What will help it evolve and grow and what elements are important? Your main mission may be raising a family together and there may be milestones along the way such as relocations, living abroad, travel, education, buying a home and family experiences.

Having a shared family goal is a great motivator. Agreeing on the goal and understanding its significance are indispensable.

> *"'Our goal is to get a house where the kids have their own rooms.' If that's the goal, any time that we talk about tactical decisions, it's like 'Okay, is this contributing to our goal or is it detracting from it?'"*

4. Develop and agree on a strategy together

When you have developed your mission, it feels really true and right for you both and you both agree, the next step is to agree on the basic strategy. Use the method that resonates best with you, and if you need guidance, think of your context, values, mission and partnership priorities. Agree on important milestones and decide what to do when you reach them.

Remain open to deviations while considering the validity and relevance of the original mission. One partner may want a different mission, or want out. This may be a distraction or an exit strategy. If you want out, then you are in charge—not so much if your partner is the instigator.

5. Identify and agree on partnership portfolios

Once you understand your context, values, and mission and develop a strategy, you can agree on partnership members' and family members' roles and responsibilities, and establishing roles and responsibilities.

> *"Parents are a gender—mum and dad—but you're both parents. Everyone has their role in the house, but responsibilities for the kids should be fluid."*

Broaden the skill range

There is a more fluid and lower energy backup plan when both partners are trained in the areas required to raise a family and the partnership is stronger. While it may not feel natural to operate outside your zone, there is great value in being stretched in the workplace and at home.

Broadening the skills range adds to the list of manageable tasks to be shared, and also deepens perspective for each of you. You understand what each other is experiencing in terms of your partnership and contribution. This leads to greater empathy and connection.

Emma explained that she and her husband have portfolios rather than roles defined by gender. They focus on their shared mission of raising their two children, and also interchange portfolios. She may take the lead and have the chief executive officer portfolio, overseeing the activities of the entire family while her husband has the chief operating officer portfolio and manages the day-to-day operations. Then, as need and circumstance dictate, they swap portfolios. Each understands the other's perspective.

In financial management of the family inflows and outflows, shared responsibilities, knowledge and decisions are a smart insurance policy against future financial distress, particularly for women. Whoever controls the money has the most power, so that sharing this skill, a sense of control and power are vital.

The big bucket of family jobs

Gender training and expectations play a huge part in the division of labour in the home. If both partners view tasks required to maintain the family rhythm as a big 'bucket' of all of the family jobs to be done, there is no opportunity for demarcation along gender lines, which also eliminates the equation of:

> I work full-time + you work part-time = you do more at home,
> or I work longer hours than you = you do more at home.

Sometimes working longer hours is a deliberate avoidance strategy—or a subconscious one.

For some people the relationship equation results in equality, while for others it becomes a huge disparity. Limiting equations like these cause disconnection in relationships. Viewing work and home as places to bring your best self, intelligence, passion, care, work ethic and perspective creates opportunities for an upward relationship spiral.

This concept was completely foreign to me until I met my current partner. He does not see any household chores as more male or female and he does not operate from the equation mindset. Nor does he recognise any equation in contribution to human flourishing and paid work. While he is a parent raising two pre-teen boys of his own and does all the household chores, there is a lot more to it. He is self-confident and secure in who he is, and is not judgmental nor negatively influenced by other people.

He is genuinely focused on human flourishing. He wants me to succeed and be fulfilled, and he wants the same for his children and all the important people in his life. As this is his primary goal, he is able to dial his ego right down and focus on the greater good. He does not keep a mental ledger of jobs and contribution.

"I just see that there are jobs to be done around the house or wherever and so I do them."

Relieve the Gender Code pressures

Pressure can build up in terms of care-giving and breadwinning. If one person manages major responsibilities, that can create entitlement and expectations. I earn the money, so I have the final say. I do all the caring, so I have the final say.

Research on sharing the load and relieving pressure reveals that women who have left work to have a child and then come back into the workforce are more confident, capable and choice-driven, which drives productivity.

Sharing caring and breadwinning provides many opportunities to work towards a shared mission and to relieve the pressure of one partner being responsible for the other.

"In my first marriage, from a historical male point of view I felt like I had to contribute. But now life's easy because I have met a woman who is more equal. We are both earning the same salary. But guys still struggle with that or if their partner is earning more. Whereas I just love the fact that I've got an equal that can have an opinion and it doesn't matter."

Mark feels since they both earn decent salaries, he is less pressured to work long hours and earn more, and that dropping the male gendered way of operating, focusing on primacy of work and financial contribution has given him back time. Time to spend with his children, time to invest in personal interests, time to share with his partner.

Use mindful language

In additional to identifying responsibilities and portfolios, being mindful of the language you are using is important. Rather than 'helping' the lead parent in the home, who is the mother more often than not, substitute 'contributing to the family mission' or simply 'getting the job done'. Looking at tasks and activities as being owned by the group to maintain the collective rhythm changes the belief that it is the lead parent or mother's job to be responsible.

While the lead parent may still carry the mental load, when there is a sense that the whole family unit plays a part, the pressure to be hyper-responsible is reduced. Also, the tendency to judge yourself is considerably reduced. You can be comfortable with others taking on responsibilities, and dial down your personal expectations. No more feeling guilty about being a bad mum because you didn't manage to complete all of the tasks on the endless to-do list!

Of course there is the outdated idea that fathers babysit the kids for mum. Dads never babysit their own kids. They are being dads.

> "When you've got a shared mission, you're all working on the mission or the family goal. You're not worrying about it because you're contributing in terms of everything you're doing. Then whoever is doing the other family tasks is contributing by keeping things ticking over. You're all contributing whatever way you can. It is everyone feeling that their contribution's valuable, whatever it is. We do that in teams at work."

Interchangeable portfolios and shared responsibilities lead to less pressure, then less stress, more clarity, more connection and more opportunities to create and build trust and true partnerships.

6. Communicate clearly and consistently

> "We discussed it before we had kids, as to how it would work, and he said it was something that he'd wanted to do. So I thought 'Okay, well that's going to work.'"

In addition to being open, adaptable and curious, the importance of honest, clear and direct communication and the power of conversation between partners, although it may lead to discomfort, cannot be under-estimated. Creating agreements rather than expectations is key, and both parties understanding what they can rely on the other for and what they can be relied upon for.

It is important to accept that there will be times when one of you will need more support than the other. This is part of the partnership deal—being there for each other. Being frank with each other about challenges and potential changes is crucial. Some couples excel at com-munication, while others go through pain and practice along the way. One participant said when she and her partner were first together and she started to earn more money they were living in rural England. The female being the major breadwinner was not normal and it was quite tough for her husband to deal with.

> "We didn't talk about it for a long time, and it festered. Then we came to the realisation that we needed to be a bit more open and honest about it all. Sometimes that involves a bottle of wine to remove the inhibitions, or going out for dinner and having a chat about things outside of our normal environment. It is all about communication, and also it's about compromise."

7. Reflect, review and reassess

> "All it takes is the little things. People need to feel appreciated. The biggest conflict that happens between partners is lack of appreciation. That's fundamentally what it goes down to. You're not doing your share of the housework... It's appreciation."

Creating and maintaining a true partnership is not plain sailing. There are so many opportunities for the rhythm to be disrupted—although sometimes this is a good thing as you may find a work–do–repeat cycle starts to eat away at you.

Periodically reviewing the health of your partnership is essential, like servicing your car or your annual medical check-up. Problems may be detected before they snowball into big issues which require money, time and a whole lot of pain to solve.

Establishing a true partnership eluded me first time round, but I didn't have this list. I have compiled it as a guide, not so that you can avoid pain and discomfort, as the experience can result in growth and strength, but to help you hurt less and navigate the tough times more quickly.

Family, paid carers and a support team

"If you are chasing that sense of being a successful professional, you have to be able to come to terms with the fact that there are a lot of resources around you whether they are paid or not paid that can help you achieve that."

Family

Family, immediate and not-so-immediate, is most often the ideal source of support for parents who work. Many parents dream of having their own parents look after their children and showering them with love and attention. For some, it seems like it's the next best option to being at home with your children.

Some mothers I spoke with have had to dial down personal expectations before accepting support from family, especially if they initially believed that childcare was a burden and it was their responsibility to find another solution.

But they moved from "Looking after my kids is my burden... I don't even want to ask them as it is too hard and I will feel needy" to "Spending time and caring for my kids is an opportunity. Everyone will benefit. I will ask, and I am okay with a no."

Once you shift your perspective, you can find a new rhythm.

Most women I interviewed did not have family support, due to geography, tensions or medical conditions, so building up relationships with paid carers, support teams and community members was crucial for them.

Paid carers and a support team

An element of guilt, worry or hesitation when contemplating the idea of paying for help is normal and often driven by internal and external expectations of what a model mother should be.

Some women wanted to be home for their kids after school, cook healthy meals and help with homework, however their jobs meant they had to outsource.

It is not possible to be everything to everyone, and you can find ways to lighten the load with nannies, cleaners and tutors, and there are upsides to outsourcing: enduring professional and personal relationships with nannies and carers, the feeling of being supported by a professional cleaner, the relief of knowing someone who cares can help your children with homework.

It is important to think of yourself as resourceful when using outside expertise and not feel guilty for paying other people to care for your children. By using a nanny or carer, you are in a better position to achieve and benefit from your professional rewards.

It can also enhance your wellbeing to give yourself permission to take a few tasks off your to-do list and allocate them to someone whose zone of genius it is.

"If I go down, we all go down. My wellbeing is just as important as my kids' wellbeing."

Sometimes too, the relationships children build with carers are overlooked.

If you can welcome other people into your children's lives as role models and to care for them, you have someone looking after you, caring for your kids and taking responsibility, which is enriching and reassuring. Your children benefit: they have a rest from you and experience a different carer's perspective, which makes them more open-minded, non-judgmental and considerate. Carers can also provide an extra layer of richness and teach children about relationship transitions and resilience.

"We've had a number of nannies. Hannah is picking the children up from school today and she will drive them around to their activities and do homework with them. She's a brilliant role model for my kids and she's young. She cares a lot for my children, but she also teaches

me. Hannah's been able to show Sarah how to approach exams and truly prepare for a research problem."

Community members and the village

"I love that Hillary Clinton quote, 'It takes a village to raise a child.' I think that's so true. There's not enough that's perfect. So you want to make sure your children are exposed to people that have the strength that perhaps you don't have."

School networks, friends, local community groups, clubs and sporting teams, churches, gyms, hobby or advocacy groups and volunteer organisations make up a support structure. Investing in community builds strong connections. While for some, the local community interactions can be claustrophobic at one level, they do provide the opportunity of bumping into people and adding a bit of variety to your day. They can also help you deepen your perspective.

"Because we've become high tech in the big cities, we've become low touch. And touch—I think what I mean is there's a sense of compassion and connection. It's so important that, as we continue to become high tech, we continue to remain high touch as well. But in the country if you run out of something and you run out of petrol, you can't do anything. You've got to ask for help. Your survival depends on it."

In Astrid's native Switzerland every village has a centre, and people come to know each other. This was not the case in the suburb south of Sydney where she was raising her children. She says that she could never have stayed at home in Australia.

Building community is not necessarily easy, as Jo has found.

"I bumped into somebody I know recently and I've not seen her for a while and she said to me 'You are so lucky, look at where life's landed you.' I said 'Actually, I haven't been lucky. I've actually worked really hard to create my family, my village, my job and what I have taken responsibility for.' People have to take responsibility for their lives, and the fact that the village doesn't just appear.'"

It is important to have socioeconomic, cultural and other forms of diversity and then inclusion. That requires clarity, intention and flexibility. It is essential to understand and acknowledge that you must dedicate yourself to building community, and think about it the same way you think about networking professionally. It is a high priority.

A solid support network and community have positive benefits, although for people who are driven and ambitious, it is not always easy to ask for help and invest in non-professional relationships.

"I had to rely on a combination of nannies and friends; also the slow process always goes hand in hand with your growth as a person, the spiritual growth. I think I've always had a lot of people around me to help me, but I was probably in the past a lot more stubborn and felt like 'Well, I'm strong enough, I don't need that, I can do it myself.'"

Peggy acknowledges that the strong community she has built is instrumental to her success. She thinks of herself as a well-oiled machine like a Ferrari and has a team of people supporting her. She shows her gratitude for their contributions and organised a party to thank them all.

"A lot of them don't know each other, but my naturopath will be there, my nutritionist will be there, my chiropractor. I have a coach who will be there. I have a good friend whom I do a lot of spiritual work with who will be there, I have another friend who helps me with styling, and how I dress for particular events and work things. So I have that beautiful network around me. I have another friend who is always there: she is the godmother of my children, and she's always there to help me with advice on my kids."

The village is supporting the mother so she can practise her skills as a hunter and raise her children.

Let's sum up support

"It's a great feeling. I think it makes it easier to lead in multiple roles when you've got that support. That makes it so much easier. When you feel like someone's got your back. And someone is going to take care of you when you've got a kidney infection. It just feels good."

Seeking, building and maintaining support, it is crucial to invest in relationships where you feel safe and completely at ease with who you are. With this solid foundation, you can create, innovate and go beyond what you thought possible. A great deal of freedom comes from feeling safe and secure. You do not have to try too hard and you're accepted and loved.

You can build true partnerships with all of the support people in your world.

20 C is for Conversations

This part of the CIRCLE is all about having conversations. Conversations you need to have, to write and execute in your own unique code and live life on your own terms.

The aim of each conversation is to establish respect to help establish a solid connection. Then you can reflect on what is needed and direct your energy and attention towards achieving the best outcomes for everyone.

Respect – Connect – Reflect – Direct

There are many important elements which contribute to meaningful and productive conversations. We will explore the top five and provide solutions that work. Conversations is in five sections:

1. Listen to understand — perspective and empathy

2. Deal with discomfort — before, during and after a conversation

3. Ask for what you need and want

4. Set and hold boundaries

5. Create agreements, don't set expectations.

Throughout the process, frame every single conversation with the intention of connecting rather than disconnecting — and it will change your life.

1. Listen to understand

> *"You never really understand a person until you consider things from his point of view... until you climb inside of his skin and walk around in it."* Atticus Finch[1]

This quote from *To Kill a Mockingbird* made a huge impact on me as a teenager, and again when I reread the book in the '90s. I have used it as a compass ever since. Perspective develops over a lifetime and is strengthened by your becoming a parent or leader. It builds rapport, trust and respect. Perspective leads to empathy.

The power of perspective

Understanding someone's perspective and what they face is not only a decent, human thing to do but it is also an effective strategy for *connection*, *communication* and *conflict resolution*. It is a powerful skill to use in all of your relationships.

Being open and present, and practicing mindfulness rather than mindlessness, listening deeply in order to understand rather than just responding helps you to truly see people. Listening to their stories and challenges, being curious and exploring what they think and feel helps to break down barriers and to connect with a broader range of people.

When your focus shifts, a whole other world opens up. It becomes difficult to judge or blame and shame people when you appreciate their perspective, and understand that, just like you, they want to be content and free of suffering—and they are trying to achieve that in their own way.

There is a difference between perception and perspective

It is important to understand the difference between perception and perspective, and how both help you formulate your view of the world.

Perception

Perception is a way of regarding, understanding and interpreting, an impression taken in through your senses. It was once thought that humans had five senses, but scientists now believe there may be between 14 and 20.

---

1   *To Kill a Mockingbird*, Harper Lee

Everyone perceives the world differently and has a different experience or reality based on how they take in information and data.

Perspective

Your perspective is the angle or lens through which you look at something, and it is shaped by experience, society, family, personal philosophy, goals and intended outcomes. Looking at something from another person's perspective, and seeing the same scene or object differently, always changes your perception of life.

Your reality can be distorted by what you want to happen. If you think of a football match, which can be a perception and a perspective minefield, your experience is shaped by the team you support. When a player kicks a goal that may be ambiguous to some but clear to the umpire, opposing team players and supporters view it differently even though everyone is looking at the same scene. Everyone perceives the same game through their senses, but perspective differs due to the desired outcome of the game.

The way you look at things is usually based on your choice of pre-determined outcomes and biases.

We see things differently close up

Needing time out after a coaching conference in Santa Monica, California, in 2017, I participated in a local street art cycling tour that included Venice Beach. It was a great way to discover more and orientate myself and I do enjoy experimenting with different ways to try and cultivate art appreciation. Also I love an adventure that involves movement, exercise and the outdoors.

Along the route, the guide talked about murals and paintings of significance. Some were huge, and we had the opportunity to view them close up and then from a distance. It was incredible how different the murals looked, and when I commented on this the guide replied *"Yes, when you are close up you see things differently to when you are far away."*

I had a light bulb moment and thought this was a great way to understand perspective. When we are close up and in a situation we see the detail, but can't quite see the whole picture clearly. When we stand back at a distance, we can see the whole picture and things make more overall sense. Both are important and the intensity and type of light we direct toward something can determine how we take it in and see it.

Do you want to see more clearly?

"I think just being exposed to a diverse range of people has made me a better person and more accepting and open, and I think who doesn't want to work for an accepting and open organisation?"

Understanding how someone operates and how they see the world, you are able to use perspective as a tool to connect, communicate, resolve conflict, problem-solve, be cognisant of the customer/client experience and create new opportunities for you and everyone in your world.

"You can't influence unless you can relate and you can't relate unless you know where a person is coming from. That's influence."

The benefits of perspective and awareness include:

- Knowing your lens and the filters you apply
- The ability to remove the filters
- Understanding other people's fears
- Opening up by osmosis
- Developing into a more rounded person and interacting with a greater range of people
- Becoming more compassionate
- Becoming less judgmental—it is harder to dislike people close up
- Feeling more connected
- Empathy flowing from understanding perspectives
- Understanding that when your perspective changes everything changes
- Understanding what people are saying beyond the words.

When you are dealing with people, your best relationship will be with someone whom you spend time trying to understand: their story, what motivates them, where they are coming from, why they have that chip on their shoulder.

If you can unbundle those mysteries, you're going to connect a lot better. If you take everybody at face value, and just say they said this, and they do that, and be very clinical about it, you may actually be missing most of the story. It's what's not being said. That's the story.

It takes work

Building your capacity for perspective needs application, dedication and discipline. You may have started your early management career and the parenting adventure differently. Perhaps curiosity was not in your toolbox. Perhaps you were or are still opinionated. Taking a certain position, do you sometimes find yourself making statements rather than asking questions?

> "Really it was about that change, about me accepting 'Okay, I've got my position. But so do other people.' If I'm genuine about treating people as human beings and as equals, then I should put my money where my mouth is."

One of the first mistakes Jodie made was to say what *she* wanted people to know as opposed to what *they* wanted to know. She eventually learned to understand the other perspectives and whether her stakeholders cared about what she was attempting to communicate—and why they should care.

> "It's really about finding what they do care about, how it's going to impact them fundamentally. I've always had a high level of empathy. I can walk a mile in someone's shoes relatively easily. So I think it's really about understanding that there are always two sides to a story. Preparing for meetings, it's about saying 'Well, what is it that I really want to know?' As opposed to 'What is it that I really want to tell them?'"

It is crucial to talk to your team about seeing things from your stakeholders' perspective.

You and your team may have plans for a solution and believe it will be beneficial. However, it is essential to ask why your customers should care and how it impacts them. If it does not, and all the proposed solution does is save you and your team some time, then perhaps it is best to keep the workload within your team rather than pass it on to the customer.

It is important to ask a person questions such as "How are you?" Or "Tell me what you were thinking at the time." Curiosity about their perspective shows they will get a fair hearing. When they feel supported they are usually more open about the issues.

Curiosity opens things up straight away.

Listen deeply to understand

> "I believe it's really important, for your own peace of mind and everyone else's, for people to feel heard, because when you're passionate, like I'm passionate about women's money matters, having three daughters, it's important for me to not just be seen as working and giving them scraps of time. I'd almost rather to be the other way around, because I feel more productive if I'm a better mum."

Listening deeply to someone with complete focus helps you to understand more about them. You can see the story behind the words and the body language and what is at the heart of an issue or experience. You become Other People Centric (OPC).

When you replace listening to respond or listening to solve with listening to understand, you park your own self-interests and rise to a higher level of the greater good, becoming more connected. You experience the sense that we are all in it together. You can move from searching for what is wrong to seeing what is strong and lifting everyone up in the process.

How to listen more deeply

Researching this book, the effect of listening has been profound. Listening to people's stories during 52 recorded in-depth interviews and hundreds of conversations gave illuminating insights into their lives. It is remarkable the wisdom and perspectives people are willing to share when they feel safe and there is no agenda.

Another huge influence is listening to programmes on ABC Radio National. Over the past 10 years I have benefited from the simple act of turning on the radio and listening to whatever programme is running live, from *Life Matters*, *The Philosopher's Zone*, *All in the Mind*, *Health*

Report, The Minefield, Late Night Live, Books and Arts and *Awaye!* to *Earshot, Blueprint for Living* and *The Music Show.*

I would not have chosen to listen to several of them, but I did and they have certainly broadened my perspective.

Why listening matters

Listening to other people's stories provides you with a window into the experiences of people you might not normally encounter.

When someone feels acknowledged, heard and understood, it is powerful. Paying them attention leads to stronger, richer relationships personally and professionally. Building trust creates opportunities for innovation and creativity.

> *"I think I'm genuinely interested in what people have to say. I know that's a big lesson from my parents who spent a lot of their time listening to others and understanding their stories, understanding their perspective, seeing their view. They didn't look through a single lens, where everything that you did and all the decisions that you made were based on a particular view."*

Seeing things from different perspectives develops a better understanding. The only way to accomplish this is to genuinely listen to what people have to say and respond so they know you understand what they mean.

When you have to understand quite quickly and move from one situation to another, you need to change communication style and the way you interact for each person.

Experience helps determine how to interact with different people and you realise that it is not about you: the focus is on the other person.

Empathy 101

Heather believes that when you take the time to listen to what people are saying, it is very hard not to be empathetic, but if you listen and communicate superficially, then you have to work at it.

> *"If you are genuinely listening and genuinely understanding and genuinely putting yourself in that person's shoes, then empathy is just a natural progression from the process.*

"I don't think it's something that you think about, try and work on. I don't sit back and think, 'I need to really understand this person and empathise with them so that I can communicate better with them.' It's more that you are listening; you are genuinely spending time with them and understanding. Ask enough questions to understand where they're coming from and then the empathy just forms a part of that. You can't not be empathetic when you know a person's story. That's why storytelling is so important."

Organisations and individuals spend millions on learning and development initiatives to build empathy, but spending more time listening and looking at things from different perspectives would create conditions where there is less need for training.

With this foundation you can be empathetic without being drawn into the emotion of a situation — empathetic enough to provide support, but not emotionally distracted.

Do you want to understand what is really going on?

Camille, a C-suite executive at one of the major banks, spends time on the front line and says *"Truly, you've got to go deep to understand what's really going on."*

She sits with people at the coalface and asks them to pretend she is not there and show her what they do every day. So she is able to see how people experience their work, which often makes her wonder who developed stupid processes. She also sits by the phones with her team and observes customers and staff first-hand.

Because she gets out and talks to people and engages with them, they feel they can say anything to her, which makes her more people-centric and a real leader. This is how she unlocks discretionary effort in her teams, drives innovation and consistently exceeds business targets.

How can you experiment?

If you were to be brutally honest, do you believe you really listen to the important people in your life? On a scale of 1–10 with one being 'hell no' and 10 being 'hell yes', what would your rating be?

And do you feel listened to often enough by the important people in your life? What is your rating on a scale of 1–10?

My four best ways to listen to understand are to stay open, be present, be receptive and ask rather than assume.

1. Stay open—dial down the judgment

This is self-explanatory and seemingly obvious, yet not easy. If you accept a natural conscious and unconscious bias, it affects your thoughts and choices and you don't resist or choose something different.

What do you look for in people? From the shoes they wear and how they present themselves—make-up or no make-up, body shape and size, height, clothes, voice pitch—what judgments do you make?

Labels provide safety and help people to live with culturally embedded codes. However when you put people in a box and stick a label on it, you tend to treat them in accordance with the instructions on that label. While you know that is what the box manufacturers (architects of the gender, relationship, workplace and government codes) believe is best, you are actually creating barriers, and limiting your capacity to deepen perspective and build connection.

What myths do you unconsciously buy into and perpetuate? Cultural myths, gender stereotypes, hierarchy determining the rules of engagement, value and power...

Thinking challenge: Your definitions are based on your own experiences. It is okay. Those are your decades of training. Knowing what you now know though, I invite you to challenge the labels and look beyond the external.

2. The power of presence

Achieving presence is another key element of listening to understand. Your attention, presence and mindfulness are a gateway to understanding and connection.

The present moment is all that exists. The past has gone. The future is imagined and may never materialise. Living in the moment and where you are right now, time becomes richer, more vivid and more meaningful.

When there is no past to bring into the present and no future to extrapolate, there is only right now. Connecting with the right now, you feel all the physical sensations through your body and a powerful presence in your physical space.

If you are not focused you are wasting your time.

"To be present is really important. I suppose it's from being a writer; you like to listen so you fully understand what the question is. You hope to add a bit of value, make an impact where you can."

This may seem simple, yet it is difficult to maintain.

"I often find when the girls talk about things that we've done or funny things that have happened, that's often when we are on holiday. And I think that's because everyone is present and you remove all those other distractions from day-to-day life."

The environment you choose to live in may lead to distraction overload. Living in a VUCA (volatile, uncertain, complex and ambiguous) world, you may be constantly distracted, constantly dealing with emails, meetings, deadlines, relationships, demands.

"It's my daily challenge and I have to remind myself that where I'm at is exactly where I need to be. I think if you say it often enough it does ring true. It helps with my impostor syndrome, and it helps me with that sense of let's make the most of the thing that we have right now, and I think it's so hard to do when everybody is constantly trying to be in a growth mindset."

It is really difficult to switch off. Who is in control though? Ultimately you are. There are probably thousands of ideas and strategies to switch off, and to digitally detox and become less distracted helps being present. But instead of *switching off* from distractions, try *switching on* to the present moment.

"I'm constantly battling and having to work much harder at keeping that sense of just be in the now. Things will grow and things will change, but just enjoy the now. I have to really make sure that I'm present."

What helps you to stay in the present moment?

Practice is the key to maintaining presence, and consciousness and mindfulness are important. It is really about being present in the moment in a structured way, which helps when your environment is challenging: like soccer training several times a week to prepare for a one-hour game. The value is in the training and the practice drills programme the skills you need.

Be aware when you are able to practise it, but not distressed when you cannot.

"I will watch my kids and take the joy in the moment, instead of letting my mind drift and do the other 50,000 things that I've got swirling around."

Thinking challenge: You may have a great deal swirling around in your mind, but can you practise being present and understand that the present moment is all that exists? Listen to someone you find challenging and see if you can stay focused!

3. Be receptive

Listening deeply to understand and deepening perspective are not natural gifts, but skills to develop.

Allan is an ex-policeman, Deputy Commissioner of the Mental Health Commission of New South Wales, Chairman of the National Police Bravery Award Committee, a recipient of the Cross of Valour and of the Medal of the Order of Australia for service to mental health organisations. He is one of 10 Australians to have received the Queen's Diamond Jubilee Medal and is a renowned inspirational speaker. Confident, strong and exuding energy, Allan learned to see people in a four-dimensional way during his 20 years as a policeman. He calls 3D the first dimension, which is face to face. The fourth dimension is what is not visible to the naked eye: people's thoughts, dreams, and feelings — their essence.

It required work to reach the point of seeing in 4D, and Allan came to realise that when the impact his outward energy had was too dominant, people shut down. He decided to turn it off, replace it with inflow energy and use what he calls 'receptor sponges'.

"The key is to be receptive to people. The stories can be distressing but I needed to be a complete receptor. I needed to listen carefully."

This approach also helped Allan to build the skill of seeing what is strong and not focus solely on what is wrong. He learned to use his 4D approach to separate the behaviours from the person and still see some good, to view them as people who had done bad things rather than bad people.

Thinking challenge: If you are a dominant person with a high degree of outward energy, can you switch it off? Can you activate receptor sponges and absorb what someone else is saying?

4. Ask rather than assume — be curious

"I don't need to have the answers; I've just got to have the questions."

Making assumptions about other people is normal and usually comes after labelling and judging. It is easier than devoting energy and attention to understanding.

But when you assume how other people will respond, react and make decisions or choices, you disempower them and elevate your own role to all-seeing, all-knowing, all-powerful. It is a way of maintaining control.

Asking questions rather than presuming you know the answers or need to provide a solution leads to greater understanding, stronger connection and more trust, which foster creativity and innovation. People will be more likely to explain their ideas when you ask questions such as:

- Can you tell me more about that?

- And what else?

- It sounds like you are saying… Is this correct?

- Can you help me understand better?

It is also important to ask what their strengths and positive attributes are, and what is strong and can be leveraged rather than what is wrong and needs to be fixed.

Vanessa sits on her hands

Vanessa is a senior executive in the car industry. She used to listen to react rather than to understand. Having made a conscious decision to focus on listening to understand, she created physical and mental cues. Now when she really wants to understand what someone is saying, she sits on her hands or clasps them together and holds them as still as possible.

Her mental cue is to ensure that the first thing that comes out of her mouth is a question rather than an assumption or a statement.

Thinking challenge: How can you listen to understand rather than just react? Can you use the physical and mental cues most relevant to the way you typically operate?

Being respectful and listening to understand are the foundation for perspective and developing the skill of being empathetic. This is a career and life asset.

2. Deal with the discomfort—before, during and after the conversation

Living life on your own terms and writing your own code may sound appealing, but the challenge—and gift—requires courage, which often involves negative emotions and difficult admissions.

The emotions may manifest before, during or after tough confessions, but upsides can be exponential and a solid way to build self-efficacy and create a new normal.

What is your comfort zone?

Discomfort is experienced differently by everyone and may range from uneasiness to agony and everything in between. There is discomfort when you are asked to complete a task and really don't want to, but feel obliged and commit against your better judgment, discomfort in saying or hearing the word 'no', feeling a failure, rejected, 'un-Liked'. There is discomfort in having difficult conversations, feedback, listening to harsh realities, stretching yourself beyond what you thought possible, not knowing the answers to painful personal challenges—discomfort in not being able to reduce the pain and suffering of loved ones.

This section is about helping you build your capacity to not only sit with these emotions but to accept and welcome them as a path to growth and a way to be more you. Think of this section as your discomfort Sherpa.

What do you do when you can't say no?

Why would you say no when you trust yourself to handle the workload associated with saying yes? My coach Pam once told me that discomfort in the moment is healthier than hanging onto resentment. Resentment not only lasts longer but it can escalate.

You may have over-committed to tasks and responsibilities which drain your energy—felt obliged or backed into a corner. People know exactly whom to ask to get a job done.

You may find yourself saying, *"I am fine, really. Yes, I will help you with the presentation to the board. I know I haven't slept in a week; I have a huge to-do list, a kids' party to plan and those bags under my eyes are really nothing to be concerned about. So I'd love to volunteer to put that report together. I'll just grab my fifth coffee of the day and I'll be good to go."*

It may seem that all is well, but on the inside you are feeling resentful, unable to say no to helping someone else's professional career at the expense of your own wellbeing—and it is taking time away from the things that bring you joy and meaning.

You may experience similar resentment in your personal life when you act out of duty and in accordance with other people's expectations. Initially you feel flattered at being asked, but then resent taking on things you are neither interested in nor suited to.

Before I became comfortable with saying no, when my middle child was in his first year of school I was talked into being a parent representative for the kindergarten year. We had just returned from China and I was struggling to get back into local life.

I knew no one at the new school, a 60-minute round trip away, and it all felt overwhelming. The president of the P&F sweet-talked me into it, saying it meant a meeting once a term with the principal and other parent reps, a parent/family social gathering once a term, a fete stall, and fundraising activities throughout the year. A mission dedicating energy and attention to people at the coalface and building school community.

It provided meaning and purpose and built supportive relationships, but every year there were more responsibilities and commitment, until I was appointed secretary of the P&F.

It was a surreal moment—I was shocked for days and still have flashbacks! In addition to that executive role, I found myself on the fete-organising committee. This was a low point, and even after working in a paid position for a not-for-profit, I have vowed never to take part in organising an event ever again!

The additional responsibilities cost me dearly in terms of professional opportunities to do more meaningful work and personally in terms of doing the things that bring me joy, but I did not want to let anyone down or let them think I was not up to it.

Have you experienced anything similar?

I use that experience as an opportunity to practise accessing my courage, sitting with discomfort in the moment and avoiding resentment in the future.

Practise saying no

If saying no is hard for you, you can practise.

Yes, there is awkwardness in the moment, but so much awaits you on the other side. You can say goodbye to that resentful feeling, and hello to productive, meaningful opportunities.

Think about:

- What am I dumping and moving away from? Resentment, wasted emotional and mental energy

- What am I gaining and moving towards? Other opportunities, space...

Why it is important to have difficult conversations

"So inevitably you're going to have a conversation where you're sitting with a whole bunch of discomfort and unrest or that person's going to be creating more discomfort for others."

Similar to saying no in the moment and the outcome being zero resentment, having tough conversations avoids complications and adverse reactions. Being direct and honest is the key to maintaining a harmonious running rhythm and a positive culture.

So why don't we have difficult conversations more often?

Some people may have had a bad experience either conducting or listening to a tough conversation and wish to avoid repeating this at all costs. Others may have had conscious or unconscious training that everything is okay if everyone is happy, as if happiness were the measure of success.

"Your mantra's got to change to, 'Everyone should be happy if they've a right to be heard.' And you're not going to solve it for everyone.

That's not what you're going into the conversation to do, but I think people tend to think, if we can just make everyone okay, then life's okay. And, unfortunately, I think that's a naïve kind of position to take."

In her book *Dare to Lead*, Brené Brown and her team asked *"What, if anything, about the way people are leading today needs to change in order for leaders to be successful in a complex, rapidly changing environment where we're faced with seemingly intractable challenges and an insatiable demand for innovation?"*[2]

The most common response was a need for braver leaders and more courageous cultures. The book details the top 10 cultural issues and behaviours identified by leaders across the world as a barrier to becoming a braver leader and building more courageous cultures. The number one behaviour was avoidance of tough conversations and sharing productive and honest feedback.

"Some leaders attributed this to lack of courage, others to a lack of skills, and, shockingly, more than half talked about a cultural norm of 'nice and polite' that's leveraged as an excuse to avoid tough conversations."[3]

How to approach a tough conversation

"I think a lot of people aren't really sure how to approach a conversation."

When you have not received consistent exposure or best practice training, starting the tough conversation is understandably hard. However there are effective ways to achieve positive outcomes.

Preparation

If a conversation is potentially awkward or challenging then preparation and thought are required. Relevant information is a way to gain a deeper understanding, as well as deciding how you would like the conversation to go, what outcome you hope for and the potential hurdles.

---

2   *Dare to Lead*, Brené Brown, pg 6

3   Ibid., pg 8

Clear the decks

Starting a conversation with a clear and open mind is a huge step toward greater understanding and positive outcomes, so there is a balance in terms of letting go of preconceived ideas and expectations.

Purpose and perspective

Understanding why you are there and that the conversation is one of many and may be uncomfortable, but the feeling is temporary and will pass and the experience is a path to growth.

Timing

The longer you wait to have the conversation, the more energy builds around it, until it takes on a whole unnecessary life of its own.

You can jump in now and have an easier conversation, or wait for fallout to fester until someone says "That was six months ago. What are you talking about?"

> "I would 1,000 per cent say that you will always end up better off. And the discomfort you feel now will be a tenth or a hundredth of what you would feel should you delay that conversation any longer."

Dare to Lead shows how to build capacity for courage by being vulnerable and sitting with the uncomfortable emotions. Courage can be "*taught, observed and measured*" and is a combination of "*Rumbling with Vulnerability, Living into Our Values, Braving Trust and Learning to Rise*". The first step is the rumbling part. The other three need this core skill.

"*A rumble is a discussion, conversation, or meeting defined by a commitment*"[4] from parties to:

- Be vulnerable

- Remain open, curious and generous

- Stay in the middle of problem identification and solving

- Take breaks and circle back when necessary

- Be fearless in taking responsibility and accountability

- Practise deep listening.

---

4   Ibid., pg 10 and 11

Why do we fear feedback?

"I've always been very open to hearing people tell me what I'm doing wrong and listening to more senior people who are comfortable giving me feedback. When they tell me I get hurt, because it's personal. But then I accept it and I do something; I pivot, and I try to do something different. Then the joy you get from an outcome changing far outweighs that pain that you felt when you got that criticism about you as a person."

Feedback can be incredibly uncomfortable and damage self-confidence. The delivery method and intention matter, but by taking yourself out of the process you can accept the feedback as information rather than an attack.

"Every time I get negative feedback or any kind of feedback, I use that to change. Not change in a bad way, but if it's feedback where someone's giving me good advice, I'll use it to change. If it's negative feedback, I'll use it as fuel. And then I go, 'Right, I'm just going to do this.'"

Taking pride in both your successes and your mistakes is crucial to moving forward, and self-belief and feedback are valuable, despite the antiquated view that all feedback is negative or bad news.

It is not good news and it's not bad news. It's just news.

This insight can be life-changing. If you accept feedback as nothing personal and more a reflection of the choices you are making, and do not blame or shame yourself, then opportunities to improve, learn, grow and connect expand.

To create that distance between the feedback and your choices, take a subject/object view.

- **Subject** — you are the subject

- **Object** — your behaviour, your work output, your communication method, the feedback.

The subject (you) is viewing the object (feedback) without any attachment. While it is a bit more tricky to practise unless you are familiar with meditation, Buddhism and consciousness, if you think of feedback as an object in the external world, like a car or a house or a piece of furniture, you can then view it from a distance and create mental space between yourself and the feedback.

Since feedback is based on the perceptions, experiences, motivations, mode of operating and intentions of the person delivering it, there is an even greater reason to distance yourself and remove personal sensitivities. Attitude varies from leader to leader and person to person, so do not base your self-image and sense of values on their perceptions and goals.

How to have feedback conversations

Feedback should be delivered with perspective, empathy and understanding. The facts should be given as you see them though, and you have to deal with the fallout and help people work through it and learn. It is not feedback when a someone unloads an issue they are angry and frustrated about.

> "But if it's genuine feedback, it's just feedback. It's just news, and I guess that's improved my communication skills both at work and in my personal life."

John, a senior executive in the petrochemicals industry said that, early in his career, he was given incredibly harsh feedback upward by a female direct report. It was the worst he had ever received—however, it also turned out to be the best, because it shifted his whole perspective on gender and proved transformational.

> "If I had not listened to that feedback I would not be where I am today."

Following the difficult conversation, he put practices in place and changed his leadership style. His team's performance improved and this became his standard. His current team ranks highest in his organisation for performance and diversity.

Difficult conversations at home

Many progressive workplaces which understand the need to build trust and psychological safety train their people to have purposeful conversations which may involve unwelcome emotion. It is equally important to conduct these at home with your partner and children.

"Having purposeful conversations supports trust, honesty and speak-up culture at work. We talk about these conversations in the workplace and they are actually important at home too. And I think we assume that you do it at home, but actually, realistically, most people probably don't. I think partly at home in your personal life it's because everyone is so busy."

There are several explanations for what may be getting in the way. Screens, and how technology is used to communicate and interact play a part. There is also the loss of the family dinner. Full schedules of school and after-school activities reduce time for conversation.

How often do you sit together with your family and have the clear-headedness and energy to conduct difficult conversations? It is not easy to hear your child has a pain point, and so you need to be in a certain headspace to be able to absorb it.

"Not having the conversations doesn't mean that you don't love your children or you don't have a wonderful family. That's not a criticism. It's just I think life is so busy that sometimes we forget. And it's easy to assume and not ask, or it's faster to assume and not ask.

"And, equally, you could be putting a whole lot of energy into something that actually isn't that meaningful to your child."

How do we do this in practice, both professionally and personally?

1. Ask questions rather than assume

2. Understand it is not about you

3. Stretch yourself to grow

4. Be okay with not knowing the answers

5. Avoid a download.

1. Ask questions rather than assuming you know the answer

"You wouldn't assume that you understood... Well, some people do. But you wouldn't assume with another adult that you necessarily know what their good points and what their pain points are."

One of the biggest barriers to all forms of communication is when people make inaccurate assumptions rather than asking a simple question. As people want more autonomy and to feel they are treated equally, they become resentful when other people presume they know what they want or how they feel. This causes instant disconnection.

However, asking a question and demonstrating you understand someone's perspective builds the connection. Being present and listening to understand rather than listening to respond or react are important skills.

2. This is not about you

"It's really important not to carry grudges and not to hate people for something they said to you once, because in business and in work life, you have to really get on with a lot of people and get a lot of different things done. You need to be able to have a really challenging conversation with them one day, but then know that they trust you the next."

Conducting the uncomfortable conversation or being asked to participate in one, it is crucial to distance who you are from the words being said. You can never fully understand how someone is feeling and what they fear unless they tell you. They may react negatively and download their fears and disappointments onto you, which can be difficult to digest. Trying to remember that this is their experience can help you overcome your own upsetting feelings.

3. Stretch yourself to grow

"While it seems hard in the moment, and it might be really uncomfortable, knowing there is another side—it will stop and right now is temporary—there's comfort in that."

Most people I spoke to believe there is always growth after personal and professional conflicts and change, and that experiencing the pain from stretching themselves beyond what they thought possible is a huge positive.

"You need to get outside your comfort zone, because you won't grow unless you move outside that comfort zone. That's another thing that people don't realise, because they like the security; they like how it

was before, because they were comfortable. And it's getting people to think... the future's not going to be better, or that you're going to get comfortable again, accepting that, but you've got to get in that uncomfortable place first to grow."

While we may intellectually accept this, it can still be difficult during the crisis moment or tough period.

If you think about your muscles when you exercise, you use them in various ways that build capacity. In strength training and using weights or your own body weight, you maintain repetitions to the point of fatigue and peak discomfort, causing microscopic tears in your muscle fibres. The process can be really uncomfortable and hard, however if you treat your muscles with respect and support your body to recover with the correct nutrition, sleep and hydration, as the fibres grow back the muscles become stronger and adapt to a progressively heavier load.

You stretch yourself, experience distress, and then you recover, repair and grow.

You become stronger.

However if you push yourself too hard and cause a large tear, then it takes a lot longer to recover. If you don't pay attention to the recovery, you can produce scar tissue. Scar tissue is not only a hindrance to performance, but it also requires a whole lot of physiotherapy.

There's a lot of uneasiness in stretching yourself, but you do recover and grow stronger. You can apply this to any physical, mental, emotional or spiritual discomfort, and any type of muscle—your self-compassion muscle, acceptance muscle, perspective muscle. The more you push past what is comfortable and stretch, the more you build and strengthen that muscle, but you will need to recover and repair.

4. Not knowing the answers

"I realised that I had to sit with the pain and disturbance of not knowing, and mentally accept that growth would be on the other side of the experience. I would joke that the greater the pain, the greater the growth. Deep in pain, deep in learning."

There are times when you feel it is all too much. You are tired, stressed and everything is overwhelming. There is so much you are trying to process that there is no more room, and only an explosion can release the pressure.

The problem is, when you are overwhelmed you do not have clarity. When you do not have clarity, you can't access the best, most reliable and trustworthy parts of yourself. It is also easier to click into judgment mode. Telling yourself that you are perfectly healthy and have intuition and instinct at your disposal is vital. The answers will come.

5. Don't download

Do the opposite to your normal pattern of behaviour: don't say anything to anyone, don't rant on social media, don't download your hurt on anyone else, but do notice how you are feeling. Sit with the feelings, not knowing when they will end, and listen to your thoughts. Create distance.

When you do this, your clarity and inner wisdom/instinct/intuition have a chance to surface.

Negative emotions are not permanent

"The experience of pain and discomfort supported with hope is a pathway to growth."

Mastering the practice of sitting in the moment with your own tough emotions is a life-changing skill. It allows you to sit with the tough emotions of others—direct reports, partner, kids, family, leaders, soccer coaches or music teachers. Allowing them to manage their own feelings of distress or pain gives them an opportunity to build their own capacity and tolerance levels, supported by coaching.

Many of us have experienced that awful feeling of seeing someone we love treated disrespectfully or cruelly. It starts with toddlers. There is usually at least one bully in a group of kids who revels in grabbing toys, pushing, kicking, biting and screaming—and that Mamma Bear instinct kicks in.

As children progress to a larger arena, you cannot protect them and have to trust in other people, aware that no one has their best interests at heart the way you do.

I remember when a schoolfriend of his accused my middle son when they were in year one of something he said he had not done, which resulted in a reprimand from the teacher. Since his worst nightmare is to be late, get a detention, be told off, break the rules or not fulfil expectations, he was desperately upset.

Tempted as I was to contact the teacher and defend him, I knew that would not end well, so I took a deep breath, said it was fine to feel that way, gave him a hug and asked exactly what had happened. Asking for clarity rather than making assumptions led to understanding. I asked why his friend had told on him, which helped him see his mate's perspective. Doing this concentrated my unhelpful feelings and allowed him to feel his, so we worked through the problem together and came to a resolution. We also built trust, and he was able to see his friend and the whole situation from a different perspective.

It turned out my son had done exactly what he was reprimanded for, and the upsetting part was that his friend had told on him. The core impact was that their friendship and trust were wrecked. From this incident, I learned:

- Never assume your child's interpretation of events is the universal truth

- Do not react while you are in a state of frustration and anger, and risk damaging other relationships

- Ask lots of questions from different perspectives

- It is absolutely possible to sit with your child's uncomfortable feelings

- Your child will be okay, and even learn from it and grow.

This approach works with everyone. Rather than clicking straight into solution mode, sit with the unease of not knowing how to fix it, understand more about the problem by asking rather than assuming, look at other perspectives and allow the solution to materialise.

Jumping to the rescue provides short-term relief, but you may be denying an opportunity to build capacity to accept unwelcomed emotions, and to grow and thrive as a result. When you truly understand the benefits associated with sitting with difficult emotions, and realise this is a way to personal growth, you will know that allowing others to sit with theirs is a way to build resilience.

Discomfort is important when writing and executing your own code, a vital skill to develop and a prerequisite for standing firm, knowing you fit into any and all arenas, and setting and holding boundaries so you can lead life on your own terms.

3. Ask for what you need and want

"You can't just sit there and wait for people to give you that golden dream. You've got to get out there and make it happen for yourself."
Diana Ross

Imagine the barriers and challenges Diana Ross faced becoming a successful, influential person in her chosen profession. She found the courage and confidence to ask for what she needed and wanted and made it happen.

"We get what we ask for, not what we deserve." Zivai

Asking for what you need and want with absolute clarity and purpose provides opportunities to work collaboratively with others, build their capacity and develop a shared mission. You also get more of what you want and value.

How do you ask for help?

Asking for help can be a huge hurdle, but it does not mean you are needy or a failure. Make asking for help and support a question where people have a choice to respond with a yes or a no rather than viewing it as a commitment where people are obliged to agree.

Before my divorce I was in the privileged financial position of being able to pay for any support I needed. Our families lived overseas or inter-state and Fred travelled constantly, so I simultaneously held the positions ranging from family CEO through to frontline worker. I believed that I had chosen to be a parent and live in a beautiful, kid-friendly location far from my parents, marry someone who would never settle in one place, and be a stay-at-home parent. I intended to honour my commitments and thought I was not only the best person for this job but the only person. I needed to excel in parenting. All my eggs were in one basket.

I wanted to be in charge of how my children were cared for even when I was not with them. When I needed some time to myself to exercise or work on projects, I reasoned that by paying I would have more influence and control than if I accepted free help. Trusted child-minders and my guardian angel Mannie, who is like a grandparent to the boys and a good friend to me, provided childcare and cleaning support. I did not ask friends to look after the boys as I made assumptions about how busy they were with their own family responsibilities—and I would have had to relinquish some control.

I also did not like owing favours or being perceived as needy.

I didn't realise it at the time, but I was completely closed as I was applying filters and judgments. I was also dealing with the slow, painful decay of our marriage.

Divorce required a complete rethink and restructure. The necessity to work again terrified me. I had to start asking for help. For free as the budget was tighter. Whom could I trust? What would they think of me? What if my children misbehaved? Would my kids be judged because they came from a broken home? I had worked so hard to make the family solid and was super-resentful of being in this situation.

I was forced to start asking for help. And I didn't like it.

The pivotal experience that opened up my world happened one Saturday morning in winter 2016. I was juggling three soccer games and could not be in three places at once, so I asked a friend I had known for five years—a nurse with three kids of her own, a husband who loves soccer, and a minivan—to give one of the boys a lift to and from the game.

It was excruciating at first and I felt so indebted that I brought a bag of fruit as a thank you, but during pick-up we had a lovely conversation and my son said that he had enjoyed the experience. So I took a step toward letting go of my own disappointment at not being there and felt a deeper connection to my friend. It also provided a launch pad for future requests for help.

Give someone a 'helper's high'

A good friend who asks for help quite a lot pointed out that when you ask someone to help you, they feel needed, wanted and important, especially when it is someone very capable asking, who seems to be in control of everything.

"When you ask someone for help you can give them a gift and an opportunity to feel needed. They are completely free to say no, but they might say yes."

It turns out that serving and helping others can be a meaningful way of increasing your sense of wellbeing. Random acts of kindness and making a difference to someone's life can lift your mood. The benefits may be more powerful than acts of generosity towards yourself. It is called the 'helper's high' and produces endorphins and dopamine. Even small acts like holding the lift, directing a car in the parking lot, helping with bags, giving directions or shouting a coffee count.

Becoming more comfortable about asking for help and support can transform your relationships and create opportunities to work and do other projects, attend events and just be yourself.

A continual work in progress

I thought I was doing quite a good job, asking people for help and being clear about my needs, creating bonds and building connections with all sorts of people. I was enjoying it all and felt open, honest and authentic.

I was wrong.

It is the final week of the long summer holidays, outside temperatures are peaking, people's tempers are fraying and all family members are sick of each other. Everyone wants to move on.

Many parents can empathise.

I am losing patience with the boys and offloading my frustration with daily rants.

"Why is there sand all over the couch, bed, toilet seat, kitchen bench...?"

"Why are there wet towels on my bed?"

"The beds aren't made."

"Why are you kids constantly fighting about every little thing?"

"Don't piledrive your brother into the sand. He can't breathe."

"I am trying to work and I can't think clearly with all of this moaning and fighting..."

I am teaching the boys important life skills such as feeding themselves, sweeping the house, weeding, emptying the dishwasher, cleaning up after themselves, and unloading and unpacking the shopping as I do not want to be a house elf. My goal is to eventually send the boys out into the world able to fend for themselves and not look for another mum to tend to them.

It is hard work.

Added to the mix swirling around in my head is the outstanding feedback about the boys from Fred and his wife Ginger. Fred visits the boys four times a year and spends a week or so with them. They had spent 10 days at the beach with their baby sister and, according to Fred and Ginger, they were so helpful, kind, caring, mature, lovely... Completely confused I asked hopefully "They must have fought a bit, surely?" I wanted Fred and Ginger to experience the real-life blended family situation!

Apparently not; they were angels.

I explode after what had seemed like a full day of fighting and boundary pushing. I sit the three of them on the stairs and ask through clenched teeth: *"It seems as though you are all focused on what you don't have rather than what you do have and there is a lot of complaining and fighting going on."*

Youngest son's response: *"Is this a gratitude talk, mum? Because if it is, I am really grateful for the fact that it is nearly my birthday. So are we done?"*

"No, it isn't. And no, we are not. I am trying my hardest to be the absolute best parent I can. There is only one of me and three of you, and I can't believe you guys are not helping more or even just cleaning up after yourselves. I don't understand why Dad and Ginger say you are so helpful and you don't fight. Help me understand why you are not like that when you are with me?"

They all look at each other and reflect. My eldest son then responds: *"Well, Mum, Dad and Ginger, they aren't used to looking after kids, and, well, they need help with that."* Pause. *"But from what I can tell, it seems like you don't need any help, Mum."* The other two agreed.

I am completely floored. I thought I was doing so well, letting go and asking for help, yet the feedback from the most important people, my own children, did not correspond to my efforts.

I give my eldest a huge hug, which the other two want in on, and thank him for his honesty. I have more work to do on the asking for help front and I realise how pervasive the "If it ain't broke, don't fix it" maxim is. Just because I have a strong focus on continuous improvement in every realm and role I operate in does not mean others do. I also realise that if people perceive that someone has all bases covered, is productive and does not bring challenges to their attention, then generally they won't offer to help.

I choose to view my kids not raising the bar in terms of their contribution to family chores as an effective energy management solution. Why waste your own energy if someone capable and willing will do things for you? I take responsibility for the part I play and, although it is yet another point to add to my list, decide in future to be more direct and ask for more regular contributions.

A bit more about asking rather than assuming

In some situations you may wish you had asked a question rather than made an assumption. Like "I assumed you would have taken the washing off the line since it was raining." Or "I assumed you knew that I was the best person for the position because I am committed, ethical, diligent and great at what I do."

Assumptions are risky, and inaccurate ones can lead to a huge expectation gap. You may assume everyone is on the same page as you since it all seems so crystal clear. To you.

Incorrect assumptions and the resulting expectation gaps can cause disconnection and even relationship breakdowns. It is extremely annoying when the response to expectation gap fallout is "I am not a mind reader. How was I supposed to know…?"

You may make assumptions for other people about how they prioritise. You may not want to ask your neighbour to watch your kids for a bit as she is so busy with her own kids. Or not ask your leader if you can work more flexibly, because he may assume you are not committed to your career.

When you make assumptions rather than asking a question or making a request, you potentially shut down an opportunity to experience something different, realise your potential and build relationship bonds.

I cannot stress strongly enough the supreme importance of asking questions rather than making assumptions.

Assume means you make an ass out of u and me!

Be clear asking for input and making decisions

An effective way to reduce stress—on team members, partners, children, leaders—is to ask for input working toward a shared purpose, a useful approach when facing multiple deadlines, questions and decisions.

> "If you've got your stakeholders engaged and they understand where you're at with everything, then nothing can surprise them. And I found that when people understand what your issues are and what you have to deal with or why you structured something in a certain way, if they understand the whole concept, then they actually support you rather than interrogate it.

> "You make them feel part of what you're doing. If that's the only way that they're contributing to the decisions you're making, then it makes it easier in the end to get that across the line."

We looked at the different ways gender plays out in the workplace, and how effective clarity can be when asking a question. As I wrote earlier, the gendered male way of operating is to process internally and present a solution, whereas the gendered female way is to process externally and work through a solution with other people. Either way of operating is perfectly okay, but being clear about how the information is to be used is crucial. Standing firm and being the decision-maker means you can explain you seek feedback and ideas and not a decision.

Leadership strategies at home

There is lot more to asking than merely making requests of others and hoping they feel a deeper meaning or purpose—essentially, the WIIFM factor: what's in it for me?

> "If people feel like we've got a good purpose and we have a strategy we're working towards, then within that they understand their role and where they belong and how it's connected to the overarching strategy with respect to the group. If I lead that way then hopefully my people can observe that, feel that, and do the same.

> "Then you can get extraordinary outcomes from a large group of people who are all aligned. Hopefully who are engaged and hopefully giving discretionary effort."

I reasoned that if it worked for a senior executive at a big four bank, then surely it could work for our family. I was not aiming for extraordinary outcomes from a large group of people; I would be content with more focused listening and consideration for others.

Who is the boss?

In the belief that motherhood is not an obligation to fill in all gaps in the domestic realm and do all the crap jobs, I tried a new approach. I acknowledged that I am the leader of the family and lead parent, but that does not mean I am responsible for all of the traditional gendered 'mother' jobs, being hyper-responsible and being the house elf. Comparing to other leadership roles, how many chief executive officers or senior executives routinely perform all of the important but mundane tasks in an organisation and fill in the productivity gaps? Even volunteer soccer coaches typically have a manager or assistant.

I took the opportunity to truly step into my leadership role in our family. I stood firmly in my place. During a Systemic Leadership Training course I had learned how place and position in the family influenced interactions, expectations and relationships. Thinking this was useful, we experimented at the dinner table with me at the head (unintentionally eldest son had claimed that spot), eldest son to my left, middle son next to him and youngest son on my right. It was remarkable how that changed the dynamic at meal times and beyond.

Mind your language

I also decided to change the language we were using. Rather than 'helping Mum' we said 'contributing to the family mission' and now I speak to everyone this way as much as possible. I will ask *"Are you helping me out or are you also spending time with your children, building your relationship?"* "Are you helping me or are you cleaning up the kitchen, which will save time and enable us to spend more time together at the end of the evening and provide an opportunity to have a dance, play a game, do Tickle Monster, have longer cuddles?"

The process of reframing the act of contribution in a beneficial way shows people they are part of something bigger and it is not all about them. It builds survival skills and strengths in family members and relieves pressure for the lead parent to do and be everything!

Go from Mission Impossible to Mission Possible

Next we created and articulated a family mission which everyone bought into at some level. We talked about how the boys all play an important role in the process each day and that their contribution matters.

The family mission approach is a constant work in progress for us, but I did receive some feedback recently.

It was the usual pre-school morning flurry of activity and I was hurriedly getting dressed and running through all of the organisational priorities for the family, and simultaneously stepping through my professional tasks for the day. It is it during these most frantic times of the day that children seem compelled to bring up the juiciest topics of conversation that you would really like to pay more attention to. Jaw droppers include:

- *"Mum, why have priests been able to be in charge of people for so long?"*

- *"Why did Eve give that apple to Adam and did she eat it first?"*

- *"Why didn't Americans include black people in their sport teams for so long? They are so good at sport."*

- *"When can we move to Hollywood so I can be closer to where movies are made and star in a movie?"*

- *"How long have you been a prophet? You seem to know a lot of helpful information about health and wellbeing."*

- *"Why did we move back from China after a year when we were supposed to be there for three?"*

- *"Mum, do you think you are the female version of Jesus?"*

They know my favourite topics and sometimes they will double and triple team me.

I was attempting to do the multi-tasking tango and time was ticking away. I sounded the morning mum alarm of "Jump in the car. We don't want a late note." One of my personal goals each school term is to be late-note-free.

Just as we were leaving I noticed we had two out of three kids in the car. The youngest was missing. I charged into the house and rounded him up. All three boys knew I needed to get them to school and catch the train into Sydney for a meeting.

I was preparing to unleash a tirade when middle child went into bat for me.

> *"Don't you get it, Luca? If you don't get ready in time so mum can get us to school and then catch the train to Sydney to have her meeting, she can't earn money. If she can't earn money then she can't save the money to complete the family mission. That means we can't go to Disneyland. You are just thinking of yourself Luca! Think about the mission."*

Wow! Middle child was totally on board with the family mission idea. It had landed for at least one out of three! I suspect his focus on the mission was more aligned with his love of gaming, but it was nevertheless a big win.

How to ask when you are last on everyone's list

As a coach, mother, friend, daughter and confidant I listen to people's perceptions and beliefs about why they cannot dedicate energy and attention to activities and pursuits that they say are important to them. Although they are aware of the positive benefits of exercise, rest, sleeping, stillness, good nutrition and pausing, they choose to mentally, emotionally and physically prioritise other people's needs and work before their own. This is okay unless it is causing depletion, frustration or unhappiness, or they want to change their way of operating.

A friend illuminated the importance of asking for what we want rather than assuming people know or care about what is important to us. She was disappointed and frustrated with the way her partner had treated her. He was carrying on a long-term affair which my friend was aware of. She chose to stay with him, although she was devastated. It is my firm belief based on my own marriage that it is never about the third person in the marriage. They serve a purpose. They may be a distraction and the marriage may recover and chart a new path, or they may be an exit strategy.

The affair ended, but the marriage continued and contained an increased load of resentment, guilt, unmet expectations and disconnection. My friend expected her husband to be remorseful and make up for his behaviour, and wished he would put her first. I tried to empathised with her, however she only saw hurdles and barriers, and was lacking in motivation. She was also dissatisfied with her body, energy levels and general wellbeing. I suggested possible solutions, but she didn't want to know.

> *"I am not like you, Danielle. You are so driven. It doesn't matter what's happening, you make sure you exercise in the mornings, whereas if the kids or my husband need me I put them first."*

There were two major parts to this revelation: she had not explained to her husband that she wanted to be put first, and she was saying she was not worth being put first as she did not put herself first! Even in something simple like a morning walk.

If you do not show that you are worthy of coming first, then how can you expect other people to know it is important to you? If people don't know what is important to you, how can you expect them to support you in your endeavours, even when they love you dearly?

When someone is exclusively focused on their own goals and mission, they are less likely to offer support to others unless they are asked. This is especially true of family members who are used to the main person of service in a family—often the mother—doing everything and being everything for everyone. The expectation level is set and, unless the person of service communicates their expectation, most people are content to continue along the same path.

How to ask when you bump yourself up the list

There is an alternative to being last on the list and a way to include your important people to bump you up.

An interviewee, Lisa, was struggling to make time for herself. One morning she couldn't do up her pants, which surprised her until she realised she had stopped exercising, but had been too busy to notice.

Realising that her kids never missed soccer or cricket, she decided that for her own mental health she needed to make sure that exercise was an important part of her day. She needed to be bumped up the list of importance, and she set about lobbying her three sons for support.

> *"So, I had a big chat to the boys, and I said 'Look, you guys get your sport in. I need to do something too, because I'm feeling uncomfortable.'*

We had a bit of a giggle about my tight pants and the fact that I was expanding, and then we just sat down and worked out when we could do it."

Lisa and her sons worked out a plan (or a mini family mission)—*Let's get Mum back into her jeans*—and she was able to prioritise and invest in her wellbeing.

"So, they all came to Pilates with me. And they were fine. They just took a book or an iPad or something. And it's against what I say about screen time on a week night, but it meant that I got to do my exercise as well. And we're a team."

I liked how Lisa framed the discussion: it wasn't just "Right, kids, you're coming with me to Pilates." They had a giggle while Lisa got them on board. They care about their mum and Lisa made sure that they knew it was important to her.

"Absolutely. It's the only way to do it, because your family is invested, and it's something else that you're putting on top of them. Or like me at work, if I don't feel that I'm appreciated. It's just about being respectful. I don't put the swing set on top of the fridge."

Having conversations and asking for what you need and want with clarity, intention and purpose can lead to positive outcomes. Bringing everyone on board, helping them become invested in the overall goal and providing an opportunity for them to understand that their contribution matters is crucial. Assumptions lead to disconnection and mistrust, whereas asking may result in the best possible outcomes.

4. Set and hold boundaries

"Boundaries—You respect my boundaries, and when you're not clear about what's okay and what's not okay, you ask. You're willing to say no." Brené Brown[5]

Boundary conversations are tough and require preparation and thought. When you have strengthened your perspective and empathy skills, built your capacity to sit with discomfort and feel as though you can ask for

---

5   *Braving the Wilderness*, Brené Brown, pg 38

what you need and want, you are in a perfect position to identify your boundaries and communicate them to build trust and belonging.

What do you think about boundaries?

"Did I respect my own boundaries? Was I clear about what's okay and what's not okay?" Brené Brown[6]

You may see boundaries as a barrier and consciously choose not to implement them in any relationships for fear of being perceived as selfish, negative, cold or distant.

But if you consistently put others first, you are showing how you expect to be treated: last on the list of priorities. This becomes the baseline or foundation as you tolerate treatment and choices at your own expense.

If you are not prepared to prioritise yourself then other people will not be prepared to prioritise you, a consistent theme with women trained by the Gender Code to serve themselves last.

"We assume that if we disappoint someone that's the end of the world. But, realistically, you have to disappoint people all the time, because if you didn't they would give you everything to do all the time. Everyone wants your attention, everyone wants your time, everyone wants your contribution, but you need to pick who you're going to give that to, because otherwise you will just completely burn out, and then you're no good to anyone."

Set and hold boundaries with your kids

It is important for your children to understand boundaries and realise and acknowledge that while they may be your primary focus, your entire life doesn't revolve around them.

Karly is clear on her boundaries with her two young sons. They know she is not keen on attending weekly school midday assemblies. She made the effort when they were receiving an award until she realised that half of the time the kids were not sure what they had done to achieve it.

Karly and her boys have agreed that if their class is hosting assembly and/or they are speaking or performing they can ask her to come. That will depend on her other commitments, but she supports and participates

6   Ibid., pg 39

in most of their other activities, which she is satisfied is enough. She will not go to everything.

> *"I'll choose what I go to. If it's really important I will go, but I think that if I am there for them all the time physically, I would like to believe I am always present in spirit and provide support, it creates the expectation that it doesn't matter what I do, Mum will be my shot in the arm, will pick up after me, run around constantly."*

Rather than lowering the bar, which sometimes does not appeal to high achievers, perhaps it is a rethink and a question. Do I even want to participate in this event, high jump, pole vault, with the bar at all? Perhaps there is another event I am more interested in trying with a success measure more meaningful to me?

It is our job as parents to set and hold boundaries and it is our kids' job to push them. Over and over and over again!

It doesn't have to be either/or

Emotion can get in the way of articulating and holding boundaries when you only view situations in polarity. Although a difficult conversation may have adverse consequences, if you say nothing you have to put up with something eating away at your confidence, your sense of freedom and hope. If you are stuck in a hard place and can't find a way out, a middle path is the key.

Communicating and holding boundaries can be an act of self-compassion and compassion for others, eliminating expectation gaps, frustrations, disappointments and fears. Using the core thing that is most important to you is a powerful motivator to work out your boundaries and have the difficult conversation.

This may be wellbeing and self-compassion, which can lead to caring for others better and improving your mood, perspective, energy levels and sense of freedom. It is also another opportunity to create relationships and trust.

> *"And leadership more than anything else, I think. Because you look after people, you're responsible for people. But if you don't look after yourself, how can you look after people? Same thing as being a mother—if you're not in a good place, you can't raise children."*

Courage to have the boundaries conversation

Boundary discussions with my ex-husband resulted in a life-changing, positive impact on my daily existence, so I am a huge fan of setting boundaries.

The conversation with Fred

Since our separation, Fred and I have gone from a hollow, resentful, love-less relationship to a respectful, supportive friendship with the shared mission of raising three sons. Fred's contribution is primarily financial and mine is everything else. Our roles are clear and, while mine is not what I signed up for, I have accepted my responsibilities and the result-ing gifts. I resent my boys not having their father as a regular part of their lives, and of course I would like to share the parenting with Fred, but that is not possible as he lives in China with his new family.

I am grateful that he places a high value on providing financially for the boys—part guilt and part Gender Code where the male is the main breadwinner. After our divorce, in order to keep being the parent I wanted to be and make up for Fred not being present, I needed Fred to maintain the high value on financial contribution and allowed him to stay in my home when he visited the boys four times a year so he could spend more time with them and save on accommodation costs. I would move out while he was there.

After frank conversations with friends and the solid support of my partner, I realised the toll it was taking on me, preventing me from break-ing free of the marriage, but the main barrier to having the conversation with Fred was fear of financial insecurity. What if he pulled the plug? What if he halved his contribution? Or stopped coming to see the boys?

I could only see two polar opposite choices. I could let him know he could no longer stay and risk the financial consequences and jeopardise the boys' relationship with him and his new family or just continue to grin and bear the constricting, shrinking feeling of powerlessness asso-ciated with his visits. The distress was eating at me constantly and I felt such a fraud—here I was coaching people to stand firm in who they are, use their spark of brilliance, sit with discomfort and rethink, but I was not modelling my own message with integrity.

With the support of the two powerful Ps, my coach Pam and my partner, I was able to have 'the conversation'.

Pam pointed out that I saw the situation as all or nothing, focusing only on these two outcomes. What if I could create a different outcome?

This was the best advice and help. I had invested a huge amount of energy in potential negative consequences and courses of action, and nothing in the outcome I wanted. Pam encouraged me to identify what I wanted and why it was important to me. I was then able to decide with clarity and simplicity what was and what was not okay.

After gaining clarity, I went through the practicalities around logistics, finances and worst-case scenarios with my partner. I knew I could rebuild my finances. I'd done it before and I could do it again.

The most precious gift was his words of support: *"Whatever happens, Danielle, you have my support and we will get through this together. I am not going anywhere and I want to help you in any way I can."*

I believed him and that belief allowed me to plan, initiate and execute the conversation quite straightforwardly.

Danielle: *"Fred, can I ask you something? It is important to me that we discuss your visits to the boys and staying in my home."*

Fred: *"Yes?"*

Danielle: *"What is okay is that you all come around for meals or visits and stay for a few hours. It is also okay to spend a day at the beach and use the house as a base."*

Fred: *"Great. I'm looking forward to staying over Christmas for 10 days or so."*

Danielle: *"What is not okay is that you all stay in my home overnight and for extended periods. What is also not okay is that you leave all your mess and belongings for me to deal with after you leave. What is also not okay is that I move out of my house and become a nomad when it is the only opportunity I have for respite and to work without parental responsibilities. What is not okay is that it is affecting my health."*

Fred: *"Oh."*

Danielle: *"Do you understand?"*

Fred: *"So where are we supposed to stay?"*

I resisted the urge to manage things for Fred and continue to enable him and his life choices.

Danielle: *"I have been house-sitting or staying with friends over the years. I am sure there are many options available to you."*

Fred: *"This is a shock. Let me think about it."*

Danielle: *"Okay."*

Fred: *"We are grateful for you letting us stay. I suppose it is getting harder for you with your work and working from home. Thanks for letting me know."*

Danielle: *"No worries."*

There was more discussion, however I kept speaking in what was okay and what was not okay language. I found this framed the discussion, avoided blame, and left no room for emotional discombobulating or dragging up past hurts and histories.

Outcome

To my relief, there was no direct financial impact. I feel as though Fred and his partner respect me more, and I certainly respect myself a great deal more. It was the most difficult conversation of my life as I felt there was so much at stake, but I was creating a lot of negative, scarcity energy, thinking about the past and catastrophising into the future. I finally broke through the emotionally debilitating last hurdle to freedom, and now I feel there is a balance of power.

That has become a basis for all difficult conversations and the others are not as difficult. Setting and holding boundaries has become a simpler process.

- *"May I make a request of you?"*
- *"It is really important to me."*
- *"This is what is okay…"*
- *"This is what is not okay…"*

Starting with what is okay can be disarming and frames the discussion positively.

Set and hold boundaries at work

"I had to train myself to be quite firm with my boundaries. I'm pretty firm now. I'll leave work at four and not at ten. If they want to call me about it, go your hardest, and no one has, but that was really hard at first. I think it was the confidence though, to say 'You know what, I am leaving.'"

Setting firm boundaries at work is important and setting structures around what's appropriate is a first step, particularly for women with a family or a partner who travels extensively (or flying solo). Being clear on availability is key, explaining that appointments can only be made at certain times. Anything that can't be scheduled can be held over.

"My children are really young, and they're not going to be young forever. And I want to be around to do those things with them, like the afterschool activities. And also, I couldn't ask anybody else to do the schedules that they have."

When you love the work you do and you are committed to giving it your best it can be difficult to change the way you operate. However when you are clear and set boundaries for your leader, team, direct reports and yourself, you will have more to give.

"I enjoy what I do and, from a contractor perspective, you get in and you get out and that's the end of it. I need that, I need everybody to know that after five, don't call me. That's past time. If I don't set those boundaries in my life I wouldn't be able to do what I do. I think that being an agile coach drains you to the ground."

Boundaries allowed Lisa to align her work and her family without an overload in terms of logistics. Her teams are all supportive.

"…family's just not negotiable for me. If you want me at something after hours, then I'm likely to have a child with me. If that's okay with whoever's inviting me, then of course I'm happy to be there. And I take them to everything. There are some things that I have boundaries around, but because a lot of my outreach work is child-focused, they have been a big part of it. So they go to openings of galleries or exhibitions or those things that I'm involved in professionally."

I have committed to a similar plan. Early on when I established my coaching business, I realised I had to include the boys. It was too hard to operate in two different worlds and strive for an illusion of control and order. They have handed out business cards at group coaching events at home, sat at nearby tables in cafés while I was conducting interviews and waited patiently when I was late for school pick-ups due to coaching sessions running over time.

Should you have a boundary conversation?

When you are able to hold a boundary, it creates the foundation and fuel source for the next one and your confidence grows exponentially. Is there anyone you need to have the boundary conversation with? Have you had one with yourself?

5. Create agreements rather than expectations

Although the gap between what was expected and what is delivered may damage your confidence, your sense of self and your relationships, a different approach can establish clear, firm agreements with consequences and leave no room for mind-reading, inaccurate assumptions or unmet expectations. Establishing and adhering to agreements also reduces unhealthy behaviour choices.

Create social contracts

> "When you form teams, you have to solve problems and deliberate quickly under pressure. They have to work well together. So we create social contracts. The social contract typically accelerates that process of identifying what is important to you and what's important to me."

I was first told about the social contracts tool by Stephanie, who works in the technology sector. When geographically dispersed teams are working on an important project with tight deadlines, or teams are assembled quickly, there is a need for clarity, so when a team is formed there is a period for them to adjust to each other so they can all hit the ground running. Sometimes that can be two days. Sometimes it can be two months.

Stephanie explained that IT teams are constantly expanding, contracting and reforming, so it is necessary to be able to work with new people effectively and pretty quickly, otherwise more time is spent learning how to work together than actually achieving anything.

Social contracts with teams are creative ways to solve communication challenges and establish the culture of the group. This is an example Stephanie shared:

- If a team member receives an email, it doesn't require an immediate response

- If a team member receives a text message, it is important to respond within an hour

- If a team member receives a phone call, pick up

- Team meetings are limited or avoided during lunch

- Team members are supported in important activities such as picking up children from school or going to the gym.

> "It can be just within your team. It doesn't have to compete with the company culture. You can make it your subculture. We still adhere to all of the values and culture of when somebody comes into work in the morning and they're bringing a coffee, sending a quick message saying 'Does anybody want one because I'm on the way.' That's the way they become a team."

An important part of the contract too is clear consequences for breaching it.

> "If we fall down, this is what's important to us. We hold each other accountable, which can be tricky."

Learning about the social contracts approach made me wonder about other agreements. Asking for what you need or want, sitting with the discomfort, and expressing what is and is not okay makes it possible to create agreements with clarity and reduce the expectation gap. These are no longer unwritten, unspoken, ambiguous expectations but informed agreements.

Is it an agreement or an expectation?

How do you know if you are setting down an agreement or forcing an expectation, and why is it important? Steve Chandler, respected personal success coach, business consultant, public speaker and the author of 30 books, works with senior executives, Fortune 500 companies and American universities to improve performance and achieve sustainable results. He believes the distinction must be made between agreements and expectations.

What are expectations?

People's expectations are based on how they would like things to play out, but the outcomes are based on experience, goals and preconceived ideas.

You place expectations not only on how you think, feel and behave, but also how others should think, feel and behave. When life does not go according to plan, an expectation gap is created which causes a combination of frustration, disappointment, anger, sadness, fear, jealousy, stress and self-doubt.

In such non-clarity, you tend to look at your external world for answers, which results in a scarcity and blame approach using outside-in thinking. Unmet expectations then become a relationship killer, when connections are severed.

What are agreements?

Agreements differ substantially from expectations as they provide you with an opportunity to take responsibility for your thoughts, decisions and behaviours and, in the process, reclaim power. Asking rather than assuming.

Agreements are mutually agreeable, co-created arrangements where all parties determine what is required and when it will be executed. They are effective in the sense that they are promises made by all contributing parties using mutual respect rather than resentment or coercion.

In creating agreements, the 'How' can be reflected on and discussed, but the focus is on the 'What' and 'When'. Consequences of not fulfilling the agreement should be outlined, and a solid agreement established based on the participating parties' words, with good intentions and all information available at the time.

What is the impact?

If an agreement is not met, the focus is on the strength of the agreement rather than the weakness or behaviours of individual contributors.

The upside is that there is no one to blame, just an understanding that the agreement was inadequate in terms of What, When and How. Therefore the agreement can be rewritten more accurately.

Expectation not met = external focus = blame person or other entity.

Agreement not met = insufficient information available to create an accurate agreement. Focus on rewriting.

Agreements eliminate frustration, anger, fear and disappointment. You access clarity and focus on moving forward.

What does 'done' look like?

If you prefer something simpler than a detailed agreement and you can't invest the energy and attention in writing one, there is a quick and dirty version:

1. Boundaries conversation — request, what is important and why, what is okay and not okay

2. Followed by describing what 'done' looks like

3. An agreement between all parties.

Articulating exactly what 'done' looks like is incredibly valuable in all relationships and realms. I use it with my children, at work, and in community groups and projects.

It is particularly effective in terms of chores. 'Done' looks like all the dirty dishes in the sink are either washed or stacked in the dishwasher. 'Done' looks like all the leaves swept up from the front driveway. 'Done' looks like all the bikes, toys, Lego and food scraps have been put away or thrown away.

It is also effective at work. 'Done' looks like completing that report and checking for errors. 'Done' looks like getting feedback from at least one team member before coming to me. 'Done' looks like following through with your team member/client/customer and getting a result.

It is necessary to be explicit in terms of what 'done' looks like or people are able to take shortcuts and use the lower energy expenditure version of a task.

21 L is for Leverage

This next section of the CIRCLE process focuses on leveraging and understanding your value and how your contribution matters, the significance of internal resources, strengths and unique wonders and ways to build on your current capacity and what you already have at your disposal. Leverage has three sections:

1. Use what you already have—your value and your contribution matter

2. Use strengths you already have

3. Build on what you already have.

1. Use what you already have—your value and your contribution matter

> *"Value yourself. It's a bit like dating post-divorce. You listen to your heart about what you want and what you believe in. If you are working for someone who doesn't value you, or you're in a marriage with someone who doesn't love you, then you can look for that person or that employer who is going to value you. You don't have to stay in the job or situation. You make your own luck."*

You already use your internal resources every day. When you understand how valuable they are, you can harness them to build expertise wherever it is needed.

Why it matters

In corporate Australia there is a focus on creating pathways and pro-grammes to propel women into senior leadership, although I think we need jet runways rather than pathways. Core to this is reinforcing the confidence of women in corporations.

It seems so simple to say "Ask more" or "Be more confident", but the Gender Code prevails in workplaces, and women are working in a system designed to favour the male way of operating. Without experience and expertise it is harder to play by the rules.

But you can break the rules. Acknowledging the value of your contribution right now, and using what you already have rather than acquiring what other people think you need is a better way to approach the challenge. You can build grounded confidence, and that leads to mastery.

Trust and confidence in yourself provide a stronger sense of personal identity, security and wellbeing, which help you make worthy choices, stand up knowing who you are, and cope in every situation—and to deserve to be in the arena with all the other high achievers.

When you think and believe you are as human as everyone in your world, everything changes. Know that you are never above and never below anyone else but uniquely and universally equal. Your strengths, attributes, way of operating and areas of mastery will be valued differently by different people in different contexts and in different cultures, but you are equally human.

Standing firm, you are able to access your untapped brilliance. Think how much of your potential you do not use. Knowing your value and building grounded self-confidence is crucial in relationships too, as imbalances result when one person is more self-assured and perceived as contributing more to any relationship. In an unequal power base, the less confident person always feels they come second.

You can recognise your value and contribution confidently and create on your own terms. Your contribution is all-important, and everything you do matters.

What is the value of your work?

When you look beyond the obvious financial reasons, work can provide a great deal of value for you and for those you lead, including:

- Autonomy
- Mastery
- Engaging with a purpose
- Feeling a higher degree of self-determination and self-worth.

People are motivated differently, and some need to feel that their contribution matters and they provide value beyond the bottom line.

When asked what a good day looks like, every single research participant included an element of improving themselves professionally, building relationships and improving other people's daily experience. A leader has the opportunity to make other people flourish and to change their lives for the better.

Understanding how you value work, what it provides for you and the difference you make, helps relieve any pressure or guilt of not living up to your ideal model of parenting. You are contributing to the essential mission of human flourishing, nurturing and supporting the emerging future through your positive impact on people in your present moment.

If you look more deeply into what you are doing and why, and appreciate how important your contribution is, then effective, meaningful contribution can be a high octane fuel source and drive positive outcomes.

Others can see your value

Does positive feedback not really register? Do you know what other people see in you? While building capacity is an inside-out approach, the recognition of mentors, sponsors, peers, leaders and direct reports can help you define your value.

When you really start to believe that your contribution is valuable, you will understand why people back you, and you can trust them because they have seen something you haven't. Then you will perform better.

> "It was a confidence booster to let me say 'Shit, I am good at this, and I do have value — and an amazing person who has been the CFO of

a successful company for 20 years and is chairman of a board and is an amazing man, thought I was amazing.' No one can allocate that person to you through a mentor programme. It just doesn't happen. It's like relationships and dating before you get married."

A senior banking executive said that when people asking her to mentor them listed the achievements and qualities they saw in her that provided a massive boost of confidence.

It is almost like a mirror being held up and can be pivotal for building confidence and validating leadership value and contribution. You start to believe that you are a high-level contributor when people look to you for guidance and you can acknowledge that the way you operate is beneficial. However it does require balance and humility to avoid ending up in an echo chamber where everyone you choose to work with thinks you are brilliant.

Can you recognise your value and contribution?

All except one person I spoke to believed they were a better leader after becoming a parent, and often a better parent for being a leader.

Although each of us is different, easily identified benefits to being a parent include the development of critical thinking, increased flexibility, adaptability and creativity, a deeper perspective and empathy, and better organisation, prioritisation and connection.

"Essentially, also it's forced me to learn to analyse and step back, which is helpful from a leadership perspective. You can't necessarily be freaking out about everything all the time. It's definitely given me a lot more patience than I would naturally have possessed. I've had to learn patience. It's also helped with adaptability, because kids don't come with a manual."

Whether you are in paid employment or not, you are using these valuable skills. I believe in this so much that I included the development skills I had honed while I was not in paid employment and being a lead parent in my LinkedIn profile! Far from switching off your strengths and talents when you become a parent, you sharpen them and develop new ones.

Parenting and leading—emotional intelligence training 101

"You really develop your emotional intelligence as a parent both in terms of skill and tempo. It is a lovely attribute to bring into the workplace."

A leader and lead parent builds strong internal resources and delivers huge value. Just managing daily responsibilities you work across the range, moving fluidly through your many roles.

Most parents who also lead at work use flexibility of thought as well as mental organisation to take on everyone's needs. The range of situations is another precious asset in terms of strengths.

A day in the life of a powerhouse

It is 9:30 on a sticky morning in mid-February. The temperature has already hit 30 degrees and the 50-metre, 8-lane swimming pool is empty and still. Penny is at her daughters' swimming carnival and has set up a small table brimming with fruit for the primary school competitors. She is a stellar cheerleader and coach, encouraging the children and chatting to their parents, and she leaves in the late morning for an Executive Women in Business lunch where she clicks into networking mode, has meaningful conversations and makes connections.

After lunch she goes to a multinational corporation to conduct a two-hour afternoon facilitation session then, slightly tired but energised by the responsive group session, she has a Zoom call with her business coach back at her home. Penny prepares dinner and eats with her two children, plays a quick game of 'guess the dance move', reads a bedtime story and joins in an unplanned, child-instigated philosophy session.

She ends the evening with school lunches for the next day and a WhatsApp group discussion and text messages with her children's soccer coach, music teacher, school teacher and other parents as she is a committee member of the school Parents and Friends.

"It's true. It does test your mental agility. With juggling, you've got multiple things. You do have to learn mental agility and excellent organisation skills. You need to get better organised. You develop a host of skills because you have to. It's that survival skill set and once you have it, it's a fantastic skill set."

I believe it is more than a survival skill. The skills, attributes, strengths and awareness we develop as parents are a priceless asset.

The huge productivity impact in your workplace

It is time people stopped saying that when a woman has a baby she is less productive, less committed to her work and less capable of leadership roles. This is completely untrue. Women who are lead parents are not interested in wasting time.

Cognisant of this, John has an outstanding approach to maternity leave and returning to work. He provides an opportunity for mothers to return to work one day a week before their maternity leave is up and they work 'on' the business rather than 'in' the business. This is an upside for him as he has a trusted team member there who is good at relationships and at sorting stuff out.

> *"You really get this incredible productivity increase from those people working one to two days a week. It's so cost-effective from a performance perspective, and also from a development perspective."*

John refers to women working 'on' the business as a development opportunity. Work becomes not all about them personally, but also what they do for the business, and every one of his teams with women with children has improved his own and the team's performance.

Having someone with good internal resources and the drive to contribute in his corner results in high performance and achieving business KPIs. Over a 20-year period he has led 32 women returning from maternity leave. One hundred per cent have returned, and all have been promoted within three years.

> *"People do it because they like it, not just 'I have to go to work today,' but because they love it. You end up with a better and stronger team as a result."*

When you view situations through a different, broader lens it can open up possibilities. What may traditionally have been seen as a potential liability can actually be a powerful productivity asset.

When you understand your value you gain confidence

However, gaining confidence and increasing the value of your contribution can lead to conflicts in relationships. Sometimes your values, hopes and dreams are no longer aligned. Your development and progress at work have a direct influence on your personal life, and ultimately result in clarity and growth.

> *"As I've gotten more confident in who I am and the value that I bring, I'm accepting that I don't have to please everybody, which is I think one of the things that women in particular are encouraged to do. It does change the way we see the world and value our relationships."*

Self-knowledge is an essential part of building grounded confidence, self-belief and a strong sense of personal identity. This is the foundation for harnessing your unique strengths and wonders.

2. Use strengths you already have

> *"I found that I had all the right skills—what I loved to do—and my skills were the perfect match to build a business. It's been such an absolute joy playing to my strengths. Running a business in this industry I've created for myself."*

An important part of the process of creating and executing your unique code is to know, understand and use your strengths. This self-knowledge is remarkably powerful. Strengths can be expanded to a far greater extent and, using that base to work on self-awareness by acquiring relatable language and looking through a clearer lens, you are able to explore far deeper.

You can build grounded confidence and self-worth, expand your thinking, access your full potential and live life on your own terms.

Do you know your strengths and unique wonders?

Understanding strengths is life-changing as it provides the opportunity to understand people better, and what strengths are at play in their lives. It changes the course of careers, and leaders who identify strengths in others help people connect and progress.

271

"When you take the time to identify and acknowledge what people are good at and what support they need, you get more out of them. But it's time-consuming. Very time-consuming."

Do you search for your strengths and 'the thing'

Exploring strengths and how you use them is an area I have focused on for many years. I have always dedicated energy and thought to discovering what I excel at and was often amongst the best, but I desperately wanted to be the best at something—a champion swimmer, top academic, netball superstar or acclaimed dancer. I so wanted to be a *Young Talent Time* member, but after I was unceremoniously dumped from the school choir for 'bad singing' that dream evaporated!

I used to wish someone would sponsor me and help me become an incredibly successful person. I just didn't know what an incredibly successful person did and the one I imagined was not a finance professional. I had met and worked with accountants for decades and was in awe of them: so committed and focused. I do enjoy seeing a story and pattern in the financial numbers, the challenge of problem-solving, continuous improvement and the team element, but being the CFO of a multinational corporation or partner in an accounting firm did not feel right.

Each time I moved countries I promised myself I would make a career change, explore other options and find the thing that fulfilled me. I did explore, and engaged in all sorts of projects and community activities, but 'the thing' eluded me and I stayed in the safe, financially rewarding space of finance.

What I did find out after doing a great many personal development activities, reflecting, taking online quizzes, doing assessments, studying, coaching as a client and a coach, upskilling and ultimately being a parent is that one of my strengths is actually understanding and identifying what I do have and using it for the best possible outcomes.

I also realised I had been trying to bridge my 'developmental gap' and dedicating energy and thought to acquiring what I didn't have, believing that if I just had more time, more support, more qualifications, more experience, then I could do more and be that incredibly successful person.

When I flipped everything around and, rather than focusing on roles and titles, looked at who I was and what strengths and abilities I was using, I found that I had been blind to what I actually did have at my dis-posal—my internal resources. I discovered I am creatively resourceful.

Shifting the focus to what is strong from what is wrong is huge—understanding that what is viewed as wrong through one lens may be strong with a lens adjustment.

Why do we focus on the development gaps?

While it is beneficial to use our strengths as a base, our weaknesses seem to take centre stage.

> "Perhaps it is part of human behaviour. I always think of that Julia Roberts movie with Richard Gere. That film where she tells him about her childhood, about how she was treated awfully, and her mother said all this awful stuff about her? And he says to her 'I think you're an amazing woman.' And she says 'Isn't it funny that the bad stuff is easier to believe?'"

It is easier to believe the bad stuff and focus on weaknesses, although they may be sabotaging your potential. There are new discoveries in science, and in particular neuroscience, thanks in large part to more women entering the profession determined to overcome the misogyny and systemic hurdles and be recognised. Current findings presented in *The Strength Switch: How the New Science of Strength-Based Parenting Can Help Your Child and Teen to Flourish*, by Dr Lea Waters, suggest the focus on weaknesses all comes down to old wiring.[1]

In order to survive over millennia, our brains were shaped by our environment to become expert pattern detectors. As we evolved, the ability to identify disruptions quickly in the usual daily patterns was nec-essary for survival. The disruptions served as clues, indicating potential danger or weakness.

It was important to be alert to the environment when an unusual rustle in the grass could be a predator lurking or the one unsmiling face around the tribal campfire an enemy. This primeval instinct developed in us a tendency to focus in on what is not quite right, which helped us weigh our chances of survival and decide whether to take action.

---

1   *The Strength Switch: How the New Science of Strength-Based Parenting Helps Your Child and Your Teen Flourish*, Dr Lea Walters, pg 8

This is referred to as 'negative bias'. It was important for survival in the harsh circumstances of the past, however the old wiring is unhelpful in today's world. Since we now conduct problem-solving, complex reasoning, higher levels of communication and cooperation, and have deep wells of persistence and expertise, the negative bias actually disadvantages us.

> "It blinds us to opportunities, keeps us from seeing the larger picture, and bars access to the expansive thinking that unlocks innovation, collaboration, adaptability, growth, success and fulfilment.

> "Attention on the negative helped us survive. Attention on the positive helps us **thrive**." Dr Lea Walters[2]

What you are strong at is probably over 90 per cent of who you are right now. Why would you rectify the 10 per cent when, if you focused your attention on harnessing the 90, you could seize opportunities, expand your thinking and unlock your potential?

It all makes complete sense when you shift your thinking and refocus the lens, then train your brain to rewire by repetition and practice.

The Dalai Lama says *"There isn't anything that isn't made easier through constant familiarity and training. Through training we can change; we can transform ourselves."*

Your Inner Mean Girl may be questioning the whole strengths approach and being a tall poppy cutter if you focus on your strengths and not your weaknesses. Does that mean you are not being authentic and providing full disclosure? In the context of strength-based parenting (SBP), Dr Lea Waters writes:

> "If anything, SBP drives home the point that our strengths make us unique, but they don't make us special—because **everyone** has strengths. There's actually nothing special about having strengths. What is special is how we learn to use them in ways that are good for us and for others."[3]

---

2   Ibid., pg 9
3   Ibid., pg 11

What you need to know about strengths

Dr Water's research, insights and practical solutions detailed in her book resonated with me and I started experimenting with my learning partners—my kids and clients. The concepts and practices are equally applicable in different roles and so it became my personal, professional and parenting Bible.

Dr Waters defines strengths as positive qualities:

- That energise us, that we perform well and choose often

- That, used in productive ways, contribute to our goals and development

- Built over time through our innate ability and dedicated effort

- Recognised by others as praiseworthy, they contribute positively to the lives of others.[4]

Taking a strength-based approach for children and adults means:

- You perform better at work

- You achieve higher levels of happiness and engagement

- You achieve and maintain greater levels of physical fitness and are more likely to make healthy behaviour choices such as sleeping, healthy eating and having regular check-ups, and you recover better from illness

- You reduce the risk of depression and increase your ability to cope with adversity and stress

- You experience greater levels of self-esteem and life satisfaction

- You have an increased likelihood of being fulfilled in your marriage and staying married.[5]

It seems like an easy choice to use a strength-based approach.

---

4   *The Strength Switch: How the New Science of Strength-Based Parenting Helps Your Child and Your Teen Flourish*, Dr Lea Walters, pg 7

5   *The Strength Switch: How the New Science of Strength-Based Parenting Helps Your Child and Your Teen Flourish*, Dr Lea Walters, pg 9

How do you identify your strengths?

There are myriad ways, and a simple, free option is the VIA strengths survey: http://www.viacharacter.org/www/Character-Strengths-Survey#

I have used it and recommend it to clients, but when I coach I prefer to identify client strengths through conversations and questions:

- What are you doing when you are at your best?

- What is working well right now?

- When you think about what you do in a day, which activities make you feel energised and excited?

- What do others come to you for?

- Which 3–5 words would family, friends and colleagues use to describe your strengths?

- When you wake up in the morning, which activities are you most excited about completing in your day?

When you are present and open, listen to understand and ask rather than assume, the strengths seem to pop out. It takes practice and repetition but is definitely achievable.

Who are your strength supporters?

"There's someone out there who's really successful, who could be male or female, who values who you are, loves what you do and would love you to work for them. If you can hold that dream and keep looking and not give up, then I think you've got a pretty good chance of finding it eventually."

Just as you set people up for success by helping them play to their strengths, developing a network of people who see your strengths is crucial—your 'strength supporters', as Dr Waters calls them, see a great deal more in you than you do.

Most people have at least one strength supporter, and others are fortunate to have more—perhaps someone who has known you for most of your life and believed in you and seen your potential: an aunt, uncle, grandparent or sibling, a teacher who helped to bring out the best in you, a sports coach or a mentor who had more confidence in your abilities than you did.

These people are in your life right now. Sometimes they are obvious and sometimes they are there and always have been, but you have not noticed them. They may not fit your defining criteria, and you may be focused on results and outcomes rather than people. The strengths support they give may be subtle and seem insignificant, but it is enormously valuable and may take you to the next stage of your definition of success.

It is equally valuable to understand your strength detractors—the people who are intentionally or subconsciously reinforcing the code you are determined to delete. They may be contributing to your feelings of self-doubt and impostor phenomenon because they still see you in the old context and have you in a box with a label stuck on it.

Strength supporters may include:

- Professional network contacts and relationships

- Mentors and sponsors

- Coaches.

Professional networks and relationships

"Girls are raised to nurture and collaborate, to work together to achieve a common outcome. We network horizontally and down. Women don't tend to network up as much. It's not as self-serving."

Networking can be polarising—some women love networking and being a part of network groups, while others loathe the idea.

If you do not see value in dedicating energy and effort to sitting around having coffee or listening to people speak at events so you can hand out your business card, and think it is contrived and feels like a self-serving sales pitch supporting the traditional male way of operating, changing the way you view networking and shifting your thinking, intentions and language may open up all sorts of opportunities.

Networking to help others

The women who enjoy and benefit from networking approach it quite differently and instead of asking "What's in it for me?" (WIIFM) they ask how they can help others and learn.

This shifts the intention away from professional aims towards contributing to a greater good, so that events become opportunities to connect rather than networking.

Over the past two years, there has been an increase in women's networking groups, events and opportunities, and a shift from networking as a competition opportunity to networking as a supportive opportunity. My view is that this is based on the female gendered training focusing on caring for other people, setting them up for success and investing in human flourishing.

Most women are good at connecting and networking, so if you have the skills, use them!

The same principles apply to relationship building, and it is important when you are having a difficult time to know that you have a reliable support network. Having a network feeds into your sense of optimism and confidence: you have a safety net, whether it's financial, emotional or professional, and that helps you in tough times.

"Creating your own business can feel like jumping out of a plane. Being part of a supportive network is like having a parachute."

Investing in the integrity of relationships is a two-way process where you give and receive. It is important to understand that giving and receiving ebbs and flows and is a long game.

"Those support networks, they're long-term relationships, or you might be giving a lot at one point, but you know that. In the future, and you don't do it from a mercenary point of view, but you know that things go around, come around; it's about building those relationships and investing in them, even if you don't see immediate returns, so to speak."

Mentors and sponsors

"I personally don't think you need to chase titles and roles and things. I think you need to chase experiences and you need to chase good leaders and good mentors, and you should work actively, actively hard, harder than you would at your job, because that's where you're going to become the best you.

"And then I think career follows."

278

The message is clear: it is crucial for your professional career growth to find good sponsors and/or mentors. They need to be people you can learn from who can convey hard truths to you. Having someone who encourages you to be you rather than a carbon copy of them is more valuable than chasing and investing in the next role.

> *"The way people get jobs and big promotions and the C-level jobs is not by responding to an ad in the paper. Someone has catapulted them into the stratosphere."*

Gender, mentoring and sponsorship

There are challenges in finding a good mentor, mentor programme or sponsor. Gender may play a part, and general patterns can be identified.

For men, traditionally mentorship tends to happen organically. A relationship is set up through sporting clubs, school or university connections or workplaces. Mentoring relationships seem to flow and happen.

Traditionally, for women more energy, attention and work are dedicated to creating mentoring relationships. When women in leadership roles were rarer, they would be partnered with older, senior men with varying degrees of success. Now there are more senior women available to be mentors, quite a bit has changed. However, my research revealed than mentoring can still seem to be about helping women navigate their way through a man's world. There are better ways to access and create opportunities, but mentor programmes do serve a useful purpose.

> *"It's lovely to tell people 'Find your own mentor,' but I think that these mentor programmes, particularly for young people in their careers, they help because people wonder how to get started and it gives them an experience."*

While it is not necessary to enrol in a formal programme, it is important to find people who influence you positively, who see what you are capable of and help you to be self-reflective.

> *"You have to realise that mentors are people of influence and come from all walks of life; there's a lot of them around, and I think being open to meeting them and accepting those opportunities is really important."*

Mentoring later in your career requires careful attention and an even greater focus. There are some very helpful programmes and resources available, which an employer can organise on your behalf.

Would you prefer a mentor or a sponsor—or both?

In a mentoring relationship, the mentor usually imparts knowledge, wisdom and experience aimed at helping the mentee advance their career by understanding the rules of the game, but this can be viewed as a deficit approach—women don't understand the rules and need help—and may be limiting. It does not necessarily create special opportunities.

"I honestly think one of the struggles that we have with women mentoring and women-only workshops is that they're often marketed on implying that we in some way have a disability and therefore we made this special training. But fundamentally I think it is about women actually leveraging off the strengths they bring to the business. It's not about closing a gap.

"Rather than, 'Let's deal with your disability or your inferiorities,' let's actually explore what it is you bring to the table and let's use that."

For some people having a mentor is helpful and provides opportunities to lay stepping stones, but being sponsored leads to catapulting their career in ways they never thought possible.

A sponsor may see something in you and provide opportunities to connect. Someone who is not in the room is talking about you and recommending you. The sponsorship relationship focuses on what you bring to the table. Your sponsor does not tell you how to play the game, but commits to getting you onto the field.

Sponsorship can play out in many different ways, but usually involves the sponsor making contact with a professionally valuable person and setting up a connection for you. While the sponsor may be older and wiser, they are more of a connector, creating new opportunities rather than cultivating a carbon copy of themselves. The sponsor will not do leg work for you. You must build up the relationship and earn your stripes and, when you have autonomy, you're running your own race and shaping your own future.

"Which is way better than mentoring. Mentoring is telling someone how they did it and what's good for them. That's not running your own race. But if you have someone sponsoring you, they see all the amazing things in you [and] they will say 'You should speak to this person. I can get you a coffee with that person,' and then that leaves it to you to run your race with it. And there's no other people's rules required."

Your experiences of being mentored or sponsored may not fit these definitions. You may be a mentor or have a mentor who operates with a combination of both. The real key is to work hard and find the person who will understand that you are amazing and can do amazing things. It is important to seek people who believe in you even before you do and help you draw on your capacity to perform and progress.[6]

What about coaches?

"When you are open to new ideas, you want to be honest and share and you are prepared to take action, working with a coach really works. It has changed so much for me."

Most of the people I spoke with had had coaching and believed it enabled them to benefit from a fresh perspective — being asked tough questions and feeling supported. They were able to deepen self-awareness and self-knowledge and view them as career assets.

Faced with challenges, coaching can help you get to where you want to be.

Most high performers in all fields have coaches — sport, acting, music, speaking, leadership, business. In order to develop excellence, it is important to have people who are masters of their craft, and who see more in you than you see in yourself, helping you.

Coaching helps you to decide what you want and what is important to you. It can help you gain a fresh perspective, understand what is working well now and how you can use that to make changes to get you to where you want to be. A coach will work with you to create an action plan or your own blueprint, and will hold you accountable.

---

6   'How to Make a Life-changing Career Move. Mentoring or Sponsorship: What Works Best for Women', ABC Radio National *This Working Life*, 10 February 2018, https://www.abc.net.au/radionational/programs/this-working-life/10218/9412424

It is vital that, if you decide to enter a coaching relationship, you are both a good fit. Most coaches request at least one 'matching' or 'getting to know more about what you want' meeting. It is a serious relationship with appreciable investment, a conscious act of self-care and self-investment.

It can be more difficult to prioritise seemingly easy activities like sitting still and meditating, reading a book or having a bath, and activities with a more structured time and financial commitment such as a massage can be easier to keep. If you use this same approach and commit to sessions with your coach where you will be listened to, focused on, guided and supported, you have the opportunity to work on your mental, emotional and spiritual health and wellbeing.

When your mind and perspective are in a great place, everything else improves. When you feel you are making progress, are in control and someone is helping to take care of you, you can build a life that you enjoy every day.

Your strengths and unique wonders in action

Imagine if you were aware of your unique wonders and could use them openly and freely every day with the confidence that you are good enough and you are giving enough.

You may use the default way of looking at your environment to define who you are: the people around you and how they treat you, the situations you have found yourself in, health scares, job challenges, deaths, disappointments, frustrations, achievements and Facebook-worthy accomplishments. All of these external factors can own you and your identity.

But you don't have to allow people, places, things and thoughts to decide who you are. You can choose to allow your wonders and how you use them define who you are and write and execute your own code so as to live your life on your own terms.

3. Build on what you already have

The internal and external resources you already have are incredibly valuable. You can build on them and leverage more.

Take risks and build your confidence

"Have faith to jump off the cliff, because you'll actually find a way to get through it."

Risk-taking behaviours are encouraged—or not—from an early age with play behaviours and socialisation of boys and girls. Babies are treated differently according to gender as early as in the womb, when the colour of the inside of the cake at gender reveal parties indicates the sex of the developing baby. Studies show that people engage in more physical play with boy babies and less so with girl babies. This pattern continues throughout childhood.

Risk-taking on any level builds confidence. Based on the Gender Code, men are encouraged to take more risks in their physical environment and view challenges through the gendered male lens of 'It's just a game'.

This teaches them how to lose and look to the next game and possibly the next win, understanding that there will be a next time. Learning from losing shows you how to develop a new plan to act differently to maximise the chances of winning next time, and that there are other options to achieve outcomes and experience that winning feeling. This builds resilience and trust in yourself and in other people.

"It's a game. It's not personal; it's just literally a soccer match. As a person tackles you and they're trying to get the ball past you, it's not about you personally. It's not because they don't like you or they do like you; it's just a game. That leads into the whole 'Just dust yourself off, have another go.' It's just about having a go."

When you are faced with a degree of uncertainty and risk, you may be hesitant to commit. But the worst that can happen is that it will fail. In that case a Plan B or C provides a safety net. This builds self-trust as you feel confident that you have anticipated all the potential issues and will adapt and change course as you navigate the challenge. This is the difference between blindly leaping off a cliff without a landing scenario and doing all the pre-leap prep work, the difference between a reckless person jumping and Navy SEALs executing a mission. Viewing a career as a game allows you to take more risks and build the confidence to know you will survive and thrive.

Let's put risk-taking under the microscope

Traditionally the focus has been more on the obvious forms of risk-taking and associated with the male gendered way of operating and levels of testosterone. However as Cordelia Fine shows in her book *Testosterone Rex: Unmaking the Myths of Our Gendered Minds*, the stories about testosterone are unjustified.

> "Testosterone affects our brain, body and behaviour. But it is neither the king nor the kingmaker—the potent, hormonal essence of competitive, risk-taking masculinity—it's often assumed to be."[7]

It is more of a part of a complex bio-cultural mix.

Cordelia Fine's research shows that women and girls can and do take risks and compete to the same degree as men and boys. Identifying sex differences depends more on what you ask women to compete at and whom you ask. She found that women are more likely to compete in familiar territory, which may be more neutral or 'feminine', such as dancing, speaking or fashion.

Wherever women and girls have built confidence and mastery in their abilities, they are more likely to be competitive and take risks. It is time to stop buying into the myth that women are not 'naturally' competitive and are more risk-averse. It all depends on context.

Having a baby is an incomparable act of risk-taking. While developed countries have a relatively low number of complications and deaths, a first-time mother has little idea to what extent her body will be transformed during pregnancy and after birth or how much pain she will experience.

> "I'm not risk-averse. I make informed risks, but my attitude is to ask for forgiveness rather than permission."

Can you push some boundaries?

> "It's just something that's evolved over time. I was always fairly adventurous as a younger person. As you mature, and you experience things, you say 'Well, I can do that. I can take that opportunity and I can give that a go. And I can push myself beyond what I thought

---

7   *Testosterone Rex: Unmaking the Myths of Our Gendered Minds*, Cordelia Fine

I could do. I can challenge my thinking and do something different.
I don't have to do the norm.'"

Pushing boundaries can be as a result of a huge adventure, or slower incremental shifts. Regardless of speed or intensity, when you push a boundary and mindfully engage with the process and outcome, your boundaries move.

Allison, now a chief financial officer of a large organisation, has travelled on her own to some of the dodgiest countries in the world. Surprised when Pakistani border guards tried to stop her crossing into Afghanistan without an armed escort, she went anyway. Her adventure there started with hitch-hiking, a boundary she pushed early on.

> *"And then all of a sudden I'm going to Afghanistan. And then I'm riding a bike 1,500 kilometres around West Africa. So as you push risks, your boundaries move. Practise pushing boundaries. If you don't, your boundaries stay where they are."*

Now that Allison has two children, she has stopped taking these types of risks, but she will still say *"Oh shit, I can do it. It's just pushing a boundary that you think is there, and you push past it and go 'Oh shit that was actually not a boundary at all.'"*

This can apply to seemingly small boundaries, like calling people you have been meaning to speak to for a long time, or asking for more work or a bit less.

> *"Just little incremental things to push boundaries, and all of a sudden you will find that your boundaries are this much taller."*

Silence the self-doubt gremlins

Do you experience self-doubt? Do you see it in others and wish you could help them?

> *"I doubt myself probably every day. It's interesting, because it's when I forget the things that I feel make me successful or it's around the people that are around me or the problems that we're solving. When I lose sight of that and I start to think about other teams or other people's opinions, or what's the right political thing to do, that's when I start to lose my way."*

Self-doubt is a feeling that is shared by many women, and the Gender Code plays a huge part. If you find yourself living in environments that reinforce an unwelcomed code of behaviour and you feel pressure to be a version of yourself that does not feel right for you, self-doubt may be a constant companion.

What helps?

Using grounding practices and mantras, you can navigate your way through tricky situations, grounding yourself in questions: "What is the problem I am trying to solve? Who am I doing this for?" This can scale up and down, depending on the context, and when you find your footing and connect with your capabilities you will be reassured that you genuinely know what you are talking about.

> *"It's not about me at the end of the day. It's funny that it ebbs and flows because, like anybody, we all look for validation. Sometimes you're the only one that's going to give it to yourself."*

Like Alex found, this insight may take you years to get to. It may not be natural and perhaps you are not yet confident enough to really believe it. Or you may already be there.

You are the only one who knows what's true for you. Validation from others is based on what is true for them or what they see in you. While this is important, it is more important to know what drives you and how to choose.

Alex's mantra, *"Don't seek validation, give it to yourself,"* is an effective way to build capacity using the inside-out approach.

> *"I think as I get older, as I get more self-assured, I definitely rely on that personal mantra. It really helps me see the light of day and figure out what's important."*

Look at your language

The language you use has an impact on your self-confidence and building on what you already have. It can be overt and clear or quite insidious. And sometimes apologies go beyond politeness.

"I think there's an element of not apologising. Because if you think about some of the language we use in terms of men and women, women are sometimes almost apologising for existing."

Have you felt at times as though you were taking up space, or you apologise for interrupting or interjecting in a meeting or conversation or you often use the word 'just'? Do you sometimes feel as though you are almost begging rather than asking for support and that you include a series of pleases and thank yous in correspondence and conversations?

When this was highlighted during the research project, I paid more attention to my own language and noticed that I used 'thank you' excessively in professional emails—and also the word 'just'. I also looked at my personal texts, social media messages and other correspondence and noticed how often I used 'just'. It definitely conveyed the message that what I had to say was not important or worthy of a great deal of attention. Of course context is everything and saying, "I have remembered just now..." is different to, "I just wanted to say..."

The most irksome revelation was that when I asked for help I seemed to plead, especially when asking a man. I was playing along with the Gender Code that says I need to be the one in charge, females are better at this organising game, and if a male helps out he is a saint. Where was my self-confidence?

Do you want to take up space?

In my marriage, and afterwards as I was rebuilding my confidence, I felt smaller and less important than other people, even when I knew something was not right and I needed to do something about it. It was debilitating, but also a foundational perspective and empathy-building tool and a window into other people's struggles and pain.

How you hold yourself is important as it sends a message about how you feel about yourself and what you want the world to feel about you. Women sometimes take up as little space as possible so as not to be in the way. The Gender Code tells us to stay quiet, thin, presentable and agreeable, so when we make a fuss we are violating the Gender Code, which makes people who adhere to it feel insecure.

"Even in meetings—I'm five foot nothing—I tend to step back, and so you've got all these people who are five foot ten and taller standing in front, talking to a board or what have you. I don't even have a physical presence. If I start talking apologetically or asking permission to speak, I become even less visible."

Rather than fighting space takers, you can become one. You can ride confidently on the road knowing you belong there, and coach yourself to feel you are equal to everyone, regardless of their gender, age, experience or position. You belong in whichever arena you choose, because you are human and we are all connected.

"As a woman, trust yourself, trust your instincts and don't let anyone put you down. Reflect. It's very important to reflect and think differently. Don't doubt yourself and put yourself down."

22 E is for Energy

Energy is your most precious resource, ranking above all your internal resources. Understanding more about where your energy comes from, exploring ways to manage it—not your time—better and how you use it now will help you create and execute your code. Energy has one section:

1. Energy, your most precious asset

1. Energy, your most precious asset

"We have all got a finite amount of time. So how do remarkable female leaders do it all and have it all? You can't be everything for everyone. It's physically not possible. You've got to do things that generate energy for you, but you've also got to direct your energy effectively."

What fuels you?

Have you ever wondered why some people seem to have a more consistent supply of energy and enthusiasm than others? Or why there are some incredible people who seem to be highly productive and appear fulfilled while doing it? Have you also ever wondered why you can feel drained of energy while listening to a conversation or being involved in a task that feels like hard work and then, a short time later, be energised by another task or conversation and even perhaps experience a flow state? Even though you haven't had any chocolate or a coffee to stimulate you.

Every single process, moment to moment, down to the cellular level in your body uses your energy. Even your thoughts and emotions require energy. You get to decide how you will use it effectively.

When you are in a state of hyper-responsibility, you need all your energy to be everything to everyone. You may be running on adrenaline, but you cannot afford to be ill.

It is only when you stop to ask yourself why that you realise how tired you are and that you are neglecting the important elements that sustain you.

Let's pull apart the energy equation

Like most people of my generation, I saw energy as driven primarily by the physical elements. It was all about input and output. Whatever we ate and drank determined the fuel available for movement activities and cognitive tasks. This was reinforced by popular culture and the media, and was supported during my Personal Training certification study. Everything changed in China.

In Beijing, I attended lectures and workshops on acupuncture and massage, and Chinese herbs and foods. The most influential and life-changing workshop was called 'Eat Sleep Breathe — Developing Healthy Habits Using Traditional Chinese Medicine'. The workshop founder, Alex Tan, taught us about the ancient Chinese ways based on Taoism, about eating and traditional Chinese diet therapy, breathing, resting and rhythms, exercise and meridians, thinking and observing, and how important these are for wellness and energy.

Alex created the course after years of studying both Western and Chinese sciences and philosophies.

> "The key focus of this approach is learning how we can live in accordance with nature to avoid illness and disease. The wisdom of the ancient Chinese can greatly assist this understanding of ourselves and our environment. My aim is to help you discover the transformative powers of ancient Eastern health practices for restoring and maintaining balance, health and happiness."

Most people attending the course hope to lose weight and be healthier; consequently the topic of diets came up often and one week we looked at the Mediterranean diet. To Alex, the significant element of Mediterranean people's health is not merely what they eat, but their entire lifestyle.

These people eat fresh food grown close to where they live or they grow it themselves. They eat healthy food at regular times. Mediterranean people sit down together and talk and walk. They tend to live in family groups and villages and provide each other with support and a sense of connection. And meals are prepared with love. I observed this when I lived and worked in central Italy years earlier.

In the food- and exercise-obsessed West, for decades the focus has been on the twin evils of calories and measuring scales and less on our lifestyle as a whole. We believe a disciplined, measurable approach to calories in and calories out should result in improved physical appearance, greater energy levels and enhanced wellbeing. This is the equation approach and we dedicate very little effort to being predictable and regular in the significant areas of our lifestyle. We fall down because most people don't establish regular routines around meal preparation and timing, eating with family and spending time together connecting, and exercising after meals: sleep, rest, recovery and play.

Perhaps there is even more to energy than we pay attention to.

What is the hidden energy source?

Not content that I had found all the answers, I wanted to understand more about our energy drivers and the motivation—or lack of motivation—to help my Personal Training clients. Childcare and money are not the issue for expats in Beijing as they are in Australia, so why did they struggle to keep their commitments?

My clients were intelligent high achievers, and living in Beijing was not for the faint-hearted. It required grit, determination, application and a sense of adventure. Why was fitness not a priority? They all told me how important it was to them to be fit and healthy, so they knew, but not all of them could apply themselves to regular sessions.

It was not a high enough priority. They all struggled with the difficulties of managing family and work while living abroad and feeling like they were doing everything well, but they were highly driven people. And even though they did not invest regularly in their health and lead a 'balanced' lifestyle, they still seemed to be achieving incredible outcomes personally and professionally.

I eventually realised that a deeper, spiritual energy source was available to them as it is to everybody: their sense of purpose and meaning. Absolutely they would have benefited from more sleep, nutrient-dense food and movement—and some did make positive changes—but connection to what was uniquely important to them was providing the fuel they needed.

When you have a strong sense of purpose, know who you are and what you stand for, you have the foundation to build a full and complete life. That gets you up in the morning and keeps you energised throughout the day.

The secrets to consistent energy

"Performance, health and happiness are grounded in the skilful management of energy." Jim Loehr and Tony Schwartz[1]

Having an awareness of the elements that contribute to your energy is a helpful first step. However, there is more to it. Understanding how your energy works and learning how to manage it more effectively can have a hugely positive effect.

Alex's Taoist principles are valuable and, taking the Western approach, the groundbreaking work of Jim Loehr and Tony Schwartz is very useful.

"Energy is the X factor that makes it possible to fully ignite talent and skill." Jim Loehr and Tony Schwartz

Their book, *The Power of Full Engagement: managing energy, not time, is the key to high performance and personal renewal*, maintains that the way to lead a fulfilled life with a consistent and reliable energy source is to adopt four key principles to manage your energy.[2]

First principle—Energy sources
You can access and use four different types of energy source:

- **Physical**—deep breathing, nutrition (quality and regularity of food), sleep (quality and quantity), degree of recovery, level of fitness, rhythmic balance

---

1 *The Power of Full Engagement: Managing Energy, Not Time, Is the Key to High Performance and Personal Renewal*, Jim Loehr and Tony Schwartz, pg 5
2 Ibid., pgs 9, 11, 13, 14

- **Emotional**—positive and negative emotions
- **Mental**—focus
- **Spiritual**—purpose and deep connection to values beyond your self-interest.

Each dynamic is essential, and influences the others to a great extent. Using one in isolation is not adequate.

Second principle—Recovery and renewal

Your energy is reduced when you over or underuse it. Dissipating much more energy than you recover or having more energy than you expend leads to depletion, burnout and depression. Purposeful energy use needs to be balanced with recovery and renewal periods.

Third principle—Habitual stretching

Pushing yourself beyond your standard limits builds energy capacity. Rather than viewing this type of stretching or stress as detrimental, it is actually the key to growth. To build strength in your muscles you need to habitually stress them, consuming energy beyond your normal limits, to create tears in the muscle fibres and support your muscles to grow and become stronger.

Think of daily high intensity interval training (HIIT) and dealing with difficult emotions. This applies in all areas of your life, physically, emotionally, mentally and spiritually. It is not only effective in terms of fitness and training. It is pushing boundaries and building muscle capacity—compassion muscles, empathy muscles, patience muscles, creativity muscles, focus muscles.

Fourth principle—Positive rituals

Exercising willpower and discipline constantly is exhausting and uses up energy. Specific routines or rituals and switching to autopilot use less conscious energy, which frees you up to focus strategically on where you use energy creatively and sustainably. Think of willpower and discipline as something you have to push yourself to do, whereas rituals are something you are pulled to do.

"There isn't anything that isn't made easier through constant familiarity and training. Through training we can change; we can transform ourselves." Dalai Lama

When you develop a rhythm by implementing these principles, you are physically energised, emotionally connected, mentally focused and spiritually aligned with your purpose and the greater good.

What are your energy challenges?

You may be challenged by all four of the principles or perhaps only one or two. Whatever it is for you, it is okay where you are right now.

I have written about the first principle — energy sources — throughout the book. We looked at the Core Four, Peggy's Pyramid, inside-out thinking, self-compassion, acceptance, using what is strong and what is most important to you. I have also written about the third principle of stretching and pushing boundaries to grow.

For many people I spoke with, recovery and renewal is a big obstacle. It is understandable: building these periods into your time can be difficult, but you need to manage your energy with periods of recovery before you are exhausted.

What do recovery and renewal look and feel like for you? They could be meditation or having stillness at times throughout the day, transitioning during the commute to and from work and between your roles, taking a circuit breaker and going for a walk at lunchtime. It could be going offline for a period in the day or for a whole day. Perhaps it is as simple as sitting by yourself and having a coffee.

"I regather myself from the weekend. But there's a bit of a routine to that. Definitely sport, watching my kids play sport. Definitely watching my daughter's touch football. Then just regather, sit out and look at my pool or go for a swim or sit and watch the jacarandas or just really simple stuff."

Some people can recover, reset and launch into the next project with higher levels of energy and enthusiasm. Others are forced to slow down after injury, illness or a health scare and that can be a life-changing experience.

Are you a sprinter or a marathon runner?

Lying face down on a cold, hard table in a small, sparsely furnished room, I am motionless as Josh prods my lower back and spine. I feel the familiar, persistent pain as the pungent smell of liniment wafts through the air and I wonder when it will all be over.

I had been pushing too hard for too long. I did not listen to my body so my body took over and I sustained a lower back injury. At the end of a three-month intensive physiotherapy treatment programme my therapist is pleased.

"You are looking much better and the rehab is working well, but don't go back to running long distances. Ever."

Elated and confused, I sense things need to change dramatically.

"What is your definition of long distances?"

Before the injury, I had been running two or three 10-kilometre-plus runs at a respectable sub-five-minute kilometre pace. I accepted these would be on hold until recovery was over, but had not contemplated never going back. Josh's view of long distance is three kilometres so I gasp and feel dizzy.

I decide to use the opportunity to rethink my approach to exercise and movement. For years I had been loath to incorporate any type of interval training into running, even though the benefits in increasing speed seemed believable and achievable. I had built my fitness identity code on the basis that I am a rhythm girl, built for comfort and not for speed. The thought of pushing to the point of intense discomfort felt wrong, but the injury had taken me to a crossroads.

So I trick myself into starting intervals and wean myself off long distances, warming up with a one-kilometre continuous run then sprinting for 30 seconds and walking for 30 seconds for the entire five or so kilometres. Technically I am not running continuously.

Initially the experience is punishing, but I am inspired by the physical results and soon able to increase overall running speed and the number of seconds of sprinting. Then I start doing weight training too, which up until then had not been part of my weekly fitness routine.

I am feeling fitter, healthier and lighter. I notice my clothes are fitting better, and after exercising I feel energised. This was different to when I was running longer distances because I would enjoy the post exercise endorphins, but after they wore off I would feel tired and slightly depleted.

I had heard about the benefits of high intensity interval training (HIIT), but could not fathom how a 20-minute HIIT workout could be more beneficial than a long run. My focus had been more on the measurable unit of time rather than effort. While the physical upside was incredible, the most life-changing benefit of my experimentation and adaptation to HIIT was allowing myself to incorporate recovery periods. And know that it was okay.

Feeling the positive effects, I wondered if I could apply this methodology to other areas of my life. I changed my thinking—that it was not necessary to flog myself relentlessly—and found the strength and confidence to experiment. I do not need to operate as a marathon runner; I can build in breaks and trust that when a recovery opportunity is near I can stretch myself.

It changed my whole perspective when I decided to become a life sprinter rather than a marathon lifer.

What initially felt like a huge blow in the form of a back injury transformed into an opportunity to pause, reflect, recalibrate and stretch. It deepened my understanding of my physical and emotional selves and how they are connected. Every interval session is still punishing but I know that will pass and I will be better equipped to face the day and thrive.

This approach works in tough times when you question your character, your values and your coping abilities. You can become stronger and know you will cope better next time. You build tolerance for physical and emotional discomfort, trust and self-belief, and you become more internally resourceful.

It can help you understand that you do not have to be afraid of the pain. The difficult feelings and emotions can be pre-conditions for healthy change.

Can you recover and renew too?

Can you build opportunities into your day, week, and month to recover with the knowledge that it will lead to building energy capacity? You may have already built recovery periods without viewing them in this context.

Can you ascribe a higher value to recovery and renewal when you believe they will help you and everyone who relies on you?

Practical ways to improve energy

To build and nurture your energy takes effort and attention. Working through the whole process and incorporating all of the principles can be challenging, but your most precious resource is at stake.

It breaks down to a three-step process:

1. Start with your CORE

2. Hold up a mirror

3. Execute your plan.

1. Start with your CORE

There is a good reason why we finish the CIRCLE guide with Energy—it completes the circle and leads back to the most important thing, the thing at your core and what you live for: your purpose. Thus you make decisions about how to use your energy—not your time but your energy. Your values, your core thing, are your internal compass and they will help you.

Deeply held values provide the inspiration and meaning to engage with life. Connecting with them and living them and your purpose provide a powerful fuel source. The more committed and guided by your values you are, the more potent an energy source they become.

2. Hold up a mirror

If you are honest and self-compassionate, you can ask yourself where you are and whether you are living the values you profess.

3. Execute your plan

Motivated by your values and being honest with yourself, you can build positive rituals into your day by determining specific behaviours and performing them at particular times. A great deal of work is needed to achieve the whole daily rhythm objective, so it is best to start with small, doable practices that work for you and may include the following:

• Eat one regular meal each day, sitting down and not working

- Reduce processed foods in the afternoon
- Tweak your bedtime routine — 15 minutes earlier each night
- Leave 15–20 minutes between meetings
- Talk to someone you wouldn't normally be in touch with
- Practise deep listening with direct reports and partner
- Take a breath before reacting.

These are very generic ideas and may not all apply to you.

The Three Things ritual

Do you find that you have a ridiculous number of jobs on your to-do list? Are you lying awake at night thinking about them? Or when you wake up in the morning, do they all seem to pop into your head and compete with each other, vying for your attention?

Deb was in the habit of trying to do and tick off 50 useful tasks in her day personally and professionally, but realised that meant she was failing to address the big things and, as a result, she felt overwhelmed. Now she focuses on a few priorities and is less easily distracted. A ritual which has been pivotal in releasing the pressure is Deb's *Morning Three Things*.

As soon as she wakes up, she makes herself a cup of tea and goes back to bed for 10 minutes to think about her priorities for the day and channel her energy.

She writes three things she would like to achieve that day in her diary and categorises them:

- One people — which may include mentoring, meetings, supporting others
- One personal — such as attending a charity event and connecting with the speaker
- One professional — for example briefing her staff for an important meeting or working on strategy.

She is goal-driven and likes to tick off achievements for a sense of accomplishment. Achieving the three things each day is good enough for Deb and it means she has had a productive day. While she still has a master list of tasks which she reviews periodically, she accepts and focuses on the three daily tasks.

"It's changed my life because I'm in a really busy area; it's very reactive, and I found that I wasn't dealing with some of the big things. I was letting my team down because I wasn't spending enough time with my people. I'm a better leader. It makes me feel better. It takes some of the stress. It becomes too overwhelming, so I just write three things down each morning in my diary."

I experimented with this myself and it is life-changing. It helps to build all sorts of muscles including patience, acceptance, prioritisation, self-compassion and focus. It is an effective use of your energy and a major benefit is that it helps you sleep better. Rather than running through all of the things you haven't managed to do throughout the day as you prepare to sleep, you are able to reflect on the three things as good enough and feel a sense of achievement. Not a sense of failure and more to do the next day.

What gives you energy and what sucks your energy?

While energy interplay principles are a helpful guide to building energy capacity, a simpler approach is knowing your energy sources and drains, which depend upon what you value and how connected you are to your motivators and purpose. What is an energy drain for you may be an energy source for others and vice versa. Drains are inevitable, but you can minimise them and find a way to refuel.

The habits, people, places, words and language and thoughts that give you energy or suck your energy are yours alone. The people I spoke with shared sources of energy and drains which you may be able to identify with.

Energy sources:

* Love and connection
* Healthy food
* Exercise
* Sleep

- Rejuvenation
- Sense of purpose
- Strong sense of self
- Focus
- Life satisfaction
- Belonging
- Collective experiences
- Value
- Self-worth.

Energy drains:

- Stress
- Unmet expectations
- Low energy
- Lack of meaning and purpose
- Externally imposed expectations
- Lack of clarity
- Loss of control
- Fears
- Anxiety
- Shame and guilt
- Insecure thoughts
- Low energy language—"I am stressed/busy/depressed".

Do any of these apply to you too?

What are your energy priorities?

How do you prioritise and decide what you will give your energy to in terms of physical, emotional, mental and spiritual deeds? What motivates these priorities?

- Duty and obligation
- Fear of upsetting others
- Feeling worthy and wanting love and connection with others
- Completing the task will bring glory
- Not completing the task will bring discomfort
- It is the right thing to do
- It is the professional thing to do
- It is expected of you
- It is the easy thing to do
- It is the hard thing to do
- Central purpose is clear and the value is obvious
- The value to be gained is aligned with your own values
- Completing the task will reinforce the value and become a building block
- It is within your boundaries
- It reinforces your self-efficacy.

Competing demands for your energy make it difficult to prioritise and maintain your values and sense of self.

Do you want long-lasting energy?

If your motivations are external—pleasing others, gaining attention or fear of rejection—this can be depleting, rather like a sugar hit: a temporary sense of excitement and increased energy levels followed by a low.

If the motivations are internal and you prioritise based on your values and a deep sense of what is authentic to you, the act may be a source of fuel and create longer-lasting energy.

Initial discomfort which may upset other people is better than living with resentment.

Choosing based on your values and what is truly important and meaningful to you helps you to lead a life you love and be authentic, self-compassionate and connected, to step outside the zone of pleasing, obligation and doing things for duty's sake.

Only you can judge your limits and motivations, but it is okay to please and act out of duty. The crucial part of the equation is the intention. Is it connected to you and who you are? Are you making the choice?

Would you like to increase your energy?

Adapted from Rich Litvin, coach and author of *The Prosperous Coach*, this exercise is a great way to get to know your energy and improve how you prioritise.

Objective: Gain clarity and insight by identifying what acts as a source of energy and what drains you of energy:

- Habits

- People

- Places

- Things

- Words and language

- Thoughts.

1. List as many habits, people, places, things, words and language and thoughts as you can think of that are an energy source, neutral, or an energy drain.

2. Take one item on the list from Sources and one from Drains and make notes as to why.

3. Tap into your energy sources as often as possible, reclassify your 'neutral' as a definite source or drain, and reduce your energy drains.

4. Commit to one week reviewing your sources and drains on a daily basis. Record them in a meaningful way.

Energy sources/fuel	Neutral	Energy drains/suck

"Energy, not time, is the fundamental currency of high performance."
Jim Loehr and Tony Schwartz[3]

Using your energy for fuel and tapping into your deep spiritual energy source can change your life. Managing your time becomes an energy drain. Prioritising and ascribing value to the who, what, where, when and how becomes second nature and you can write and execute your own code and live on your own terms.

---

3   *The Power of Full Engagement: Managing Energy, Not Time, Is the Key to High Performance and Personal Renewal*, Jim Loehr and Tony Schwartz, pg 4

Epilogue—A new world

The Gender Code is real.

Cultural beliefs established throughout history have created the myths and stereotypes that fuel the patriarchal system, giving women a supporting role. None of this is relevant in today's world.

It is clear that women as a gender are not naturally suited to being nurturers and carers, just as men are not naturally suited to being breadwinners. Rather than being innate, this is part of the culture.

However, the Gender Code is so strong that you may have subconsciously bought into the cultural myths, and even driven them personally without understanding how much they raise personal expectations and create extra pressure to perform.

Redefine having it all

Amongst the pressures we women face, the pressure to have it all is most common and has the greatest impact. For decades women have aspired to the ideal of a thriving, fulfilling career combined with a happy family and good relationships. The ideal career looks like success in focus, results, progression, and being able to dedicate all available resources to work. In terms of family and relationships, the ideal means being the perfect mum and partner, which may be all of the most attractive aspects of mums and partners curated to create a mythical person.

The reality is, however, an either/or approach and deep divisions. Work/life, career/family, career/partnership. This has left women thinking it is necessary to straddle two worlds, and constantly juggle to achieve balance or attempt to integrate them. This leads to huge expectation gaps.

The ideal of having it all just does not deliver. In this book I have broken the Gender Code for you.

Life on your own terms

Rather than basing your life on the outdated Gender Code and unrealistic expectations (yours and other people's), define what you want and let go. It all starts and ends with you.

You may decide to change your definition. It is absolutely okay. You can go from struggling and juggling to writing and executing your own code so life works for rather than against you.

Key to this is knowing what is most important and what drives you, the right foundation to build on.

If you acknowledge that your contribution in all of your roles is valuable, but that you are used to putting other people's needs before your own, nurturing people and relationships, creating conditions which allow others to succeed, and developing empathy, perspective, critical thinking, flexibility, prioritisation, adaptability, then you will realise that these highly sought-after skills are sharpened as you evolve. As a parent and/or carer, you can bring these human flourishing strengths into the workplace and realise your full potential.

As you create and build, go easy on yourself. Strive for excellence rather than perfection; release performance pressures, look after your own wellbeing and reward yourself along the way. Build confidence in who you are and move from feeling invisible to being powerful.

Where do you want to go?

To live on your own terms and create your unique world requires energy and experimentation, reflection, innovation and connection. It also takes courage, daring, belief, determination and hope. It may feel lonely and difficult at times, but other women will be supportive. You are not alone.

Women working together for the greater good are one of the most powerful forces of nature. There are networks, strategies, solutions and people waiting to help you.

The opportunities for you to be who you uniquely are and flourish are limitless and everyone in your world benefits. I am excited about what the present and the future hold for you.

Acknowledgements

When I start reading a new book, one of the first things I do is turn to the acknowledgments page because before I embark on the adventure — and commitment — of reading I like to know a bit about the process the author undertook and peer through a window into their world.

Each time I read this section I am struck by the amount of support, personally and professionally, the author has received from others.

I used to wonder how they managed to have so many people contribute, what motivated them to do so, and I would think that if I ever wrote a book there was no way I could draw on others and ask for help to a similar extent. It would be all up to me.

However, through the experiences of writing this book I have learned that the creative process is not a one-person game. Similar to managing life, there are many elements at play in creating a book. Collaboration, crafting and shaping require many talents from people with significant wisdom and expertise.

Acknowledging and benefiting from the unique strengths and commitment of the people involved in this mission has changed my world and how I see it.

The first thank you must go to Pam Dibbs, my coach, who three years ago was able to see a great deal more in me than I could see in myself and formulated the idea of a research project. The next major thank you is to Jaqui Lane, The Book Adviser. Using her straight-talking approach and decades of experience, Jaqui helped me shape a big bunch of research, experimentation and a whole lot of ideas into a book. Jaqui's consistent, solid support has been crucial and I am forever grateful.

This book adventure deepened my admiration and respect for people who write and edit as a profession — in particular Clare Wadsworth, my editor—who was not only incredibly patient and giving but also managed to artfully 'detox' my words and make them sound like me, but better. Siobhan Doran also held up a mirror and helped me reshape the manuscript at a crucial stage with her generosity and skill as a writer and editor.

There is a long list of people who have made this book a reality and contributed in different ways. Thanks go to Jacqueline Nagel, my business mentor, who not only sees the value and potential in my work but is adept at articulating it in a way that makes sense to people who need to hear it. I am also extremely grateful to the incredible people who let me into their world and gave me permission to have honest conversations, and to my family, friends, colleagues and local community members who have all buoyed me and been cheerleaders when the mission felt like an ultra-marathon.

A huge amount of thanks goes to my three sons for their inspiration and involvement along the way. They have been phenomenal learning partners and provided moments of awe by asking great questions and connecting the mental dots (although they are in no rush for the next book project to start).

To my partner and possibly number one fan, Peter, for his steadfast, reliable support and true belief that I can accomplish whatever I set out to do. As a result of his love, strength and centredness, he has given us both the gift of knowing what it means to be a flourishing member of a true partnership: the crucial first step to gender equality.

Appendix

The genesis of the Gender Code, page 8—The burning questions

1. What does a good day look like?

2. What percentage of your days are like this?

3. What gets in the way of having good days?

4. What are the biggest challenges you face as both a leader and a parent? Is this common to other women you know and are there other common themes you notice?

5. What works well in being a woman leader and having a family?

6. How do you prioritise your day? What influences your decisions?

7. How do you transition from work to home?

8. What sources of support do you have?

9. What are the essential elements that build connections with other people and create healthy relationships?

10. What does community mean to you?

11. How are your health and wellbeing?

12. What are you doing when you are in a flow state or losing track of time?

13. What do you wish you had known or understood years ago that could help other people?

14. What are your greatest hopes for leaders of the future?

Chapter 9 — Productivity and caring pressure release
Human flourishing tasks exercise

I have tried this exercise a few times and it became laborious. The point is that your effort, energy and attention are valuable. Even a mental list will help you feel less overwhelmed and resentful.

But rather than focusing on what you are missing out on or not doing, you can see the positive work you do.

Day and time	Task	Why it is important
Monday Early morning	Help kids get ready for school and drop at the train station.	Give guidance, have conversations and practise organising.
Monday Mid morning	Organise transport for kids, after-school sport x 3.	Create opportunities for participation and friendships.
Monday Afternoon	Drive son to the airport.	Create an opportunity for him to build resilience and independence and spend time with my parents.
Monday Afternoon	Christmas shopping for family at the airport.	Think of others, what to give them — when I really hate shopping.
Monday Afternoon	Research different activities/groups for children.	Seek opportunities for children to experiment and try new things, and have fun.
Monday Evening	Plan, shop, unload shopping, prepare meals.	Provide physical nourishment for family.

CPSIA information can be obtained
at www.ICGtesting.com
Printed in the USA
LVHW011202180620
658104LV00001B/3